DAVID COPPERFIELD

THE GARLAND DICKENS BIBLIOGRAPHIES
(General Editor: Duane DeVries)
Vol. 8

GARLAND REFERENCE LIBRARY
OF THE HUMANITIES
Vol. 280

DAVID COPPERFIELD
An Annotated Bibliography

Richard J. Dunn

WITHDRAWN

GARLAND PUBLISHING, INC. • NEW YORK & LONDON
1981

Library of Congress Cataloging in Publication Data

Dunn, Richard J., 1938–
    David Copperfield, an annotated bibliography.

(The Garland Dickens bibliographies ; v. 8) (Garland
reference library of the humanities ; v. 280)
    Includes index.
    1. Dickens, Charles, 1812–1870. David Cooperfield—
Bibliography. I. Title. II. Series. III. Series:
Garland reference library of the humanities ; v. 280.
Z8230.D87 [PR4558]   016.823'8   80-9023
ISBN 0-8240-9322-4   AACR2

Printed on acid-free, 250-year-life paper
Manufactured in the United States of America

CONTENTS

Part III. Biography and Bibliography

PREFACE
How to Use This Bibliography

As an annotated bibliography of *David Copperfield* editions, adaptations, reviews, criticism, and appreciative and biographical commentary, this book should serve both the Dickens specialist and the more general reader. The bibliography has three main divisions—Text, Studies, and Biography and Bibliography—each divided into several sections. Within the sections entries are arranged alphabetically by author, the exceptions being editions (chronological listing), stage plays (chronological listing followed by commentary arranged alphabetically by author), films (chronological listing in the first entry followed by commentary arranged alphabetically by author), musical adaptations (topical listing), reviews (chronological listing). Entries are numbered consecutively throughout, and the index identifies authors and subjects by entry number. Parenthetical numerical references within the entries provide cross-references to other entries, but full cross-referencing is not practical and users should consult the author-subject index.

The following remarks concerning the scope and arrangement of the bibliography, along with a judicious use of the table of contents and index, should help the user to locate materials. The bibliography covers the years 1849 to early 1980. It does not attempt to list the many translations and foreign-language studies which are listed by Ada Nisbet (777). "Other Dickens Works Bearing on *David Copperfield*" includes only the two works which relate most directly, and users should also consult the many entries in the "Criticism" and "Biographical Studies" sections which discuss the relationship of *Copperfield* to various other writings of Dickens. "Editions over Which Dickens Retained Control" includes all of the editions which editors and students must consult to establish an authoritative text. Scholarly discussion of these editions is included in "Commentary on the Text." Because it is impractical to list all of the subsequent editions or to mention all of the abridgments, the section "Subsequent Editions Containing New Introductory or Textual Matter" includes only those editions with new introductory or textual material, and that material is listed in the appropriate "Criticism," "Appreciations," and "Biographical Studies" sections. All of the currently available classroom editions are described. In the various adaptations sections, it has been necessary to be selective because many adaptations are lost and because there have been so many amateur and provincial adaptations. For notice of the many anthology pieces drawn from the novel and also for verse tributes to *David Copperfield* and its characters, subjects which I have not included, readers should refer to Kitton (775) and Miller (776).

The "Criticism" section is the bibliography's largest section, containing entries for articles, pamphlets, dissertations, parts of books, and books. Dissertations listed include only those whose abstracts in *Dissertation Abstracts International* (formerly *Dissertation Abstracts* and *Microfilm Abstracts*) clearly indicate attention to *David Copperfield*. For the major books, the bibliography includes lists of selected reviews. In a few instances, the breadth of an author's critical discussion has demanded two entries, one in "Criticism" and one in another section. In using the "Literary Influences and Parallels" section, users should consult the index for further notice of influences and parallels in other sections of the bibliography.

PERIODICAL ABBREVIATIONS

AI	American Imago
AL	American Literature
BJRL	Bulletin of the John Rylands University Library of Manchester
CL	Comparative Literature
CritQ	Critical Quarterly
DA	Dissertation Abstracts
DAI	Dissertation Abstracts International
DiS	Dickens Studies
DSA	Dickens Studies Annual
DSN	Dickens Studies Newsletter
EA	Etudes Anglaises
E&S	Essays and Studies by Members of the English Association
EIC	Essays in Criticism
ELH	Journal of English Literary History
ELN	English Language Notes
ES	English Studies
ESA	English Studies in Africa
HSL	University of Hartford Studies in Literature
JEGP	Journal of English and Germanic Philology
L&P	Literature and Psychology
MLN	Modern Language Notes
MLQ	Modern Language Quarterly
MLR	Modern Language Review
MP	Modern Philology
MQR	Michigan Quarterly Review
N&Q	Notes and Queries
NCF	Nineteenth-Century Fiction
NSN	New Statesman and Nation
PMLA	Publications of the Modern Language Association of America
REL	Review of English Literature
RES	Review of English Studies

SEL   Studies in English Literature, 1500–1900
SNNTS   Studies in the Novel
SoR   Southern Review
TLS   [London] Times Literary Supplement
TSLL   Texas Studies in Literature and Language
UTQ   University of Toronto Quarterly
VN   Victorian Newsletter
VQR   Virginia Quarterly Review
VS   Victorian Studies
YES   Yearbook of English Studies
YR   Yale Review

INTRODUCTION

To list, much less describe and evaluate, a reasonably complete collection of information about *David Copperfield* may seem the most quixotic undertaking since Mr. Pickwick "traced to their sources the mighty ponds of Hampstead, and agitated the scientific world with his Theory of Tittlebats." I do not foresee that any user will read this entire bibliography; by referring to the user's guide, table of contents, and index, anyone seeking information about the novel should be able to locate readily what he or she specifically needs. The purpose of this introduction is not to present a long-belated report to the Pickwick Club concerning the most essential or even the most eccentric information that has turned up in the course of my research. Instead, I offer a number of conclusions this work has led me to about *David Copperfield*, its author, its popular audience, its critics, and its adaptors.

Although *David Copperfield* has occasionally been mishandled critically, the novel also has received sensitive and intelligent treatment over the years. The latest commentator upon *David Copperfield*'s convincing portrayal of the childhood mind, the most recent explorer of its psychology or symbolism, or the most thorough new study of it as autobiographical fiction or as a part of some larger literary tradition more often refines rather than originates points of critical discussion. Thus, despite demonstrable shifts in the direction and emphasis of Dickens scholarship, people writing about *David Copperfield* have long known its major issues (although one generation may treat casually what another stresses). The subject headings in this bibliography's index describe most of these issues: the theory and practice of autobiographical fiction, the characterization of the narrator-hero, the question of heroism posed by the book's opening sentence, the treatment of minor characters (especially of women, eccentrics, and morally ambiguous people), the thematic and stylistic functions of memory, the relationship of *David Copperfield* to a number of other works. There is no question that the novel's own abundance of subjects for study and argument has led, for better or for worse, to an abundance of commentary, probably more than exists for any other Dickens novel. If, therefore, we speak of a "Dickens Industry" among academics and more general readers, it is fitting to acknowledge the industriousness of the "*Copperfield* Shop." The worst to be said of this criticism is that it is sometimes seriously distorted by errors, some so blatant that they probably will be recognized and not affect most readers' understanding of *David Copperfield* or of Dickens. The best to be said (and this bibliography indicates in its annotations how much sound work has been done) is that the "*Copperfield* Shop" has not been so much a cottage industry as a corporate endeavor to produce a variety of useful approaches to one of the world's great books. The novel's own abundance and the breadth of its appeal as a popular favorite and as a book for study demand that the reader examine a variety of approaches to comprehend it. The best introduction serious readers can have to the book is an introduction which touches upon the novel's genesis, the history of its composition, the circumstance of its serial appearance, the place Dickens gave it in his own later evaluation of his works, and the regard other writers have had for it.

From Dickens's own remarks about the novel we know that *David Copperfield* is one of his most intimate works. His trial titles, including such terms as "confessions," "disclosures," "last will and testament," and his consideration of "Charles Copperfield" as a possible name for the narrator-hero—all point toward this intimacy. The intimacy in large part concerns the book's autobiographical nature, but it also involves the serial writer's emotional attachment to a work evolving from his monthly reacquaintance with what he called the creatures of his brain. Biographers and critics have long noted the book's genesis in the autobiography Dickens began in the 1840's, and they also have linked *David Copperfield*'s recollective form to Dickens's 1848 Christmas Book, *The Haunted Man*. The novel's personal quality accounts for much of the charm it has had for generations of readers, but this personal quality has complicated critical interpretation. The issue is not simply that of how fully autobiographical *David Copperfield* may be or of how charmingly Dickens reveals or conceals the facts of his own life. The critical questions concern the novel's coherence, the completeness of its characterization, and the meaning of its stress on the loving heart and on fond memories. There has been ongoing debate about whether the book changes direction after David's childhood, whether the David who so vividly recalls his life before finding some security with Betsey Trotwood becomes a vague and shadowy character in the remainder of his story. Also, there has been much discussion of just what the novel says about love, especially about David's increasing need to temper his emotion with will, and just what the book shows about memory as an escape or as a complex psychic reconstruction with significant implications for the novel's narrative form. To these questions the fact of Dickens's personal closeness to the novel is essential. Whether David is or is not Dickens, whether other characters are figures from his past (and in some cases his present) given new forms and fortunes in the story, the point is that *David Copperfield* the novel became a living entity and remained one to its author.

Until John Forster's biography of Dickens appeared in the early 1870's, few readers realized how much of *David Copperfield* was autobiographical. But even after Forster published extensive samples of Dickens's abandoned autobiography, revealing the blacking factory experience as the source for David's work at Murdstone and Grinby's and also naming a number of character prototypes, critics recognized a difference between the novel's idealization of David and Forster's more forthright portrayal of Dickens as a complex and sometimes disagreeable man. It is important to keep this disparity in mind, because *David Copperfield*, however it may fascinate modern readers as a confessional fiction or as an instance of a psychologically intensified autobiographical novel, is not simply the "Copperfield Confessions," the "Copperfield Disclosures," or "The Last Will and Testament of David Copperfield." A number of commentators have stressed Forster's notice of Dickens's surprise when Forster pointed out to him the reversal of his own initials in the name "David

Copperfield." He should not have been surprised, we might argue, because in the trial titles and trial names for the hero he obviously had revealed a closeness to his own life. But by the time he had advanced to the writing of his book he had settled for a title more resembling the conventions of eighteenth-century English fiction than signaling a nineteenth-century author's slightly veiled confessions. The serial parts used Dickens's most elaborate version of the title and made a parenthetical nod toward privacy, although the parenthetical qualification may also recall the efforts of earlier fiction titles to pass themselves off as various authentic documents rather than to advertise themselves as fictions. Dickens's full title, used on the covers of the monthly parts, was *The Personal History, Adventures, Experience, & Observation of David Copperfield The Younger of Blunderstone Rookery (Which He never meant to be Published on any Account)*. For the single-volume edition Dickens shortened the title to the more direct *The Personal History of David Copperfield*. Forster, who in his first volume had claimed that Dickens took "all the world into his confidence," later realized that the biography may have led readers to assume too much of a "full identity of Dickens with his hero . . . and of a supposed intention that his own character as well as parts of his career should be expressed in the narrative."

But to acknowledge that Dickens may have left out or distorted much of his life in *David Copperfield* and to grant that he was sensitive to his audience is not to discount the book's intimacy. Throughout his career Dickens maintained the performer's and serial writer's close, sometimes sentimentally sticky, relationship with his audience. Dickens's difficulties in *David Copperfield* with the portrayal of Miss Mowcher (which he had to alter when the original complained of his evident intentions), his hesitation over Dora's death, and his inclusion of the satirical chapter on prison reform indicate his sensitivity to his readers' interests. But in *Copperfield*, more than in any of his other novels, Dickens is emotionally involved with his characters. Principally his involvement is with David, and from the extent to which Dickens's nostalgia permeates his hero's recollections, it is obvious that his emotional tie is with David the child:

> When my thoughts go back, now, to that slow agony of my
> youth, I wonder how much of the histories I invented for

> such people hangs like a mist of fancy over well-remem-
> bered facts! When I tread the old ground, I do not wonder
> that I seem to see and pity, going before me, an innocent
> romantic boy, making his imaginative world out of such
> strange experiences and sordid things! (Chapter 11)

The intimacy Dickens had with David is spurred by the recollective process; Dickens's making of this imaginary world, even
though he calls it David's remembrance, necessarily evokes
Dickens's own wonder and pity. Well may he wonder, as he himself again invents a "history," at how inventive the child had
been. The novelist's intimacy, however, does not rest simply with
David. As Forster showed and as later scholars have substan-
tiated even when taking some issue with Forster, Dickens portrayed a number of his father's traits in Mr. Micawber. More-
over, as we have learned more not only about Dickens's devotion
to Maria Beadnell, his first serious love, which inspired his portrayal of David's attraction to Dora, but also about his wife, his
sister-in-law who died in his arms when she was only sixteen, and
his other sister-in-law upon whom he became increasingly dependent, we recognize amalgamations of these people in his
novel's female characters. The point is not simply one of how
extensively his characterization draws upon the actual people in
his life, because in the course of his writing the characters take
on so much of a life of their own for him that upon completion
of the work Dickens admits some distress; he feels "as if he were
dismissing some portion of himself into the shadowy world,
when a crowd of the creatures of his own brain are going from
him for ever." No doubt wisely, Dickens does not resurrect his
characters or perpetuate them from book to book as does Anthony Trollope. Nearly two decades after *David Copperfield* first
appeared, Dickens generalized his fondness for the novel's
characters into a sense of his parental fondness for the novel
itself, which had become a metaphorical child in his imagination:
"Like many fond parents, I have in my heart of hearts a favourite child, and his name is DAVID COPPERFIELD."

The coincidence of the author's favor with that of the con-
siderable critical acclaim during the past one hundred and thirty
years does not in itself say a great deal about Dickens's novel.
And it is a somewhat awesome task to approach *David Copperfield*

within the larger context of the whole shelf of "Dickens's Works," each of which seems imposingly thick. Yet even if one tries to isolate *David Copperfield*, one is still first impressed by those qualities which upon consideration prove to be qualities which typify Dickens throughout his work. Verbal abundance is certainly one of these primary features in his work. *David Copperfield* has an incessant flow of words; its world comes into being through description and dialogue. Defying language's finite nature, the novel's language can hardly contain the life of *David Copperfield*'s world even as words create and sustain it. Dickens's verbal genius is expansive and optimistic; but if he had written at a later period, say as a contemporary of Kafka or of Beckett, the effect of his verbal dynamics would have been quite the opposite of what it is.

The novel's language is mainly that of and about its distinctive characters—the rich dialect of Mr. Peggotty, the lamentations of Mrs. Gummidge, the babblings of Mr. Dick, the sniveling of Uriah Heep, but most of all the grandiloquence of Wilkins Micawber. Micawber never is capable of declaring anything "in short." Were he ever capable of terminating his rhetorical flights satisfactorily it seems that he would have no existence. Complex and intriguing as the characters' verbal lives are in *David Copperfield*, Dickens's descriptive writing is equally rich. Rather than add to the recognition given the magnificent "Tempest" chapter, in which prose achieves the synesthesia we usually expect from poetry, or from impressionist music and painting, and rather than comment further on many small details such as Dickens's magnificent figurative portrayal of Jane Murdstone (and of all unyielding spinsterhood) in his description of her hard black purse, I want to mention the larger matter of what Dickens's descriptive methods suggest about the nature of his art. That art's abundance, I have been arguing, is not self-contained in the way we find the documentary journalism of Henry Mayhew contained in his *London Labour and the London Poor*. Filled as Dickens's novel is with detail, his fictional world is not simply a metaphoric model of any "real" world. John Romano, in a recent and controversial study, *Dickens and Reality* (New York: Columbia Univ. Press, 1978), applies Roman Jakobson's idea of metonymy to describe the linguistic surface of Dickens's novels.

Romano's point is that unlike metaphor, which encapsulates, metonymy is open in form. As Romano says, in aspiring to such form "the realist intends that our experience of his novel will converge horizontally, as it were, with our experience of life." This is not the place for a complete theoretical discussion of whether Dickens is a metaphorical or metonymical realist (Romano finds often both), but the distinction may help to sharpen the impression most readers have of *David Copperfield*'s verbal abundance.

Because of their importance as primary features, as the very personality of the novel, I have stressed *David Copperfield*'s intimate quality and its verbal abundance. It may be argued whether any novel is better than another simply because an author devotes a great amount of emotional energy and retains a strong attachment to it, yet one cannot deny the importance of the book's intimacy as a major characteristic of the novel. Another primary characteristic, the novel's portrayal of memory, is, like the novel's intimacy, linked to the autobiographical nature of *David Copperfield*. There are a number of paradoxes involved in the portrayal of memory in autobiographical writing. Whereas autobiographical writing may be presumed to be revealing, it often employs a number of disguises. Whereas it is centered in the person remembering, it often manipulates personal memory in ways that lessen the importance of the person who remembers. While we may expect the writing to focus on the *person* remembering, it may actually stress the *things* remembered. And while the spot of time held by memory's focus may be lucidly portrayed, the meaning may be unclear or mysterious. It is interesting to find that working without the advantages (or perhaps encumbrances) of more recent sophisticated critical tools and also lacking the biographical facts supplied by John Forster and later biographers, even the earliest reviewers and commentators sensed in *David Copperfield* some of the paradoxes of autobiographical writing that continue to fascinate us. These paradoxes are not unique to *David Copperfield*, for they recur in other major nineteenth-century works.

Both Wordsworth's *Prelude*, which appeared before the serial run of *David Copperfield* was complete, and Tennyson's *In Memoriam*, also published in 1850, openly declare their philosophical reasons for making personal memories public. These poets differed from Dickens not only in that their grand intentions were more evident than were Dickens's in *David Copperfield*, but also in that Wordsworth and Tennyson were able to structure their works carefully during years of manuscript revision. Students of Wordsworth's and Tennyson's finished poems have the advantage of having available for their consideration the poets' many revisions, shifting of individual parts, and changing thematic emphases. The 1850 *Prelude* and *In Memoriam*, along with the materials relating to their creation, thus reveal their authors' choices, if not always their intentions. The information to be gleaned about *David Copperfield* is far less abundant. Dickens, it is true, had some period of preparation for writing *David Copperfield* in that he had procrastinated, written, and finally abandoned an autobiography before beginning the novel. But in the actual writing of *David Copperfield* in 1849 and 1850, he worked furiously for each month's deadline, and in his case there are only brief notes, number plans, and proof corrections to help readers reconstruct the novel's inception and the history of its composition. Given these differences, not to mention the obvious temperamental variations among the writers, it is remarkable that *David Copperfield*, *The Prelude*, and *In Memoriam* all so effectively use imaginative memory to generalize personal history into spiritual, psychological, and aesthetic experience meaningful to their immediate audiences and for all time. Dickens may appear to stress more the products than the processes of memory, but this may in part be explained by the nature of the novel form, which permits more detailed description and includes more characters than do Wordsworth's and Tennyson's long poems. The content of what David recalls may seem to concern him a great deal, but it does not blind him to the psychological and aesthetic effects of remembering. His act of remembering has its most impressive artistic statement in the "Retrospect" chapters where he uses the historical present tense to suspend the past in the process of loving recollection. Also, the book artistically portrays the disturbing effects remembering has upon the narrator. David occasionally admits feeling as if he had missed some opportunities and wasted others, and his greatest turmoil comes in the "Tempest" chapter, where his description of the external scene serves also to describe his state of mind:

> It was a murky confusion—here and there blotted with a colour like the colour of the smoke from damp fuel—of flying clouds, tossed up into the most remarkable heaps, suggesting greater heights in the clouds than there were depths below them to the bottom of the deepest hollows in the earth, through which the wild moon seemed to plunge headlong, as if, in a dread disturbance of the laws of nature, she had lost her way and were frightened. There had been a wind all day; and it was rising then, with an extraordinary great sound. In another hour it had much increased, and the sky was more overcast, and it blew hard. (Chapter 55)

Recent *David Copperfield* criticism has seized upon the novel's portrayal of memory in action as a principal topic for discussion and matter for comparison not only between Dickens and Wordsworth and Tennyson but also between Dickens and Proust. Earlier discussion of the novel, however, tended to regard *David Copperfield* as the high point of Dickens's career and the culmination (and farewell) to his sentimental humor and optimistic storytelling. But whether readers regard the novel as a prelude to a darker Dickens or as a climax of an earlier, brighter Dickens, *David Copperfield* is an important transitional novel, not simply an autobiographical tangent to his development as a novelist. Although the general trends of *David Copperfield* criticism are those which I have already identified, there have been notable exceptions. Some of the earliest commentators recognized Rosa Dartle, Steerforth, and even Mr. Dick as effective characterizations of troubled souls. Some of the more recent commentators have "rediscovered" the novel's marvellous humor and well-modulated sentimentality.

The novel's experimentation with sustained first-person narration and its opening question of the central character's claim to heroism affect the ranking that critics have given *David Copperfield* among Dickens's works, and these questions also remain basic to the continuing debate about the coherence of *David Copperfield*'s structure. Few great literary works have received such praise for the opening parts and such mixed reception for the rest. The account of David's childhood and the story of his life before he runs away to Betsey Trotwood in Dover has been admired by every generation of Dickens critics. Here childhood lives. Here both the physical and moral dimensions of life remain forever enlarged by the child's perspective. Here, too, is a world of little things—the designs on Peggotty's workbox and the exquisite tenderness of David's attraction to Little Em'ly. After the powerful climax of David's humiliation at Murdstone and Grinby's, the story shifts. With a new name, new clothes, and new friends at Dover, David begins a new life that now seems to the reader less David's own life than his history as it is deflected into the stories of the people around him—Steerforth, Heep, the Strongs, Dora, and Agnes. Distinguished novelists have wished that Dickens had ended his book sooner; one, Robert Graves, revised the story in a regrettable abridgment which he called *The Real David Copperfield*; and another, Somerset Maugham, published a less radical condensation. Dickens's own reading version and other stage adaptations necessarily shorten the story, but as the many editions continually in print suggest, the entire novel yet holds up for the readers who have the patience or leisure time for long books.

As *David Copperfield* moves from its strong and rapidly paced early chapters toward its slower later sections, David changes as the focus of his narrative interest shifts from him to other characters. Several qualities help to unify the novel's distinct parts. There are recurrent characters and recurrent imagery, but most of all there is the quiet, sometimes too unobtrusive, presence of David the man remembering. One of Dickens's rejected titles included the notion of a "Copperfield Survey of the World as it Rolled." In the early parts time seems compressed (and sometimes suspended) in the fugitive sensations of childhood. Later parts roll perhaps too slowly and discursively for some readers' tastes, but in these sections we find some of Dickens's most accomplished writing, especially in his delicate modulation of sentiment and satire when portraying the courtship, marriage, and separation of David and Dora and in his "Tempest" chapter, which must stand as one of Dickens's very best descriptive efforts. Admittedly, *David Copperfield* has its loose, dead, or frayed ends, but to admit its flaws is not to declare the work seriously fragmented. The story of the Strongs seems too obviously a built-in finger post to David's need to discipline his heart. Dickens's shift in plan when presenting Miss Mowcher; the relative caution with which he portrays Martha, the fallen Em'ly, and Rosa Dartle; and the chapter on modern prisons—all are recognizable weaknesses.

Just as an awareness of the novel's intimacy, verbal abundance, portrayal of memory, first-person narration, and problems of structural unity are important to the first-time reader and to the serious student of *David Copperfield*, so is an acquaintance with the various biographical, topographical, and textual studies an aid to the reader's understanding. The best biographical, topographical, and textual studies bring special interests to bear on a better understanding of *David Copperfield*, but the worst seem uncritical and diversionary. We don't have to look far to find a biography that becomes a rewrite of *David Copperfield*, neglecting the important distinction the novel itself maintains between autobiography and fiction. We may sometimes be invited to join excursions that leave the novel forever to seek quixotically for Betsey's actual cottage. Even more objectionably, a few "textual" studies fail to attend at all to Dickens's text in their zeal to claim *David Copperfield* as Dickens's deliberate revision of Old and New Testaments or as his version of the *Oresteia*. Because of the uneven quality of the biographical, topographical, and textual studies, the reader should be wary and critical and apply to these studies *David Copperfield*'s own warning against enthusiasts of many persuasions. The most impressive commentators—the great Dickens biographers, John Forster and Edgar Johnson; the closest students of the novel's serial publication, text and reception, John Butt, Sylvère Monod, and George Ford; the authority on the illustrations, Michael Steig; and the meticulous editors, Nina Burgis and Trevor Blount—all avoid single-minded approaches.

It is one of the embarrassing ironies of Dickens studies that despite the surviving number plans, manuscript, corrected proofs, and early editions, we have until recently lacked a definitive text for this novel. However, 1981 finally brought a definitive edition in the Clarendon *David Copperfield*. Dickens scholars have also been hampered in having to rely on the very incomplete Nonesuch Edition of Dickens's letters, but the superior Pilgrim Edition of the letters should soon reach the years relevant to Dickens's work on *David Copperfield*. Certainly we cannot predict immediate critical awakenings following the publication of the definitive text and the relevant letters, but at the very least these additional authoritative resources may discourage new errors and mistaken interpretations.

My major task in this bibliography has been to provide descriptive annotation for the criticism, textual study, and biographical materials concerning *David Copperfield*, but I have also listed and annotated various materials not ordinarily considered by critics of Dickens. *David Copperfield* as a popular classic has been adapted frequently for stage, film, and radio. The novel and its stage versions have inspired musical numbers, and the book and its characters have led to a number of curiosities— novels which bring back Mr. Micawber, political pamphlets, poems, any number of political cartoons, a popular music group billed as "Uriah Heep," a "David Copperfield" magician in this year's television programming, and advertising based on *David Copperfield* characters. I have been more selective than exhaustive in sampling this material, trying to include enough to demonstrate the novel's broad and continuing appeal. The advertising is one sign of the imaginative life the novel has spawned beyond its original covers, and an interesting study might be written about the commercial uses and abuses of Dickensian creations such as Mr. Micawber as spokesman for Woodcock's Wind Pills and Van Houten's Cocoa. However, it seems that the advertisements belong more to the history of modern advertising than to a survey of the novel's popularity, and accordingly I have not included the advertising among the many adaptations and appreciations I cite. All the adaptations and curiosities included in the bibliography demonstrate the ability of Dickens's imagination to carry beyond his book's covers through the agency of his many adaptors.

In addition to the scholarly and popular responses to *David Copperfield* which I have mentioned, there have been a number of eccentric responses to this novel, which itself so humanely tolerates eccentricity. One negative early reviewer used *David Copperfield* as an "example" of Dickens's disrespect for the rightful authority of schoolmasters. A later *David Copperfield* lover projected its characters into the trenches of World War I. Ignoring the fact that Dickens's female characters were inadequate representations of Victorian womanhood, an antifeminist has cited both Dora and Agnes as today's models of fascinating young womanhood.

As this bibliography shows, a number of writers have fondly recalled their acquaintance with *David Copperfield*. Some have admitted an influence the novel had on them, and some have mentioned it as an exception to their usual distaste for Dickens or for Victorian novels. Joyce gently parodies Dickens. Kafka draws freely on *David Copperfield*. Henry James delights in identifying its country locales. And even aesthetic Bloomsbury expresses its regard.

Having already considered the popular and the scholarly reactions to *David Copperfield*, the adaptations and the eccentric outgrowths, and the responses by contemporary and later writers, we must finally consider the place Dickens himself gave to *David Copperfield* in his own later evaluations. After its early publication, *David Copperfield* continued to be a point of reference as Dickens described his increasing restlessness and marital dissatisfaction. Having met Maria Beadnell again in 1855, Dickens reflected back on *David Copperfield* and told Forster that "no one can imagine in the most distant degree what pain the recollection [of Maria] gave me in *Copperfield*." Forster, in a chapter called "What Happened at this Time. AET 45–46," shows Dickens explaining the events leading up to his separation from his wife in 1858 in language very similar to the phrasing in *David Copperfield*. Dickens speaks of his "unhappy loss or want of something," and, most tellingly, of "the so happy and yet so unhappy existence which seeks its reality in unrealities, and finds its dangerous comfort in a perpetual escape from the disappointment of heart around it." These statements to Forster and the fact that Dickens had much difficulty in the late 1850's adapting the novel for what was to be one of his favorite public readings suggest that *David Copperfield* continued to have a profound significance for him. In 1860, when starting *Great Expectations*, the only other of his novels to use a first-person narrator throughout, Dickens reread *David Copperfield*, ostensibly to prevent unconscious repetition; but given the recurrence of many of that novel's most private anxieties of Dickens's life during the 1850's, and given his deliberate drawing upon the novel's language in describing his problems to Forster, it is somewhat surprising that he might fear *unconscious* duplication of his earlier work. His public declaration of *David Copperfield* as his "favourite child" came late in his life, in the preface to the Charles Dickens Edition in 1867.

Just as Dickens himself retained an emotional investment in *David Copperfield*, so too have later commentators admitted strong feelings about it. There is little excuse for the self-indulgent discussions which misunderstand the novel and ignore the excellent criticism of it. But it is delightful to find excellent criticism admitting emotional attachment to *David Copperfield*—Matthew Arnold expresses delight at finally having the opportunity to write about Dickens; more modern critics, such as George Ford, Sylvère Monod, and Harry Stone, respond sensitively to the novel's rich subjective life. Having for this bibliography traced *David Copperfield*'s critical and popular reputation, I see the need for the rejection and revision of critical commonplaces about *David Copperfield*, yet I find myself more tolerant than I anticipated of the critical repetitiveness produced by decades of study, and especially by the acceleration of the critical machinery in the past quarter of a century. As my own views of the novel change, I find that my respect for Dickens's genius grows. The novel and its critics and commentators show me that *David Copperfield* is a book with brilliant surfaces and intriguing depths. Remaining accessible to the common reader as well as to the student, *David Copperfield* continues to stimulate discussion about issues basic to our understanding of Dickens, his times, and the literary form to which he so significantly contributed.

ACKNOWLEDGMENTS

By its nature a bibliographic volume is a massive acknowledgment to the works it includes; through the annotations to my entries I attempt to acknowledge the best scholarship and to distinguish it from lesser work. Because this is the first of the Garland Dickens bibliographies, I have had much occasion to consult Duane DeVries, general editor of the series. I greatly appreciate his helpfulness at all stages of my work. During the early stages of my project I had the assistance of research support from the Graduate School of the University of Washington, Seattle. The staff of the University of Washington Library, especially Bernadette Gualtieri and Ruth Kirk, have helped me to obtain many difficult-to-locate materials. For her help in compiling my working list, especially for dissertations and editions, I thank Elizabeth Tachikawa. In London I was greatly helped by David Parker, curator of the Dickens House and guide to its many riches. A number of scholars have responded generously to my queries about their own work; many have provided offprints and have made suggestions concerning materials I might otherwise have overlooked. Thus I owe particular thanks to Jerome H. Buckley, Nina Burgis, Pierre Coustillas, Angus Easson, Moira Ferguson, George H. Ford, Bert G. Hornback, Jacob Korg, Coral Lansbury, Leonard F. Manheim, Michael Slater, Michael Steig, and Harry Stone. To Mary Dunn, who indexed this book, I owe most loving gratitude.

Part I
TEXT

DAVID COPPERFIELD IN PROGRESS

DICKENS'S LETTERS CONCERNING THE NOVEL,
HIS NUMBER PLANS, MANUSCRIPT, AND PROOFS

1. Dickens, Charles. *The Letters of Charles Dickens*. Ed. Walter
   Dexter. 3 vols. Bloomsbury: The Nonesuch Press, 1938,
   passim.

   Letters concerning *David Copperfield* appear in the second
   and third volumes; Dickens's early letters to Maria Beadnell
   appear in the first volume. (See also 77, 715, 726.) For a
   sense not only of Dickens's views of his work in progress
   but also of his subsequent regard as much as ten years after
   the book appeared, the letters are useful. His first mention
   of *Copperfield* comes in his 23 February 1849 proposal of
   title variants to John Forster--see also the trial titles
   bound with the manuscript (2). At first the writing went
   slowly, but after serial publication began in May 1849,
   Dickens's enthusiasm mounted. On 25 June 1849 he asked Mark
   Lemon to have a clean handkerchief ready for the end of the
   third number, which Dickens described as "simple and quiet,
   but very natural and touching." In July he boasted to Forster
   of having "ingeniously, and with a very complicated inter-
   weaving of truth and fiction," worked his autobiographical
   fragment into his story. After he moved to the Isle of Wight
   in the summer, he reported on his working habits. On 22
   August 1849 he accepted Forster's suggestion that he change
   the detail for Mr. Dick's delusion from the bull in the china
   shop to King Charles's head. A letter of 21 December 1849
   mentions the changes he agreed to make "in the natural progress and current of the story" to appease Mrs. Hill, the
   prototype of Miss Mowcher. When queried about Blunderstone,
   Dickens reported on 29 December 1849 that he had chosen it
   for the sound of the name (a letter of 27 August 1853 con-
   firms this point). In the same letter he declared that Little
   Em'ly "must *fall*," but he hoped to put the plight of such
   women before the public "in a new and pathetic way." When
   the novel had been appearing for more than a year, Dickens
   acknowledged that he was pleased with the "bright unanimity

about Copperfield [sic]" (13 July 1850), and he announced
that he had "carefully planned out the story, for some time
past, to the end." On 17 September 1850 he claimed to have
"my most powerful effect in all the Story on the Anvil"
(presumably the storm scene that he had finished two days
earlier). One of his better-known remarks appears in a
letter to Forster dated 21 October 1850: "I am within three
pages of the shore; and am strangely divided, as usual in
such cases, between sorrow and joy. Oh, my dear Forster,
if I were to say half of what Copperfield [sic] makes me
feel to-night, how strangely, even to you, I should be
turned inside out! I seem to be sending some part of myself
into the Shadowy World...." Subsequent letters mention his
sending of the last materials to the publisher, announce
his dedication of the book to the Honorable Richard and Mrs.
Watson, and mention the *Copperfield* banquet in 1851. On 10
February 1855 Dickens informed Maria Winter (formerly Maria
Beadnell) that he opened her letter "with the touch of my
young friend David Copperfield when he was in love," and
five days later he told her that she "may have seen in little
bits of 'Dora' touches of your old self." In January 1855
he asked Forster, "Why is it, that as with poor David, a
sense comes always crushing on me now, when I fall into low
spirits, as of one happiness I have missed in life, and one
friend and companion I have never made?" Sometime in the
winter of 1855, concerning his reunion with Maria, Dickens
recalled the intensity "of the feeling of five-and-twenty
years ago" and acknowledged that he could not believe it
would have been better had he not been separated from her
but "no one can imagine in the most distant degree what
pain the recollection gave me in Copperfield [sic]." Writing
to Maria again on 22 February 1855, Dickens spoke of his
abandoned autobiography: "A few years ago (just before
Copperfield [sic]) I began to write my life, intending the
manuscript to be found among my papers when its subject
should be concluded. But as I began to approach within sight
of that part of it [concerning the "wasted tenderness" of
his love for Maria], I lost courage and burned the rest."
In a letter of October 1860 he mentioned having reread the
novel and having been "affected by it to a degree you would
hardly believe." His purpose was "to be sure I had fallen
into no unconscious repetitions" when beginning *Great Expectations*. For Dickens's letters concerning his reading adaptation of *David Copperfield* see Collins (78). For a sampling
of the yet unpublished letters concerning *Copperfield*, see
Michael Slater's *Catalogue of the Suzannet Charles Dickens
Collection* (London: Sotheby Parke Bernet, 1975). These letters
are to be published in the Pilgrim Edition of Dickens's

letters, but the Pilgrim volumes have not yet reached the
years during wich Dickens worked on *David Copperfield*.

2. Dickens, Charles. *Personal History and Adventures of David
    Copperfield*. Bound manuscript and number plans. 4 vols.
    (originally in 2 vols.) [1849-1850]. In the Forster Collec-
    tion at the Library of the Victoria and Albert Museum,
    London.

The first volume includes fourteen pages of various titles
Dickens considered. Forster reprints some of these in his
biography of Dickens (730) but does not provide the full
list. The titles show Dickens trying various names for his
hero: "Mag," "Thomas Mag," "David Mag," "Charles Copperfield." Dickens's uncertainty over the way he wished to
describe his work is indicated by titles including such words
as: *The Last Will and Testament* ..., *The Last Living Speech
and Confession* ..., *The Copperfield Survey* ..., *The Copperfield Records* ..., *The Copperfield Disclosures* ..., and
The Copperfield Confessions.... All Dickens's memorandums
and number plans for the serial parts, except those for the
first part, are bound with the manuscript. Those for the
first number, which John Butt first thought lost (8), are
bound separately in one of the Library's manuscript volumes
of Dickens's letters to Forster. At the end of the second
volume of the novel's manuscript there is a list of chapter
headings, Dickens's 1850 preface, and errata. The manuscript
is in remarkably good condition, probably because it is
accessible only by special permission. The manuscript is
available on microfilm as "Manuscripts of the Works of
Charles Dickens from the Forster Collection in the Victoria
and Albert Museum, London," Film 96738 (London: Micro Methods,
1969), reels 4-5.

3. Dickens, Charles. *David Copperfield*. Corrected proofs.
    2 vols. 624 pp. [1849-1850]. In the Forster Collection
    at the Library of the Victoria and Albert Museum, London.

Includes two sets of galley proofs for the first three
chapters and page proofs for the remainder of the novel.
These are the proofs Dickens corrected for the monthly numbers and used for the 1850 first single-volume edition
(38) and for the Tauchnitz Edition (37). There are a few
attached manuscript slips containing inserted material,
but most of Dickens's proof corrections are in the margins.
The forthcoming Clarendon Edition (72) will describe in
detail Dickens's proof corrections, but even cursory examination of the proofs shows that he changed a few chapter titles,
changed his plan and added the detail of King Charles's

head for Mr. Dick's obsession, and made cuts when monthly
numbers were too long. One of his more interesting marginal
notes concerning these cuts comes at the end of chapter
thirty-seven when he informs the printer that "you must
somehow get all this in." The deletions are restored to the
text in the 1962 Signet Edition (67). The 1958 Riverside
Edition (63) publishes the deletions in an appendix.
Microfilm of the proofs is available as "Annotated Proofs
of the Works of Charles Dickens from the Forster Collection
in the Victoria and Albert Museum, London," Film 96739 (London:
Micro Methods, 1969), reel 3. Also, the Widener Library
at Harvard University has a set of corrected proof sheets
for Chapters 34-64, along with preliminary pages, including
the Preface.

COMMENTARY ON THE TEXT

SCHOLARSHIP CONCERNING THE PUBLICATION, TEXTUAL MATTERS, ILLUSTRATIONS

4. Bromhill, Kentley, pseud. [T.W. Hill]. "Phiz's Illustrations
    to *David Copperfield*." *Dickensian*, 40 (1943), 47-50; 40
    (1944), 83-86.

    Describes the cover design and each of the forty plates
    with brief evaluations. For example, Bromhill says that Plate
    Twenty-two is "just what an 'illustration' should be, realising
    ... pictorially not only a close adherence to the text,
    but also conveying the spirit in which the chapter was
    written."

5. Buchanan-Brown, John. *Phiz! Illustrator of Dickens' World*.
    New York: Charles Scribner's Sons, 1978, pp. 133-147.

    Unlike Cohen (11) or Steig (31), Buchanan-Brown provides
    no discussion of the *Copperfield* plates, but he reproduces
    thirteen of them, including the title page and two sketches
    for "I make myself known to my Aunt."

6. Butt, John. "The Composition of *David Copperfield*." *Dickensian*,
    46 (1950), 90-94, 128-135, 176-180; 47 (1950), 33-38.

    Examines the internal evidence of the monthly numbers to
    reconstruct some of the stages in the composition of *David
    Copperfield* month by month. Butt discusses the number plans,
    characterization, plot lines, and proof corrections, arguing
    that the novel is not designed as deliberate autobiog-

raphy. See also Butt's chapter on *Copperfield* in *Dickens at Work* (8).

7. ———. "*David Copperfield*: From Manuscript to Print."
   RES, NS 1 (1950), 247-251.

   Compares the manuscript with the corrected proofs to show how Dickens worked with his printer. Butt shows that having to set from the much-corrected first draft, the compositors made remarkably few errors, but modern editors must take into account deletions and additions made to the corrected proofs of the serial parts. In 1958 the Riverside Edition (63) published Dickens's deletions as an appendix, and the 1962 Signet (67) Edition restored the deletions to their proper places in the text.

8. ———. "*David Copperfield* Month by Month." In *Dickens at Work*. By John Butt and Kathleen Tillotson. London: Methuen, 1968, pp. 11-12, 114-176.

   First published in 1957; the preface to this 1968 edition adds a description of the first number's plan, which Butt had assumed missing at the time of his earlier edition. Butt publishes number plans for each of the monthly parts and comments extensively on them. He describes his study's high quality and importance to anyone interested in Dickens's design for each part: "Though it is impossible to convey in print all that the number plans reveal, in their manuscript form, of hesitation and decision, of haste and excitement, and often of afterthought squeezed into what might seem the least inconvenient space unfilled, our transcription is as exact as it is practicable to make it." See Butt (242) for additional annotation.

9. ———. "Dickens's Notes for His Serial Parts." *Dickensian*, 45 (1949), 129-138.

   Describes Dickens's working notes and provides photocopies of the notes for the third, fourth, and seventh parts of *David Copperfield*. Butt shows how Dickens's chapter notes rough out the chapters and summarize contents to put him in the mood to start the next part. The left-hand sides of Dickens's sheets contain more haphazard notes, with questions and replies to himself.

10. ———. "Editing a Nineteenth-Century Novelist (Proposals for an Edit_on of Dickens)." In *English Studies Today*. Ed. G.A. Bonnard. Berne: Francke Verlag, 1961, pp. 187-195.

Points out the problems of using the Charles Dickens
Edition (42) as the copy text for modern editions of *Copperfield*. Butt cites a passage from the fifth chapter where
one of the typesetters of the Charles Dickens Edition
mistook Dickens's "without imagining" and set "without
inquiring." As an example of what Butt calls "incorrect
revision by the author," he shows that in the first chapter
Dickens substituted "taking" after the printer mistook the
verb to be "picking" when the manuscript had Betsey Trotwood "jerking the cotton out of one ear like a cork." Butt
does not think it practical for a definitive edition to
record all of Dickens's manuscript and proof deletions,
but he "should like to see recorded in *David Copperfield*,
ch. 29, that the song Rosa Dartle sang had at one time been
'The Last Rose of Summer' before the title was removed, and
that the sermon to which the love-sick David listened in
ch. 26 had at one time begun 'In the first chapter and
first verse of the Book of Dora, you will find the following word Dora.'"

11. Cohen, Jane R. *Charles Dickens and His Original Illustrators*.
     Columbus: Ohio State Univ. Press, 1980, pp. 100-107.

Treats "comprehensively Dickens's personal and professional relations with his first artists." The *Copperfield*
section is not so extensive as Steig's in *Dickens and Phiz*
(31), but Cohen frequently acknowledges debts to Steig
(489), Harvey (22), and other critics. Cohen observes that
Dickens never took Browne into his confidence concerning
the novel's autobiographical nature; nevertheless, the
illustrator and novelist worked with "unusual empathy ...
to portray David's memories, and, at the same time, to
suggest the development of his perceptions as he tells the
story." She shows that Dickens greatly appreciated Browne's
efforts; and stimulated by Dickens's approval, the illustrator included many meaningful details in illustrations
that commented on individuals and episodes. Cohen's discussion of the illustrations indicates how simple pictorial
objects comment on the hero's childhood; later the artist
suggests "sexual implications by postures, gestures, and
lines as well as emblems, which would have offended Victorian sensibilities if put into words." Cohen notes that
the illustration of Miss Mowcher makes clear Dickens's
original purpose for the character, and also she finds
telling detail in the sensitive plate of the fallen woman,
Martha. Cohen's well-illustrated book provides one of the
better brief discussions of how the *David Copperfield*
plates add "psychological, emotional, and moral depth" to
the text.

12. Cowden, Roy W. "Dickens at Work." *MQR*, 9 (1970), 125-132.

Considers the manuscript revisions in discussing how Dickens juggled his means of expression while maintaining the fundamental structure of his thought in *David Copperfield*. Cowden observes that Dickens sometimes added factual details, but mainly he rephrased to accomplish the step from fact to emotional realization of fact.

13. "*David Copperfield*." In "A New Dickens Bibliography." *Dickensian*, 39 (1943), 149-151.

Describes the history of the novel's composition and notes the locations of manuscript, proofs, and original drawings.

14. [Dexter, Walter]. "The Favourite Child." *Dickensian*, 39 (1943), 158-159.

Reproduces an advertisement for *Copperfield*'s original monthly numbers.

15. D[exter], W[alter]. "The Long and the Short of It, Being Some Observations on the Titles Originally Used and of Those in More Common Request at this Present Time. The Whole Embellished with Examples Taken from the ORIGINALS." *Dickensian*, 35 (1939), 265-268.

Briefly describes the difficulties Dickens had in choosing a title for *David Copperfield*.

16. Dexter, Walter, and Kentley Bromhill, pseud. [T.W. Hill]. "The *David Copperfield* Advertiser." *Dickensian*, 41 (1944), 21-25.

Discusses the advertiser--which contained between four and thirty-two pieces of advertising--as an integral part of each serial number.

17. Eckel, John C. "*David Copperfield*." In *The First Editions of the Writings of Charles Dickens: Their Points and Values*. London: Maggs Brothers, 1932, pp. 77-79.

Revision of 1913 Chapman and Hall edition, describing only the 1850 Bradbury and Evans *Copperfield* (38) and noting that the relatively disappointing sales of 25,000 led to Dickens's starting of *Household Words* (35). Eckel notes that Bradbury and Evans Editions following the November 1850 printing omit the 1850 date on the vignette title page. For a more complete discussion of the early editions see Gaskell (19, 20).

18. Fraser, W.A. "The Illustrators of Dickens. II. Hablot K. Browne." *Dickensian*, 2 (1906), 181-182.

   Regards the early illustrations as being better and more interesting drawings than the later ones, in which there seem lapses in Browne's memory because of his slight changes in the appearance of Mr. Peggotty. See also Alex J. Phillip's "Blunders of Dickens and His Illustrators," *Dickensian*, 2 (1906), 294-296.

19. Gaskell, Philip. "Dickens, *David Copperfield*, 1850." In *From Writer to Reader: Studies in Editorial Method*. Oxford: The Clarendon Press, 1978, pp. 142-155.

   Describes the textual history of editions published in Dickens's lifetime. Gaskell states that the 1850 edition remains a satisfactory copy text because Dickens surely allowed for compositors' alterations of the manuscript. He notes that because the number plans, manuscript, author's proofs, and some of the author's revisions survive, collation is relatively easy, but there may be occasional problems with compositors' alterations that Dickens either did not catch or that he corrected with a reading different from that of the original manuscript. Gaskell includes a passage from the fourth chapter which exemplifies such problems.

20. ———. "The Textual History of *David Copperfield*." In *A New Introduction to Bibliography*. Oxford: The Clarendon Press, 1972, pp. 384-391.

   Uses *David Copperfield* as an example of how nineteenth-century compositors followed copy with surprising accuracy. Gaskell points out that the novel's early textual history is almost complete. He provides a useful table of the six editions published in Dickens's lifetime and traces a brief extract from Chapter 64 from manuscript through these six editions. For the novel as a whole Gaskell finds "the highest rate of substantive error ... in the original typesetting from the manuscript," with a norm of "about 1-2 errors per page, of which Dickens found and corrected just over half in proof." He shows that the substantive errors increase in the setting of the fourth edition (Cheap Edition of 1858) from the first edition and in the setting of the fifth (Library Edition of 1859) and the sixth (Charles Dickens Edition of 1867) editions from the fourth edition.

21. Gibson, Frank A. "A Trifle on Titles." *Dickensian*, 58 (1962), 117-119.

Gibson thinks that Dickens cynically paid little attention to titles, but he regards the final *Copperfield* title
as a fortunate choice. For more detail on Dickens's trial
titles see the bound manuscript and number plans (2).

22. Harvey, John. "Dickens and Browne: *Martin Chuzzlewit* to
    Bleak House." In *Victorian Novelists and Their Illustra-
    tors.* New York: New York Univ. Press, 1971, pp. 142-151.

    Finds an extensive use of tableau as the chief feature
    of the *David Copperfield* illustrations and demonstrates
    how text and illustrations support one another. Like Steig
    (31) but in less detail, Harvey discusses the iconography,
    tracing a vein of Christian sentiment in the paintings in
    the background of various illustrations. Harvey notes that
    the plate introducing Miss Mowcher uses a Faust picture
    to foreshadow events Dickens later changed when he revised
    this character's role. Harvey also provides a detailed
    reading of how the "Our Housekeeping" plate epitomizes the
    David-Dora relationship.

23. Hatton, Thomas, and Arthur H. Cleaver. "*David Copperfield.*"
    In *A Bibliography of the Periodical Works of Charles
    Dickens: Bibliographical, Analytical, and Statistical.*
    London: Chapman and Hall, 1933, pp. 251-272.

    Provides a detailed description of each monthly part and
    information about the wrappers, illustrations, and adver-
    tisements. Hatton and Cleaver publish a facsimile of the
    front wrapper and list each of the advertisements. They
    note that the original forty illustrations were etched in
    duplicate and that the copies are distinguishable from the
    originals only "by the changing signature of Phiz as well
    as by other slight variations." The initial printing of
    monthly parts distributed the duplicated plates indis-
    criminately; thus "several copies of the nineteen parts
    would be required to complete a collection of the eighty
    plates."

24. Hawes, Donald. "David Copperfield's Names." *Dickensian*, 74
    (1978), 81-87.

    Discusses the process Dickens went through in determin-
    ing an appropriate name for a durable yet malleable hero
    and considers how the various nicknames other characters
    give David fit the stages of his search for identity. See
    also Alan S. Watts's reminder that Mr. Dick, and not Betsey,
    hit upon "Trotwood" as a Christian name for David, in
    Dickensian, 75 (1979), 35.

25. Kidson, Frank. "The King Charles's Head Allusion in *David
     Copperfield*." *Dickensian*, 2 (1906), 44.

     Simply notes Dickens's proof sheet change from the bull
     in the china shop to the detail of King Charles's head for
     Mr. Dick's obsession.

26. "King Charles in the China Shop." *Dickensian*, 45 (1949),
     158.

     Photostat of the proof correction showing the change of
     Mr. Dick's obsession from the bull in the china shop to
     King Charles's head.

27. Millhauser, Milton. "*David Copperfield*: Some Shifts of
     Plan." *NCF*, 27 (1972), 339-345.

     Thinks it likely that Dickens first intended the Dr.
     Strong-Annie-Jack Maldon triangle as a January-May story
     of betrayal paralleling the betrayal of Little Em'ly and
     suggests that textual evidence and the working plans show
     a shift of direction. Millhauser finds evidence for some
     change in Dickens's use of Murdstone's associates, Quinion
     and Passnidge. Sylvia Manning (408) cites evidence from
     Dickens's earlier *The Cricket on the Hearth* to qualify
     Millhauser's argument about the January-May story.

28. [Staples, Leslie]. "Shavings from Dickens's Workshop:
     Unpublished Fragments of His Novels." *Dickensian*, 48
     (1952), 158-161.

     First publication of ten short fragments cancelled from
     the *David Copperfield* proofs. Later the 1958 Riverside
     (63) and 1962 Signet (67) Editions include them.

29. Steig, Michael. "Cruikshank's Peacock Feathers in *Oliver
     Twist*." *Ariel*, 4 (1973), 49-54.

     Notes that in two of the *David Copperfield* illustrations,
     Plates 4 and 24, Browne followed Cruikshank in the conven-
     tional use of peacock feathers as signs of pride. He also
     notes that Browne often included these feathers "in situ-
     ations where the idea of misfortune is clearly applicable."

30. ———. "*David Copperfield*, Plate 1: A Note on Phiz and
     Hogarth." *DSN*, 2 (1971), 55-56.

     Supplements Steig's article "The Iconography of *David
     Copperfield*" (491) by showing that Browne may have had
     Hogarth's "The Sleeping Congregation" in mind when he
     designed the first plate for *David Copperfield*.

31. ————. *"David Copperfield*: Progress of a Confused Soul."
     In *Dickens and Phiz*. Bloomington: Indiana Univ. Press,
     1978, pp. 113-130.

     Incorporates Steig's earlier articles in the best study
     of how Dickens worked with his illustrator and of the type
     of contributions Browne made to Dickens's novel. Attend-
     ing to the iconography of the illustrations and regarding
     them as integral to the text, Steig applies his insights
     about the illustrations to his study of the novel as a
     whole. For more complete annotation see 489.

32. Stevens, Joan. *Some Nineteenth Century Novels and Their
     First Publication*. Wellington, N.Z.: R.E. Owen, 1961,
     pp. 17-23.

     Discusses the various ways writers were influenced by
     the methods of publication for which their books were
     destined. Stevens provides a chart of events and charac-
     ters introduced in each number of *David Copperfield* in
     support of her discussion of how readers may "recapture
     something of the original effect."

33. Vann, Jerry D. *"David Copperfield* and the Reviewers."
     DA, 28 (1967), 3159A-3160A (Texas Tech., 1967).

     Suggests that reviewers' opinions may have prompted
     Dickens's high incidence of changes in the serial numbers.

OTHER DICKENS WORKS
BEARING ON *DAVID COPPERFIELD*

34. Dickens, Charles. "An Appeal to Fallen Women." In *The
     Heart of Charles Dickens*. Ed. Edgar Johnson. New York:
     Duell, Sloan and Pearce, 1952, pp. 98-100.

     Johnson publishes Dickens's 28 October 1847 draft for
     a pamphlet for women in prison who might be subjects for
     rehabilitation at Urania Cottage, the home Dickens helped
     manage for Miss Coutts. As various commentators have noted,
     Dickens sounds far more harsh toward fallen women in this
     "Appeal" than in his characterization of Martha and Em'ly
     in *David Copperfield*. He asks these women "to be in firm
     control over yourself, and restrain yourself; to be gentle,
     patient, persevering, and good-tempered." In return, he
     hopes the home may offer "peace of mind, self-respect,
     everything you have lost." Johnson states that between

1847 and 1853 Urania Cottage received fifty-six inmates,
many of whom later emigrated to Australia.

35.   ————. *Household Words. A Weekly Journal.* 1 (30 March––
      21 Sept. 1850). 620 pp.; 2 (28 Sept. 1850––22 March 1851).
      620 pp.

Each page of the magazine states that it is "Conducted
by Charles Dickens," and indeed his extensive editing and
occasional writing for *Household Words* comprised the bulk
of Dickens's journalistic effort during the final eight
months of *David Copperfield*'s serial publication. The individual items were published anonymously but have been
identified by Anne Lohrli in *Household Words: A Weekly
Journal 1850-1859* (Toronto: Univ. of Toronto Press, 1973).
"A Preliminary Word" by Dickens (30 March 1849) expresses
a number of sentiments that concur with those in *David
Copperfield*––resistance to mechanism, the romance inherent
in the familiar, echoes of the past. Various subsequent
pieces expand specific concerns of the novel. There are
a number of articles on Australia and emigration: Caroline
Chisholm and Dickens, "A Bundle of Emigrants' Letters"
(30 March 1850); Samuel Sidney and John Sidney, "Milking
in Australia" (30 March 1850); Samuel Sidney, "An Australian
Ploughman's Story" (6 April 1850); Caroline Chisholm and
Richard H. Horne, "Pictures of Life in Australia" (8 June
1850); Francis Gwynne and W.H. Wills, "Two Letters from
Australia" (3 Aug. 1850); Samuel Sidney, "Family Colonisa-
tion Loan Society" (24 Aug. 1850). Prison reform, especially
the Pentonville experiment, which Dickens mocked in the
novel also receives attention in *Household Words*, in Dickens's "Perfect Felicity. In a Bird's Eye View" (6 April 1850)
and "Pet Prisoners" (27 April 1850) and in W.H. Wills's
"The Great Penal Experiments" (8 June 1850). Dickens's
"A Child's Dream of a Star" (6 April 1850) presents one of
his most idealized statements about childhood and thus will
interest readers studying the portrayal of childhood in
David Copperfield. Two articles by W.H. Wills substantiate
two more of the novel's concerns; "The Schoolmaster at Home
and Abroad" (10 April 1850) laments English schoolmasters'
general irresponsibility; and "A Good Plain Cook" (4 May
1850) does not mention Dora but argues that daughters of
the well-to-do should acquire "such principles as would
enable them to apply prompt correction to the errors of
their hired cooks."

EDITIONS
OVER WHICH DICKENS RETAINED CONTROL

36. Dickens, Charles. *The Personal History, Adventures, Experience & Observation of David Copperfield The Younger of Blunderstone Rookery (Which He never meant to be Published on any Account).* London: Bradbury & Evans, May 1849–November 1850. 624 pp.

Issued, as were all Dickens's longer novels, in twenty monthly parts with the nineteenth and twentieth parts combined in a final double number. The monthly parts had green covers, and the Penguin Edition (69) includes a facsimile of the cover design. Each number included two illustrations by Hablot K. Browne and contained a "Copperfield Advertiser" of varying length, the longest being thirty-two pages. Text for the numbers was limited to thirty-two pages, and it was necessary for Dickens to make some cuts in the proofs to fit his allotted space; these were not restored until the recent Riverside (63) and Signet (67) Editions. One of Dickens's last-minute choices was the exact title. Robert Patten (444) cites an *Athenaeum* announcement of 31 March 1849 as evidence that Dickens had made his final title choice by then, but the new novel had been advertised as late as April 1849 in that month's number of Thackeray's *Pendennis* as *The Copperfield Survey of the World as it Rolled.* The true title appeared in the May 1849 *Pendennis* advertisement. The final monthly number includes the first single volume's title page, frontispiece, dedication, table of contents, and preface. See Nina Burgis's introduction to the forthcoming Clarendon Edition (72) for detailed discussion of the serial parts and of other editions published in Dickens's lifetime.

37. ———. *The Personal History, Adventures, Experience & Observation of David Copperfield The Younger of Blunderstone Rookery (Which He never meant to be Published on any Account).* 3 vols. Leipzig: Tauchnitz, 1850. 624 pp.

Set, in English, from Dickens's corrected proofs for the serial parts. Gaskell (20) cites the Tauchnitz Edition in his chart of early editions, but the fullest discussion is P.H. Muir's in "Note No. 53: The Tauchnitz *David Copperfield*, 1849." *Book Collector*, 4 (1955), 253–254. Muir provides the following pertinent information about the Tauchnitz Edition: The first Tauchnitz volume includes chapters 1–16 and is dated 1849. The second, with chapters 17–37, may be given the approximate date of April 1850.

Volume three contains the remaining chapters and the preface
and dedication. The Tauchnitz Edition uses the elaborate
title of the parts issue, not the shorter form of the
English single-volume first edition.

38.   ———. *The Personal History of David Copperfield*. London:
       Bradbury and Evans, 1850. 624 pp.

First single-volume collection of the monthly parts
(including the original forty illustrations), which were
concluded in November 1850. This edition's title consider-
ably shortens the title of the monthly parts (36) and makes
possible a number of title options for later editions. Subsequently the novel would appear occasionally under *David
Copperfield*, the short title Dickens himself used on this
edition's vignette title page. The full title page of this
edition reads as follows: "*The Personal History of David
Copperfield*. By Charles Dickens. With Illustrations by
H.K. Browne. London: Bradbury & Evans, 11, Bouverie Street.
1850." As, of course, it had in the monthly numbers, the
title on the first page of the first chapter appears as
*The Personal History and Experience of David Copperfield
The Younger*. Later editions sometimes use this version of
the title. Browne's frontispiece illustrates Betsey Trotwood's arrival at Blunderstone as described in the first
chapter. His vignette title page shows Little Em'ly on
the beach with the Peggotty house behind her. A number of
commentators have noticed that the text gives no authority
for Browne's having drawn the boathouse as upside-down.
Dickens's dedication reads: "Affectionately Inscribed to
The Hon. Mr. and Mrs. Richard Watson of Rockingham,
Northamptonshire." His Preface, dated October 1850, declares the mixture of pleasure and regret he feels at the
conclusion of his work. More apologetically and perhaps
more defensively than in his recent letter to Forster (1),
Dickens makes public his emotional connection with this
book by saying, "It would concern the reader little, perhaps, to know ... how an Author feels as if he were dismissing some portion of himself into the shadowy world,
when a crowd of the creatures of his brain are going from
him for ever." Before concluding by looking forward to
the time when his next serial work appears, he declares
"that no one can ever believe this Narrative, in the reading, more than I have believed it in the writing." Dickens
later twice changed this preface: in the 1858 Cheap Edition (40) and the 1867 Charles Dickens Edition (42).
Dickens made no changes from the serial parts for this
edition but included errata. Eckel (17) provides collation

useful for collectors of this first edition. Gaskell (20) provides a diagram relating this edition to the first American edition (39), the Tauchnitz Edition (37), and other editions Dickens controlled during his lifetime. Nina Burgis gives close attention to this edition in the introduction to her forthcoming Clarendon Edition (72).

39. ———. *The Personal History, Adventures, Experience & Observation of David Copperfield The Younger of Blunderstone Rookery (Which He never meant to be Published on any Account)*. New York: John Wiley, May 1849–March 1850 (first eleven monthly numbers); and G.P. Putnam, April 1850–Nov. 1850 (last nine monthly numbers). 624 pp.

The initial two monthly numbers for this first American edition were set from the corrected proofs for the English monthly numbers; the remaining American monthly numbers were set from the English monthly numbers. Each American monthly part had two engravings by J.W. Orr and Brother after H.K. Browne. Each part appeared in buff-colored wrappers without the original cover design. An apparently pirated serial issue was published in Philadelphia by Lea and Blanchard during 1849–1850. It appeared in yellow covers and had plates by W.F. Gihon after H.K. Browne. For the subsequent history of American editions of *David Copperfield*, see Wilkins (778).

40. ———. *The Personal History of David Copperfield*. Cheap Edition. London: Chapman and Hall, 1858. 515 pp.

Published without illustrations except for a new frontispiece by Browne; set in double columns. The publishers claimed that there had been extensive revision, but Dickens did not make many changes. To his original preface he added, "The foregoing remarks are what I originally wrote, under the head of PREFACE TO THE PERSONAL HISTORY OF DAVID COPPERFIELD. I have nothing to add to them, at this time. June, 1858." See Patten (195) for information about the reception and sales of this edition.

41. ———. *The Personal History and Experience of David Copperfield the Younger*. Library Edition. 2 vols. London: Chapman and Hall; Bradbury and Evans, 1859. 446 pp.

Appeared as volumes fifteen and sixteen of the Library Edition, a collected edition of Dickens; with no illustrations other than one of David and Little Em'ly on the cover page; using the same preface as the Cheap Edition (40), but omitting the date at the conclusion of the preface;

set in double columns. Each volume has its own numbering
of chapters; the first volume includes the first twenty-
nine chapters; and the second volume begins by renumbering
the thirtieth chapter ("A Loss") as the first of its thirty-
five chapters. Nina Burgis collates this edition with others
published in Dickens's lifetime in her forthcoming Clarendon
Edition (72). See Patten (195) for information about the
reception and sales of this edition.

42. ————. *The Personal History of David Copperfield.* The
     Charles Dickens Edition. London: Chapman and Hall, 1867.
     553 pp.

Has frontispiece engraving of J. Watkins's photograph of
Dickens and includes eight of the original forty illustrations. In the prospectus for this set of Dickens's works
the publisher announced its object to be "Legibility,
Durability, Beauty and Cheapness." *Copperfield* was projected as the seventh volume, and it was priced at three
shillings and sixpence. Dickens provided descriptive head-
lines for the right-hand pages, and these will be listed
in the forthcoming Clarendon Edition (72). The prospectus
stated that Ticknor and Fields was Dickens's authorized
American publisher for this edition (Ticknor and Fields
published it in 1867 with illustrations by S. Eytynge).
The preface to the Charles Dickens Edition incorporates
much of the 1850 preface but deletes its final paragraph
and adds: "So true are these avowals at the present day,
that I can now only take the reader into one confidence
more. Of all my books, I like this the best. It will be
easily believed that I am a fond parent to every child of
my fancy, and that no one can ever love that family as
dearly as I love them. But, like many fond parents, I have
in my heart of hearts a favourite child. And his name is
DAVID COPPERFIELD."

SUBSEQUENT EDITIONS
CONTAINING NEW INTRODUCTORY OR TEXTUAL MATTER

43. Dickens, Charles. *The Personal History of David Copperfield.*
     2 vols. (xiv-xv of the New Illustrated Library Edition).
     New York: Hurd and Houghton, 1877.

     Introduction by Edwin P. Whipple (529).

44. ————. *The Personal History of David Copperfield the Younger*. London: Macmillan, 1892. xxv + 819 pp.

    Introduction by Charles Dickens the Younger (283). Reprinted a number of times in England and America.

45. ————. *The Personal History of David Copperfield*. 2 vols. (14-15 of the Gadshill Edition). London: Chapman and Hall, 1897.

    Introduction and notes by Andrew Lang (381). Includes the original illustrations. This is a reasonably reliable text used often by critics before the New Oxford Illustrated Dickens Edition appeared in 1948 (60).

46. ————. *The Personal History, Adventures, Experience & Observation of David Copperfield The Younger of Blunderstone Rookery (Which He never meant to be Published on any Account)*. London: Gresham Publishing, [1900]. xiii + 591 pp.

    Introduction by William K. Leask (745).

47. ————. *David Copperfield*. 3 vols. (4-6 of the Autograph Edition, a limited edition). London: George Sproul, 1903.

    Introduction by George Gissing (323), bibliographical note by F.G. Kitton, and frontispiece and illustrations by Henry M. Brock.

48. ————. *The Personal History and Experience of David Copperfield the Younger*. School Edition. London: Adam and Charles Black, 1903. xxiv + 889 pp.

    Introduction and notes by A.A. Barter (219).

49. ————. *The Personal History of David Copperfield*. Vol. 12 of Biographical Edition. London: Chapman and Hall, 1903. xxiv + 695 pp.

    Introduction by Arthur Waugh (765).

50. ————. *The Personal History of David Copperfield*. Everyman Edition. London: J.M. Dent, 1907. xx + 822 pp.

    Introduction by G.K. Chesterton (255). Republished several times as the Popular Edition without the introduction.

51. ————. *The Personal History and Experience of David Copperfield the Younger*. Boston: Ginn and Company, [1910]. xxxvii + 906 pp.

    Introduction and notes by Philo M. Buck, Jr. (238).

52.   ————. *The Personal History and Experience of David
       Copperfield the Younger.* 2 vols. New York: Macmillan,
       1911.

       Introduction and notes by Edwin Fairley (297).

53.   ————. *David Copperfield.* 2 vols. (3-4 of Waverly Edi-
       tion). London: The Waverly Book Company, 1912.

       Introduction by Hall Caine (243). Reissued as the Metro-
       Goldwyn-Mayer Edition in a single volume in 1935 with plates
       from the MGM film (122).

54.   ————. *The Personal History of David Copperfield.* Oxford:
       The Clarendon Press, 1916. viii + 1036 pp.

       Introduction by E. Kibblewhite (371). Includes the orig-
       inal illustrations.

55.   ————. *The Personal History of David Copperfield. With
       Critical Appreciations Old and New.* Edited by G.K. Ches-
       terton, Holbrook Jackson, R. Brimley Johnson. Readers'
       Classic Edition. Bath: Cedric Chivers, 1919. 823 pp.

       This edition has a large collection of introductory
       materials. See the "Criticism" section for the annotations
       of the appreciations written especially for this edition
       by William Archer (211), Jules Claretie (258), Theodor
       de Wyzewa (282), Ford Madox Hueffer (348), Holbrook Jack-
       son (352), Émile Legouis (387), Alice Meynell (417). Lo-
       cated in various sections of this bibliography are the
       listings (and annotations) of the original sources of the
       materials excerpted for this edition from previously pub-
       lished materials by Charles Kent (80), David Masson (180),
       Matthew Arnold (185), H.A. Taine (199), Hall Caine (243),
       G.K. Chesterton (253), George Gissing (321), Frederic
       Harrison (339), William Dean Howells (347), Andrew Lang
       (381), G.H. Lewes (389), A.C. Swinburne (501), Sir Adolphus
       William Ward (522), Jerome K. Jerome (562), Edwin Pugh
       (638), John Forster (730), Sir Frank Thomas Marzials (750).
       It has not been possible to locate the original sources
       of other comments reprinted in this edition, and these
       comments are listed and annotated in the "Criticism" sec-
       tion: Ferdinand Brunetière (237), R. du Pontavice (289),
       Anatole France (309), Émile Hennequin (341), Dr. Julian
       Schmidt (475). The comments by Amédée Pichot and Anne
       Thackeray Ritchie are too brief and repetitive of other
       comments to merit separate listing in this bibliography.

56. ——. *David Copperfield*. 2 vols. The Modern Readers' Series. New York: Macmillan, 1928.

Introduction by Allan Nevins (436).

57. ——. *David Copperfield*. Condensed by Robert Graves. New York: Harcourt, Brace and Company, 1934. xxxi + 490 pp.

American version of Graves's abridgment, *The Real David Copperfield* (167).

58. ——. *David Copperfield*. New York: Dodd, Mead and Company, 1943. 850 pp.

Introduction by May L. Becker (548).

59. ——. *Charles Dickens' David Copperfield*. Ed. W. Somerset Maugham. Philadelphia: John C. Winston, [1948]. xxiv + 423 pp.

Introduction by Maugham (414).

60. ——. *The Personal History of David Copperfield*. New Oxford Illustrated Dickens Edition. London: Oxford Univ. Press, 1948. xix + 877 pp.

Introduction by R.H. Malden (400). Includes original plates. This has been a frequently reprinted standard hard-cover text but will be superseded by the Clarendon Edition (72).

61. ——. *The Personal History, Adventures, Experience & Observation of David Copperfield the Younger of Blunderstone Rookery (Which He never meant to be Published on any Account)*. Modern Library Edition. New York: Random House, 1950. xv + 923 pp.

Introduction by E.K. Brown (234). Includes brief bibliography, Dickens's final version of the preface, and the original illustrations. This is a popular classroom edition, frequently reprinted as a paperback.

62. ——. *David Copperfield*. Collins' Classic Edition. London: Collins, 1952. 798 pp.

Introduction by Norman Collins (261).

63. ——. *David Copperfield*. Ed. George H. Ford. Riverside Edition. Boston: Houghton Mifflin, 1958. xx + 678 pp.

Introduction (306), textual and bibliographical note,
sketch of Dickens's early life, facsimile of monthly parts
cover, Dickens's final preface. Ford's is the first edition
to return the passages cut by Dickens from the proof sheets,
placing them in an appendix. Ford notes that Dickens himself never chose to put these passages back in his novel
and thinks it not appropriate for a modern editor to re-
incorporate them into the novel (as the Signet Edition
did later). Ford fully describes the serial publication
format and uses the Charles Dickens Edition (42) as his
copy text. With large, clear print but no illustrations,
this has been a popular classroom edition.

64.   ———. *David Copperfield.* New York: Pocket Books, 1958.
      xvii + 845 pp.

Introduction by Joseph Mersand (416). No illustrations,
but includes brief bibliography and Dickens's preface to
the Charles Dickens Edition, presumably the copy text for
this edition (42). A random comparison with other paperback editions shows more corruption (especially in accidentals) in this edition.

65.   ———. *The Personal History, Adventures, Experience &*
      Observation of David Copperfield The Younger of Blunder-
      stone Rookery (Which He never meant to be Published on
      any Account). Ed. Edmund Fuller. Authoritative Modern
      Abridgment. New York: Dell, 1958. 416 pp.

Brief editor's note explains that the purpose of abridgment is to bring the novel "within the possible limits
of a low-priced, mass-market edition." Fuller thinks the
long wrap-up of the Victorian ending and the many "orgies
of sentimental detail, embellishment, and digression are
not palatable in our time." Therefore, he cuts the book
to forty-seven chapters, but he retains the original first
fifteen chapter divisions. Unlike Robert Graves (167), he
does not adjust plot or characterization, and he works
to maintain the flavor of Dickens's language. One of the
most notable cuts is his elimination of most of the "Retrospect" material.

66.   ———. *David Copperfield.* Macmillan's Classics. New
      York: Macmillan, 1962. 850 pp.

Afterword by Clifton Fadiman (296).

67.   ———. *The Personal History, Adventures, Experience &*
      Observation of David Copperfield The Younger of Blunder-

stone Rookery (Which He never meant to be Published on any Account). Signet Edition. New York: New American Library, 1962. 880 pp.

Afterword by Edgar Johnson (356). The first edition to restore to the text the passages Dickens deleted in proof. The 1958 Riverside Edition (63) included these passages in an appendix, but this Signet Edition designates them by brackets at their proper places in the text. Asterisks before the appropriate chapter numbers indicate the original monthly part divisions. This popular paperback text includes Dickens's final preface but contains no illustrations. Johnson adds a selected bibliography of Dickens's other writings and of biography and criticism.

68. ———. *David Copperfield.* New York: Airmont, 1965. 734 pp.

Text apparently based on the Charles Dickens Edition (42) because it includes Dickens's preface to that edition. This paperback gives no evidence of editorial collation or emendation, no illustrations, no indication of monthly part divisions. The typeface is small and of poor quality. There is a brief introduction by Mary M. Threapleton (507).

69. ———. *The Personal History of David Copperfield.* Ed. Trevor Blount. Penguin Edition. Harmondsworth: Penguin Books, 1966. 957 pp.

Paperback based on the 1850 single-volume edition (38) and collated with the Charles Dickens Edition (42) with slight modification of accidentals according to Penguin's style. Roman numerals in the table of contents and asterisks in the text indicate the monthly part divisions. This edition contains twenty-three of the original forty illustrations, a brief biographical note, extensive critical introduction, a note on the text, a short bibliography, and notes (some drawn from T.W. Hill, 623). Blount provides interesting supplemental information in the notes (for instance, a listing of the popular songs mentioned in the novel). The jacket illustration uses a detail from E.R. Smyth's "Yarmouth Jetty." The frontispiece has a facsimile of the serial parts cover, and a facsimile of the 1850 edition's title page follows the editor's introduction. Blount's critical introduction is excellent (228).

70. ———. *David Copperfield.* London: Pan Books, 1967. xviii + 874 pp.

Introduction and notes by Arthur Calder-Marshall (245).
This paperback has some of the original illustrations,
Dickens's final preface, a list of Dickens's other works,
and brief suggestions for further reading. Calder-Marshall
designates the serial divisions by placing the appropriate
arabic numbers above the chapter headings which began the
monthly parts. His notes are principally textual glosses,
providing useful information about unfamiliar terms and
identifying various literary and topographical allusions.

71. ———. *David Copperfield*. 2 vols. Ultratype Edition.
     London: Franklin Watts, 1971.

     Introduction by Angus Wilson (533).

72. ———. *David Copperfield*. Ed. Nina Burgis. Clarendon
     Edition. Oxford: The Clarendon Press, [1981]. 864 pp.

     Scheduled for 1981 publication, this will be the defini-
     tive edition. The copy text is the first edition in monthly
     parts and the 1850 single-volume edition, collated with
     manuscript, proofs, Cheap (40), Library (41), and Charles
     Dickens Edition (42). Burgis notes that for the first
     number only there are variations in the Wiley and Putnam,
     New York, parts edition (39). Burgis's appendices provide
     number plans, trial titles, and the running heads from the
     Charles Dickens Edition. As do other Clarendon editors of
     Dickens's novels, Burgis devotes her introduction to a
     discussion of the novel's composition and publication and
     to a description of the text, including samples of errors
     corrected from the manuscript.

DICKENS'S READING ADAPTATIONS

73. Clemens, Samuel L. *The Autobiography of Mark Twain*. Ed.
     Charles Neider. New York: Harper and Brothers, 1959.
     175 pp.

     Speaks of attending a Dickens reading in 1867. Clemens
     reports that Dickens read with great animation; "he did
     not merely read but also acted. His reading of the storm
     scene in which Steerforth lost his life was so vivid and
     so full of energetic action that his house was carried
     off its feet, so to speak."

74. Collins, Philip. "Dickens' Public Readings: Texts and
     Performances." *DSA*, 3 (1974), 182-197.

Cites the *David Copperfield* reading as an example of how
Dickens devised and shaped his scripts. Collins observes
that many admirers thought it Dickens's most impressive
reading, especially the concluding storm scene. Collins
expands much of this article in the introduction to his
edition of the readings (78).

75. "The Contemporary Manchester Press on Dickens's Visits."
     Dickensian, 34 (1938), 141-142.

Reprints a *Guardian* review of Dickens's 1861 reading
of *Copperfield*. The reviewer had regretted Dickens's
compression of the novel for the reading and wished there
were more sunshine than the dark ending scene provided.

76. Dickens, Charles. "David Copperfield." In *The Readings
     of Mr. Charles Dickens: As Condensed by Himself*. Boston:
     Ticknor and Fields, 1868. 59 pp.

Includes Dickens's statement that "the edition bearing
the imprint of Messrs. Ticknor and Fields is the only
correct and authorized edition of my Readings." For further
details about this reading, see Collins (78).

77. ————. *David Copperfield. A Reading, in Five Chapters,
     by Charles Dickens. With a Note on the Romantic History
     of Charles Dickens and Maria Beadnell*. Ed. John H. Stone-
     house. London: Henry Sotheran, 1921. xvi + 104 pp.

This edition is reprinted from the privately printed
edition of 1868 (76) and publishes a facsimile of the original five-chapter version (see Collins, 78). Stonehouse's
introduction has nothing to do with the reading but concentrates instead on Dickens's early letters to Maria
Beadnell, in which Dickens asked her to reconsider her
rejection of him. Stonehouse thinks these letters account
for Dickens's inability years later to continue his autobiography beyond the point of Maria's rejection. It is
impossible to judge Stonehouse absolutely wrong in this
speculation, but as more complete biographical study shows,
a number of factors affected Dickens's termination of the
autobiography. See, in particular, Patten (444).

78. ————. "*David Copperfield*." In *Charles Dickens: The
     Public Readings*. Ed. Philip Collins. Oxford: The Claren-
     don Press, 1975, pp. 213-248.

The definitive edition of Dickens's *Copperfield* reading
text. Collins's informative introductory matter quotes
Dickens's 1861 letter stating the difficulties he had in

making a continuous reading text from *David Copperfield*.
This was a problem obviously shared by many of the stage
adaptors. Collins discusses many aspects of Dickens as
reader of his own works and should be consulted by anyone
needing information on the general subject. He notes the
Copperfield reading as Dickens's favorite and cites many
contemporary responses and subsequent memories of it. He
observes that this reading, first done as a two-hour performance ranging over much of the novel, was more ambitious
in scope than Dickens's readings from other novels. Collins
clarifies the reading's content, which had been published
earlier by Ticknor and Fields (76). He outlines the reading's six chapters: (1) Childhood memories of the Peggotty
family evoked by David's and Steerforth's visit to their
house; (2) David's visit to the Peggottys on the night of
Em'ly's elopement; (3) David's love for Dora and the
dinner he gave for Traddles and the Micawbers; (4) Mr.
Peggotty's tale of his quest for Em'ly; (5) David's courtship and marriage to Dora; (6) The great storm and the
discovery of Em'ly. For Dickens's own summary of the reading see Tomlin (81). Collins notes that Dickens first gave
this reading on 28 October 1861 and over the years repeated
it seventy times.

79. Fitzsimons, Raymund. *The Charles Dickens Show: An Account
     of the Public Readings 1858-1870*. London: Geoffrey Blis,
     1970, pp. 76-78, 171-172. Published in America as *Garish
     Lights: The Public Reading Tours of Charles Dickens*.
     Philadelphia: J.B. Lippincott, 1970.

     Briefly summarizes the content of the *Copperfield* read-
     ing and acknowledges its great popularity. Fitzsimons
     speculates that the force which drove Dickens through the
     strenuous reading tours is evident also in his portrayal
     of David's will to succeed. Also Fitzsimons notes signs
     of Steerforth's recklessness in Dickens's determination
     to carry on even in poor health.

80. Kent, Charles. "*David Copperfield*." In *Dickens as Reader*.
     London: Chapman and Hall, 1872, pp. 120-130.

     Describes the content of Dickens's *Copperfield* reading
     and calls it one of the most impressive Dickens delivered.
     Kent also cites Dickens's private mid-1860's comment that
     David Copperfield was "incomparably" his best book. Kent
     resents the necessary cuts from novel to reading version
     and discusses some of the condensation of details. He notes
     that although the reading evoked much laughter its most

striking effect came in the tragic storm scene. As Kent recalls, Dickens's dramatic reading of the storm "was more than an elocutionary triumph—it was the realisation ... of a convulsion of nature when nature bears an aspect the grandest and the most astounding." See also Collins (78).

81. Tomlin, E.W.F. "Newly Discovered Dickens Letters." *TLS*, 22 Feb. 1974, pp. 183-185.

Among some newly discovered Dickens letters Tomlin locates a handwritten summary of a six-chapter reading version of *David Copperfield*. Tomlin thinks that although the letter's date is uncertain, the summary may be of the reading version Dickens wanted to produce as early as 1855. This is the only known instance of a summary of a Dickens reading in Dickens's own hand. See also Collins (78), who acknowledges the importance of Tomlin's discovery.

82 Williams, Emlyn. "Some Youthful Reminiscences from the Personal History of David Copperfield." In *Readings from Dickens*. London: William Heinemann, 1954, pp. 53-63.

Williams does not use Dickens's own reading version (see Collins, 78) but rather makes his own two-part selection from David's Canterbury schooldays and from David's and Steerforth's encounter with Miss Mowcher.

STAGE ADAPTATIONS

CHRONOLOGICAL LISTING

83. Almar, George. *Born With a Caul; or, The Personal Adventures of David Copperfield*. Strand Theatre, London. 29 Oct. 1850.

Appearing before the novel's serial run was completed, this play centers on Steerforth and Em'ly, with Steerforth rescued from the sea to marry her. Morley (118) called it a loosely contrived work; he mentions a character not in Dickens's novel, one "Hurricane Flash," who in the play kills Mr. Murdstone. Fulkerson (114) gives a detailed summary of the content and calls it "an outlandish play." See Taverner (200).

84. Rivers, H. (or possibly J. Courtney). *David Copperfield the Younger of Blunderstone Rookery*. Surrey Theatre, London. 13 Nov. 1850.

Morley (118) attributes this version to H. Rivers;
Fulkerson (114) names Courtney; and Nicoll (116) does not
indicate an author but dates the first performance as 11
November 1850. Appearing the same month as the novel's
serial run finished, the adaptation was a series of tab-
leaux. According to Morley, it had a run of only ten per-
formances.

85. Stevens, Mrs. H.N. *David Copperfield*. Harvard Atheneum,
    Cambridge, Mass. 27 Nov. 1850.

    Morley (118) notes the performance of John Gilbert as
    Micawber.

86. Brougham, John. *David Copperfield. A Drama in Two Acts*.
    New York: Samuel French, n.d. 24 pp. Also published as
    David Copperfield: A Drama in Three Acts. London: John
    Dicks, n.d. 24 pp.

    Both versions are three-act plays; the title page of
    the New York edition is inaccurate. The play was performed
    first at Brougham's Lyceum in New York on 6 January 1851,
    but there may have been a variant earlier performance at
    Barnum's Museum in Philadelphia on 6 November 1850 (see
    Morley, 118). The play begins with Betsey's and Mr. Dick's
    decision that it is time to do something for David, who
    is just leaving the Wickfield house, where Uriah Heep is
    gaining power. The play includes both the Micawber-Heep-
    Wickfield and Steerforth-Em'ly stories but omits the child-
    hood of David and also the character Dora. Morley notes
    that Brougham's play appeared in opposition to W.K. North-
    all's *David Copperfield*, which opened at Burton's Theatre
    in New York on 30 December 1850. It may, therefore, be
    Northall's play that Fawcett (111) mistakenly attributes
    as Brougham's in 1851. Yet another American version with
    the *David Copperfield* title had a one-week run at New York's
    Bowery Theatre, opening the same night as Brougham's play.
    Before Halliday's adaptation (90), Brougham's is the only
    version Charles Dickens the Younger mentions as having
    "any importance." (283)

87. *Little Em'ly*. Marylebone Theatre, London. 1858.

    Listed only by Fawcett (111).

88. Burnand, F.C. *The Deal Boatman. A Serio-Comic Drama in
    Two Acts*. London: Thomas Hailes Lacy, [1864]. 34 pp.

    First performed at Drury Lane, London, on 21 September
    1863. Set in 1748 and using the outline of the Little

Em'ly story, this play concerns the elopement of Mary, adopted daughter of Boatman Jacob Vance, with Edward Leslie, nephew of the wealthy Sir John Houghton. On the eve of the date set for her marriage to Matt Bramble, a pilot's apprentice, Mary runs off with Edward, and her uncle swears vengeance, cursing the gentleman "that talked and laughed and was hearty with me, and robbed me of the treasure of my life." This line, especially, points up the similarity of Vance and Daniel Peggotty, who in *Copperfield* expresses much the same sentiment about Steerforth. The play's second act brings a complete reversal. Mary turns out to be Sir John's daughter, and he blesses her marriage to Edward. Jacob Vance finally approves the union also. Describing himself as a "rough-and-ready sort," he says he is delighted to kiss "a real born lady." Fulkerson (114) cites this play as an example of how an adaptation may circumvent the problem of presenting David as a changing and reflective character--simply by omitting him as Burnand does from *The Deal Boatman*. See Taverner (200).

89. Rowe, George F. *David Copperfield*. The Olympic Theater, New York. 21 May 1866.

Because Rowe played Micawber, a role he repeated in other adaptations, this version probably centers on the Micawber story.

90. Halliday, Andrew. *Little Em'ly (David Copperfield). A Drama, in Four Acts*. New York: DeWitt, n.d. 44 pp.

First performed at the Olympic Theatre, London, on 8 October 1869. This popular version is noteworthy because Halliday had consulted Dickens about the adaptation. In a letter to Halliday dated 2 January 1869 Dickens says he had gone over Halliday's notes and found "the usual difficulties in the endeavour to put so long a story in so short a space." Dickens would have liked Halliday to end the play on the Yarmouth beach, getting in what he wanted of Rosa Dartle and Em'ly before that scene. Dickens further noted that it was most important to Mr. Peggotty's character that Halliday should show Peggotty "merciful with, and sorry for, Martha; and that he should never bully her." The printed version of the play contains a lengthy synopsis. Like Brougham in an earlier adaptation (86), Halliday includes a large number of characters and incidents. Although he did not exactly follow Dickens's advice about the ending, he did follow it concerning his portrayal of Mr. Peggotty. Charles Dickens the Younger termed this "a remarkably good adaptation" (283). T.E.

Pemberton objects that the play does not have David present
as a mind reflecting on and coloring the whole, although
Pemberton notes he is present "on the boards, in a strange
coat and gilt buttons" (120). Fulkerson comments that despite some defects, Halliday's play proves that "subplots, tense scenes, and fascinating characters ... could
be divorced from their context" of the massive novel (114).
Halliday's success stimulated a number of the subsequent
Little Em'ly plays (see Morley, 118). The *Illustrated
London News* (4 December 1869, p. 561) published a plate of
a scene from the play that depicts the downfall of Heep,
and the caption remarks that "of the novelties of the
season perhaps the present drama of 'Little Em'ly' is the
most successful."

91. *David Copperfield*. Grecian Theatre, London. 3 Oct. 1870.

    Mentioned by Pemberton (120) and by Morley (118), who
    describe it as a two-act American version, but neither
    commentator provides further details.

92. Brooke, E.H. *Little Em'ly's Trials*. Sadler's Wells, London.
    4 March 1871.

    Mentioned by Nicoll (116), who cites no author; listed
    by Pierce (121), who thinks it the work of Brooke.

93. Wood, Murray. *Lost Emily*. Surrey Theatre, London. 8 March
    1873.

    Mentioned by Morley (118).

94. Hamilton, George. *Em'ly*. Albion Theatre, London. 30 April
    1877.

    Mentioned by Morley (118).

95. Collette, Charles. *Micawber*. Imperial Theatre, London.
    May 1881.

    Listed by Pierce (121) as a comic drama in five scenes.
    Morley (118) describes it as a one-act rearrangement of
    Halliday's *Little Em'ly* (90) and dates the first perfor-
    mance as 6 June 1881.

96. Warren, T. Gideon, and Ben Landeck. *Em'ly*. Adelphi Theatre,
    London. 1 Aug. 1903.

    Mentioned by Morley (118) and Pemberton (120); a four-
    act play which had a brief run.

97. Jackson, Harry. *Hearts of Gold*. St. Paul, Minnesota: n.p., 1903.

    Listed by Pierce (121).

98. ————. *What Women Will Do*. St. Paul, Minnesota: n.p., 1903.

    Listed by Pierce (121). According to the Lincoln, Nebraska, *Daily Star*, this was a melodrama that appropriated the story of Em'ly, Steerforth, and Daniel Peggotty from Dickens's novel. The newspaper account has strong praise for the great dramatic situation of two women, "Rosa Dottle and Emely [sic]."

99. Chambers, H. Kellett. *Dan'l Peggotty*. King's Theatre, Hammersmith (London). 11 March 1907.

    Mentioned by Morley (118).

100. Caruthers, Lillian A. *Mr. Peggotty; or, Little Em'ly*. Toronto: n.p., 1908.

    Described by Pierce (121) as a play in four acts.

101. Harry, Frederick T. *Little Em'ly*. Cripplegate, London. 15 Feb. 1909.

    Gilbert Thomas reviews this production in the *Dickensian*, 4 (1909), 74-76. The review gives a detailed summary and says that the play "came far short of being representative either of the infinite variety of Dickens or even of the particular book in question."

102. Holland, Mildred. *David Copperfield*. New York: n.p., 1909.

    Mentioned by Pierce (121).

103. Friend, A.R., and M.H. Mueller. *David Copperfield*. Milwaukee: n.p., 1910.

    Described by Pierce (121) as a five-act play.

104. Wood, Metcalf. *Wilkins Micawber*. Empire Music Hall, London. 27 Nov. 1911.

    Mentioned by Morley (118).

105. Parker, Louis. *The Highway of Life*. Wallack's Theater, New York. 26 Oct. 1914.

After failing in New York, this large-scale adaptation played in London as *David Copperfield* at His Majesty's Theatre beginning 24 December 1914. See B.W. Matz's review in the *Dickensian* (117). A special reprint of the Chapman and Hall Popular Edition of *David Copperfield* in 1915 was designated as "His Majesty's Theatre Edition" and includes a number of photographs of the London cast.

106. Evelyn, Walter F., pseud. [Walter Dexter, A. Evelyn Brookes-Cross, and Frederick T. Harry]. *David Copperfield*. Played in Birmingham in February 1922 and then toured other cities, appearing in London at the Lyceum on 6 June 1923.

The typescript of this three-act version is available at the Dickens House, London. The play centers on the Steerforth-Em'ly story. It follows the novel closely and ends with David and Agnes deciding to marry and the Miccawbers preparing to emigrate.

107. Linda, William. *David Copperfield: A Dramatization of Charles Dickens' Favorite Novel*. Minneapolis: The Northwestern Press, 1935. 128 pp.

Production notes and advertising hints are included in this reading version of Linda's play. In "A Letter from the Author of the Play" Linda claims that his purpose is to turn the novel "into a play that would be easy for amateurs to produce." He designs his three-act adaptation for a cast of six men and seven women and concentrates entirely upon the Murdstone, Trotwood, Heep, and Wickfield stories, with Clara Peggotty, Mr. Dick, and Mr. and Mrs. Micawber having large roles. Linda makes some curious changes of character roles to facilitate his plot streamlining. He makes Micawber an old acquaintance of Murdstone, exaggerates Betsey Trotwood's wealth, and brings Uriah Heep into the action early.

108. Ravold, John. *David Copperfield. A Play in Three Acts*. New York: Samuel French, 1935. 108 pp.

The preface claims that "no essential element of this glamorous story has been omitted and many of them have materially gained through theatrical compression." But the play does omit Steerforth, Little Em'ly, and Mr. Peggotty while retaining lesser figures such as Jack Maldon and the Strongs. Staged as a novel in the process of its own completion, the play begins with David's return to the Wickfield home as a successful writer at work on his autobiography. He tells Agnes he is not certain how it

will end. Then begin a series of flashbacks, starting with
David's birth. Breaking back to the present for transition
between the first act's nine scenes, the story carries
forward through the arrival of the Murdstones, David's
mother's death, his meeting with the Micawbers, and his
flight to Dover. The second act introduces Uriah Heep,
the Strongs, and Dora. The final act opens with an ailing
Dora, who gives some secret advice to Agnes and then dies.
Micawber exposes Heep, and the play concludes back in the
present with Agnes revealing that Dora has asked her to
look after David. Learning this, David is able to complete
his story. Despite the lack of the Steerforth-Little Em'ly
complication, this is one of the more comprehensive stage
versions. It does not depend entirely on Micawber for its
effect; it controls the melodramatic and sentimental parts
of the story; and it presents a credible, if not introspective, adult David.

109. Bruce, Edgar K. *Meet Mr. Micawber*. Rudolf Steiner Hall,
     London. 13 Nov. 1945.

     Mentioned by Morley (118). Bruce played Micawber.

110. Williams, Guy R. *David Copperfield*. London: Macmillan,
     1971.

     Reviewed in the *Dickensian*, 67 (1971), 178.

COMMENTARY

111. Fawcett, F. Dubrez. *Dickens the Dramatist: On Stage,
     Screen, and Radio*. London: W.H. Allen, 1952. 278 pp.

     Describes many aspects of the adaptations of Dickens's
     works and discusses Dickens as actor and public reader.
     Appendix A lists numerous adaptations. Fawcett's book
     gives a more popular than scholarly account of Dickensian
     dramatizations and does not have separate, detailed dis-
     cussion of *David Copperfield*.

112. Fitz-Gerald, S.J. Adair. *"David Copperfield."* In *Dickens
     and the Drama*. London: Chapman and Hall, 1910, pp. 232-
     245.

     Mentions two major subjects for adaptation--the Micawber
     incidents and the "pathetically domestic, with Little
     Em'ly and the rugged Peggotty as a striking background."
     Although Fitz-Gerald cites a number of the better-known
     stage versions of *Copperfield*, he does not discuss many of
     them in detail. For a more complete study see Morley (118).

113. ———. "*David Copperfield* on the Stage." *Dickensian*,
      10 (1914), 228-234.

      Mentions a number of productions and classifies them
      according to their focus on the Micawber incidents or on
      what he considers the "pathetically domestic" material
      of Little Em'ly and the Peggottys.

114. Fulkerson, Richard. "*David Copperfield* in the Victorian
      Theatre." *Victorians Institute Journal*, 5 (1976), 29-36.

      Detailed discussion of the Almar (83), Courtney (84),
      Burnand (88), and Halliday (90) adaptations. Fulkerson
      talks about why the novel was difficult to adapt, and he
      thinks much more distortion was required to bring it to
      the stage than had been necessary with Dickens's earlier
      works. Fulkerson's principal point is that as a *Bildungs-
      roman* and as a first-person narrative, the novel required
      a more interpretative dramatization than the popular con-
      ventions of nineteenth-century theater permitted. He con-
      cludes that because of this limitation, the Victorian
      dramatic adaptations of *David Copperfield* did not portray
      David as a major character.

115. Lazenby, Walter S., Jr. "Stage Versions of Dickens's Novels
      in America to 1900." *DA*, 23 (1962), 2250 (Indiana, 1962).

      Notes that by 1848 Americans were producing their own
      adaptations of Dickens's novels and that *Oliver Twist* and
      David Copperfield were the most popular when brought to
      the stage. Lazenby credits John Brougham (86) with develop-
      ing the new technique of blending comedy and melodrama.

116. Nicoll, Allardyce. *A History of English Drama, 1660-1900*.
      A Hand List of Plays. Cambridge: Cambridge Univ. Press,
      1959, vol. 5, pp. 80-81.

      Useful discussion concerning the effect in the nineteenth
      century of a developing novelistic art on the theater.
      Nicoll grants the generally poor quality of *Copperfield*
      plays but observes that "contemporary fiction was develop-
      ing a style different from that of the early nineteenth
      century. Love of incident and grotesque characterization
      had appealed in the past; now a deeper psychological note
      and a franker treatment of intimate domestic life became
      the fashion. How much the imitation of this on stage con-
      tributed to the development of the characteristic problem-
      play may readily be realised." Nicoll's hand list of plays
      includes only a few of the many *Copperfield* adaptations.

117. M[atz], B.W. "The New *David Copperfield* Play." *Dickensian*, 11 (1915), 16-17.

     Finds the Louis N. Parker adaptation (105) a propitious diversion from depressing wartime conditions. Matz remarks that the play has a "real Dickens atmosphere, and the real Dickens creations." He thinks it should drive playgoers to read the book. Matz does regret Micawber's return from Australia in the play as the only serious distortion of the book.

118. Morley, Malcolm. "Stage Appearances of *Copperfield*." *Dickensian*, 49 (1953), 77-85.

     The most authoritative discussion of the subject. According to Morley, after *Oliver Twist* and *The Cricket on the Hearth*, *David Copperfield* is the most frequently dramatized Dickens work. Morley describes many of the early stage appearances in England and America, providing many details about casts and reception. It is evident that Morley, a student and collector of plays, has read nearly all of the surviving scripts.

119. "A New *David Copperfield* Play: Bransby Williams as Actor-Manager." *Dickensian*, 18 (1922), 75-77.

     Lauds Williams's performances in the touring company of *David Copperfield*, a play written by Walter F. Evelyn and in which Williams played both Mr. Micawber and Daniel Peggotty (106).

120. Pemberton, T. Edgar. *Charles Dickens and the Stage*. London: George Redway, 1888. 260 pp.

     A source for many of the later, more complete discussions of Dickens on stage. Pemberton has strong praise for Rowe's Micawber in the Halliday adaptation (90) and provides a long list of the various adaptations of the Little Em'ly story.

121. Pierce, Dorothy. "*David Copperfield*." *Bulletin of Bibliography and Dramatic Index*, 16 (May-Aug. 1937), 52.

     Lists twenty-two adaptations between 1850 and 1935; there is some disparity of dates for plays that are also listed by Nicoll (116) and Morley (118), but Pierce includes a few American adaptations not listed elsewhere.

FILM ADAPTATIONS

122. Zambrano, Ana L. "Feature Motion Pictures Adapted from
      Dickens: A Checklist--Part I." *DSN*, 5 (1974), 108.

      Brief descriptions of seven film versions of *Copperfield*
      including: (1) The 1911 Vitagraph (USA), a three-reel
      black and white silent film; (2) The 1912 Pathé (French),
      a black and white silent film; (3) The 1912 Frank Powell
      (England), also in black and white and silent; (4) The
      1913 Hepworth (England), a six-reel black and white silent
      film; (5) The 1922 Nordisk (Denmark), a seven-reel, black
      and white silent film; (6) The award-winning 1935 MGM
      (USA), a sound film in black and white with a running time
      of 133 minutes; (7) The 1970 Omnibus (USA), in color with
      a running time of 118 minutes. This most recent film was
      presented on television in the United States and was re-
      leased as a feature film in Europe.

123. A.E.B.C. "*David Copperfield* on the Screen." *Dickensian*,
      31 (1935), 223-225.

      Finds the MGM film (122) faithfully reproducing the most
      salient narrative features and recreating the period at-
      mosphere. This reviewer expresses some uncertainty whether
      W.C. Fields plays Micawber or Micawber plays Fields, but
      even with a few distortions of character, Fields is a
      comic success.

124. Curry, George. *Copperfield '70: The Story of the Making
      of the Omnibus-20th Century-Fox Film David Copperfield*.
      New York: Ballantine Books, 1970. 210 pp.

      An exceptionally complete account of the conception and
      development of this production. Curry also publishes the
      complete script. Curry's work should interest students
      of literature as well as of cinema because of his accounts
      of key adaptation decisions. He discusses the impossi-
      bility of crowding the novel's full vision of life on
      the screen but notes that the film writers produced a
      shooting script full of character and incident that re-
      mained literate in atmosphere and dialogue. Highly cine-
      matic in handling transitions from present to past, the
      film centered on a subject relevant to the 1970 audience--
      David's adult efforts to come to terms with himself. The
      adaptors justify their stress of this theme by the novel's
      mention of David's regret for past errors (especially in
      Chapter 58, "Absence"). Curry gives an interesting account

of the script development, which restored many significant details and bits of dialogue to suit the many famous actors (Ralph Richardson, Dame Edith Evans, Susan Hampshire, Laurence Olivier). Curry notes that the filmmakers' concern for authenticity extended even to the design of the Peggotty house, for the film follows the text in showing it hull down, not upside-down as in Phiz's illustration. This paperback book is out of print and is not available in many libraries.

125. "David Copperfield." *Films and Filming*, 16 (Feb. 1970), 32-33.

   Pictorial review of the 1970 film version.

126. "*David Copperfield* on the Cinematograph." *Dickensian*, 9 (1913), 268.

   Brief review of the Hepworth adaptation (122), praising it for following the story and for using the actual places of the book's setting.

127. Deschner, Donald. "David Copperfield." In *The Films of W.C. Fields*. New York: The Citadel Press, 1966, pp. 106-111.

   Deschner's well-illustrated article on the 1935 film (122) contains synopsis, cast, credits, and excerpts from reviews in the *Nation*, the *Literary Digest*, *Commonweal*, and the *London Mercury*. The reviews take some exception to Fields's poor enunciation and his difficulty with "Micawber's rolling periods" and offer some speculation about how successful Charles Laughton, who was offered the part, might have been.

128. Estabrook, Howard. *Metro-Goldwyn-Mayer Presents Charles Dickens' David Copperfield*. [Hollywood, 1934].

   Estabrook's screenplay of Hugh Walpole's adaptation is available only at the Library of Congress.

129. "The Love Stories of David Copperfield." *Dickensian*, 20 (1924), 175.

   Reports a 9 July 1924 screening of a film, "The Love Stories of David Copperfield," and comments, "To anyone not an ardent student of Dickens's works, this would probably have proved an agreeable and pleasing entertainment." According to the reviewer the film makes many distortions of the text.

130. Powell, Dilys. "Postscript: Dickens on Film." *Dickensian*,
      66 (1970), 183-185.

      Regrets the fragmentation that comes when stage plays
      compress the expansive Dickens novels. Powell prefers
      the 1935 MGM film of *Copperfield* (122) to plays because
      it captures more of the novel's original vitality.

131. Zambrano, Ana L. "*David Copperfield*" in "Audio-Visual
      Teaching Materials: A Dickensian Checklist--Part II."
      DSN, 7 (1976), 110.

      Lists various 16mm films and filmstrips. See also her
      checklist of feature films (122).

132. ———. "*David Copperfield*: Novel and Film." *HSL*, 9
      (1977), 1-16.

      Regards the novel as simultaneously presenting "multiple
      Davids at different moments of time." Zambrano regards
      the narrative "I" as the regulatory force, modifying
      time and also the readers' reactions to the scene. Thus
      she argues that David, as focus of attention, is never
      completely passive. She says that in the 1935 MGM film
      (122) the Dickensian characters come to life, especially
      W.C. Fields's Micawber. Zambrano thinks that Delbert Mann's
      1970 film (122, 124) uses the element of time as the
      structural focus and creates a more egocentric David than
      did Dickens. The more recent film reflects what she calls
      "a topical concern of the 1970's over the generation's
      disenchantment with establishment mores and the struggle
      to achieve self-identity." She includes a list of feature
      film adaptations, 1911-1970. See also her Checklist (122).

                       RADIO ADAPTATIONS

133. *David Copperfield*. Various British Radio Adaptations.

      A number of adaptations have been broadcast, but there
      is little detailed information about many of them. Occa-
      sionally the *Dickensian* mentions radio plays: in December
      1940 and January 1941 Audrey Lucas produced a serial
      radio drama of *Copperfield*. Sometime in the spring of
      1944 the BBC Children's Hour presented a serialized
      adaptation. In June 1951 the *Dickensian* remarks, "We were
      treated to an abbreviated *David Copperfield* on a few
      week-nights." In the *Dickensian*, 53 (1957), John Greaves
      negatively reviews a series of thirteen half-hour install-

ments aired in late 1956 and early 1957. Also in December
1973 or January 1974 Radio 4 presented a new serializa-
tion. The script for one radio program, broadcast in
January-February 1946, by BBC Overseas Services, is at
the Dickens House, London. The script, entitled *Mr. and
Mrs. Micawber*, has an introduction noting similarities
between John Dickens and Micawber. The script presents
excerpts from *Copperfield* beginning with David's first
meeting with Micawber, does not have Micawber's denunciation of Heep, but does have Micawber considering emigration.

134. *David Copperfield*. American Forces Radio and TV Service.
      RU 33-6, 3B [1976]; RU 7-8, 3B [1978].

      Radio drama recorded for use by the American Armed Forces
      only. Series: Playhouse 25.

MUSICAL ADAPTATIONS

135. Hill, T.W. "A Catalogue of the Miller Collection of
      Dickens Music at the Dickens House." *Dickensian*, 37
      (1940), 48-54.

      Both the novel and its stage adaptations inspired a
      number of songs and other musical pieces. Many have not
      survived, and the few available copies often are incom-
      plete. Nearly all are undated. The largest collection is
      in the Dickens House, London. Miller's *The Dickens Student
      and Collector* (776) lists much of the music, but Hill's
      is the more complete catalogue. The following entries
      are arranged according to the music's subject.

AGNES

136. "Agnes."

      The Dickens House has only part of the title page of
      this ballad with the signature "Thornton Clarke to his ??,
      1857." Hill dates this as early as 1850.

137. Irving, George V., and Gerald Stanley. "Agnes, or I Have
      Loved You All My Life." London: Jullien, n.d. 4 pp.

      Inscribed to Charles Dickens. A headnote states, "The
      subject of this ballad is taken from the beautiful passage
      in 'David Copperfield', page, 163. 'In the dawn of youth's

bright morning, When blissful visions shone, childhood's
years with joy adorning. My heart was all your own....'"
In Dickens House collection.

138. Jefferys, Charles and J.H. Tully. "Dora to Agnes." London:
      Charles Jefferys, n.d. 7 pp.

      Listed by Miller (776) and cited in a handwritten list
      of Dickens music by William R. Hughes. The Hughes list,
      but not the song itself, is in the Dickens House.

                              DORA

139. Birdseye, George W., and M. Keller. "Goodnight Little
      Blossom." Boston: Oliver Ditson, 1868. 5 pp.

      Uses passage from Chapter 48 as headnote: "We made
      quite a gay procession of it; and my child wife was the
      gayest there. But sometimes, when I took her up, and felt
      that she was lighter in my arms, a dead blank feeling came
      upon me, as if I were approaching to some frozen region,
      yet unseen, that numbed my life. I avoided the recogni-
      tion of this feeling by any name or by any communing with
      myself, until one night, when it was very strong upon me,
      and my aunt had left her with the parting cry of 'Good-
      night Little Blossom!' I sat down at my desk alone, and
      cried to think O! what a fatal name it was, And how the
      blossom withered in its bloom upon the Tree!" In Dickens
      House collection.

140. "'Dora's Waltz' and 'Dora's Song' Composed and Dedicated
      to Doady, by 'The Dearest Girl in the World.'" Dublin:
      S.J. Pigott, n.d. 5 pp.

      Three-verse song, adapting a passage from Chapter 44
      concerning Dora's efforts to assist David at his desk.
      A photo of the song cover appears in the *Dickensian*,
      70 (1974), 19, and Angus Wilson includes a sheet of it
      in *The World of Charles Dickens* (533). In Dickens House
      collection.

141. Glover, Stephen. "Little Blossom." London: Charles
      Jefferys, n.d. 4 pp.

      Listed by Miller (776), who attributes the words of
      this song to Charlotte Yonge.

142. Lavenu, L. "The Dora Polka." London: Jullien, n.d. 6 pp.

      In Dickens House collection.

143. Linley, George, and Gerald Stanley. "Dora, or the Child-
      Wife's Farewell." London: Jullien, n.d. 4 pp.

      Ballad inscribed to Charles Dickens, Esq. Uses a passage
      from Chapter 53 as a headnote: "'I said that it was better
      as it is!' she whispers as she holds me in her arms, 'Oh,
      Doady, after more years you could not have loved your
      child-wife better than you do; and after more years she
      would so have tried and disappointed you, that you might
      not have been able to love her half so well! I know I was
      too young and foolish. It is much better as it is!'" In
      Dickens House collection.

144. Mason, Henry. "Little Blossom." Polka Mazurka for the
      Piano Forte. New York: William Hall and Son, n.d. 5 pp.

      Listed by Miller (776).

145. "S.L." and T.G.B. Halley. "The Parting of David and Dora."
      London: Cramer, Beale, n.d. 5 pp.

      Dedicated to Miss Dolby and containing a passage from
      Chapter 48 as a headnote: "My aunt had left her with the
      parting cry of good night little blossom I sat down at
      my desk and cried to think Oh! what a fatal name it was
      and how the blossom withered in its bloom upon the Tree."
      In Dickens House collection.

                              EM'LY

146. Harper, W.H. "Little Em'ly Polka." London: B. Williams,
      n.d.

      Listed by Miller (776) and apparently different from
      Severn's version (147).

147. Severn, W.G. "The Little Em'ly Polka." London: Simpson,
      n.d. 5 pp.

      In Dickens House collection.

148. Smith, Dexter. "Little Em'ly." Boston: White, Smith and
      Perry, 1871. 5 pp.

      Listed by Miller (776).

149. Thomas, J.R. "Little Em'ly." London: Metzler, n.d.

      Listed by Miller (776).

OTHER CHARACTERS

150. Chevalier, Harold, and Herbert J. Brandon. "The Wooing
      of Barkis." In *Second Cycle of Songs from Dickens*.
      London: F. Pitman Hart, n.d.

      The Dickens House collection has only the cover page.

151. Hopcraft, Editha. "Barkis is Willing." In *Four Dickensian
      Ballads*. London: Dex Ltd., n.d.

      The Dickens House collection has only the cover page.

152. Lewis, Idris. "Mrs. Gummidge."

      Listed in the Dickens House card catalog.

153. Linley, George. "Clara." London: Cramer, Beale, n.d. 5 pp.

      Listed by Miller (776).

154. Martin, William, and James W. Etherington. "Peggotty the
      Wanderer." Ballad. London: Chappell, n.d. 4 pp.

      Listed by Miller (776).

155. Minot, Elizabeth. "Little Davy." In *Songs for Dickens
      Lovers*. Boston: n.p., 1927. 11 pp.

      In Dickens House collection.

156. Winterbottam, J. "The Micawber Quadrille (on popular
      airs)." London: Weippert & Co., n.d. 9 pp.

      The Dickens House copy has the cover missing, but the
      music is annotated as being part of the Halliday *Little
      Em'ly* play (90), which would place the date at 1869. For
      the same play Winterbottam composed "Little Em'ly Valses."
      London: Charles Jefferys, n.d.

                        DAVID COPPERFIELD

157. Colmar, Charles. "The Copperfield Quadrilles." London:
      T.E. Purday, n.d. 5 pp.

      Listed by Miller (776).

158. Wilson, W. "The David Copperfield Polka." London: B.
      Williams, n.d. 4 pp.

In Dickens House Collection. One sheet is reproduced
in J.B. Priestley's *Charles Dickens and His World* (756).

MISCELLANEOUS ADAPTATIONS

159. Armour, Richard. "*David Copperfield*, or up from poverty."
      In *The Classics Reclassified*. New York: McGraw-Hill,
      1960, pp. 129-146.

      Ridicules the academic preoccupation with David's
      Oedipus complex. Armour jokingly dismisses the critical
      defenses of the novel's fragmented structure, and he
      exaggerates the book's sentimentality as he summarizes
      the story.

160. Bloom, Ursula. *The Romance of Charles Dickens*. London:
      Robert Hale, 1960. 186 pp.

      A biographical novel (true facts and fictitious con-
      versations) inspired by the Charles Dickens-Maria Beadnell
      story. In passing Bloom mentions that Dickens and his
      wife visited Suffolk to explore the Blundeston-Yarmouth
      setting [but there is no evidence that Mrs. Dickens did
      accompany her husband]. Bloom contends that the return
      to the past in *Copperfield* provided Dickens an escape
      from domestic bickerings and tragically led him to fall
      in love over again with Maria. [If so, then the "tragedy"
      was short-lived, for when Dickens met Maria again in
      1855, he found her to be a ridiculous person.]

161. Coalfield, Jonathon, pseud. *Micawber Redivivus; or How
      He Made a Fortune as a Middleman, Lost the Confidence
      of an Enlightened People and Succumbed to Direct Supply*.
      London: King's Cross Printing Works, [c. 1870]. 122 pp.

      A parody adaptation protesting the "1-5 shillings per
      ton added to most coal sold in London by the middlemen
      during the last ten years." Swindled by an American in
      Australia, Micawber returns to England and takes up resi-
      dence in "Hallucination Buildings." He decides to rejoin
      the coal trade, this time not at Medway but at the mines.
      Coalfield accompanies him to Pinxton in Derbyshire. There
      is a detailed description of the mine and its operation.
      A crisis arises when Micawber gains a reputation for
      practicing "the questionable tactics that are made use
      of among the lowest class of coal dealers." Convinced

of pernicious price fixing, the Pinxton Company publishes
pamphlets about the abuses, and Micawber loses his fortune
when the company begins selling coal directly. Once more
he must emigrate to Middlebay. The identity of Coalfield
has not been established, but the pamphlet is illustrated
by W. Graham Simpson, who could have written it. Summarizing this work in "Micawber Redivivus," *Dickensian*,
13 (1917), 178-180, Willoughby Matchett dates it in the
1860's or 1870's.

162.   Cooper, T.P. "How Dickens Helps the Trader." *Dickensian*,
       24 (1928), 267-271.

       Traces the frequent use of Micawber's aphorisms and
reflections in advertising of the 1920's.

163.   Dexter, Walter. "Dickensian Peeps into *Punch* VII."
       Dickensian, 33 (1937), 103-109.

       Reproduces a number of *Punch* cartoons including Tenniel's
famous Gladstone-Micawber illustrations of the 1880's,
his "Political Mrs. Gummidge," and several more recent
illustrations from the 1920's. Briefly surveys the mention of *David Copperfield* in *Punch* from October 1849
through the 1920's.

164.   Dickens, Charles. *David Copperfield*. New York: Classics
       Illustrated, 1948. 44 pp.

       Classics comics version; includes a short biographical
sketch of Dickens that mistakes Dickens's birth date as
17 February 1812; illustrated by H.C. Kiefer.

165.   Fellows, Charles. *Mr. Chippendale of Port Welcome*. London:
       Hutchinson, 1905. 334 pp.

       A curious novel inspired by Dickens's characterization
of Mr. Micawber. Fellows begins with the observation that
an author's consignment of a character to a colony is
the equivalent of the character's promotion to heaven.
But the history Fellows constructs for his Micawber
character, Mr. Chippendale, is one of a man yet beset
with worldly difficulty. An inveterate letter-writer,
Chippendale, like Micawber, keeps looking to the future;
"the well-meaning fellow was constitutionally incapable
of taking an accurate view of anything." J.W.T. Ley
notes that Chippendale, "in everything but name, is the
immortal Micawber." *Dickensian*, 1 (1905), 203-205.

166. Fells, M. *David Copperfield: Abridged Version to Accompany a Series of 60 Lantern Slides*. London: Newton, [1927]. 63 pp.

Fells's foreword grants the difficulty of satisfactorily abridging the novel. His attempt is a curious cross between a summary in a study guide and a film version. Fell's commentary includes brief sections of dialogue. With slides, the adaptation is designed to take about two hours. A copy of this rare work is in the Dickens House, London.

167. Graves, Robert. *The Real David Copperfield*. London: Arthur Baker, 1933. 424 pp.

Contains a brief foreword announcing Graves's intention to abridge and "modernize" the novel to rid it of Dickens's verbage and to address directly those issues Graves thinks Dickens treated too indirectly. Graves modifies the plot to include a private meeting between David and Em'ly in the fifty-third chapter. He retains the original fifty-second chapter as an appendix to show "the sort of writing in exchange for which *The Real David Copperfield* is now offered." Fred H. Higginson, in *A Bibliography of the Works of Robert Graves* (Hamden, Conn.: Archon, 1966), pp. 57-58, describes the differences between *The Real David Copperfield* and the condensed version of the novel which Graves published in America as *David Copperfield* (57). In "The Real Dickens," *Dickensian*, 29 (1933), 170-172, Walter Dexter describes *The Real David Copperfield* as a "curious hotch-potch of Dickens and Graves with all the poetry of Dickens eliminated." Dexter publishes a few textual comparisons between Dickens and Graves and asks readers to make the obvious preference of Dickens. Graves's letter of reply in the *Dickensian*, 30 (1934), 231, defends his work as "critical, not imitatory."

168. Gray, W. "Charles Dickens Surrounded by Characters from *David Copperfield*." In *Dickens in Cartoon and Caricature*. Comp. William G. Wilkens. Boston: The Bibliophile Society, 1924, p. 206.

Black and white reproduction of Gray's 1870 oil painting.

169. Huish, Margaret. "David Christie Murray." *Dickensian*, 43 (1947), 91-92.

Points out that Murray's first novel, *A Life's Atonement* (London: Griffith and Farran, 1880), was an uncon-

scious plagiarism of *David Copperfield*. According to
Huish, "No critic apparently noticed the fact, and Murray
himself was completely unaware of it until years later."
Cursory examination of Murray's novel suggests a more
subtle than direct resemblance to *Copperfield*.

170. Joyce, James. *Ulysses*. New York: Random House, 1934, pp.
      412-413.

In the "Oxen of the Sun" passages Joyce parodies the
language of the David-Dora story: "she wishes only one
blessing more, to have her dear Doady there with her to
share her joy .... O Doady, loved one of old, faithful
lifemate now, it may never be again, that faroff time of
the roses! With the shake of her pretty head she recalls
those days. God, how beautiful now across the mist of
years!"

171. McLean, Robert. "Public Examination of Wilkins Micawber,
      Esq." In *Diversions of an Articled Clerk*. London: Law
      Notes Publishing Offices, 1892, pp. 32-39.

Humorous sketch of an elderly but still cheerful Micawber being questioned for bringing on his own bankruptcy
by rash and hazardous speculation. McLean's Micawber
pleads the misfortune of having left a successful life
in Australia to attempt new enterprises in England. These
involved a poor investment in an evening paper, a treatise
which did not sell ("How to get Wealthy and Keep So"),
a novel, and a play. The downfall came when Micawber
entered business with *Martin Chuzzlewit*'s Montague Tigg
and lost what remained of his Australian earnings.

172. Nankivell, Edward J. *David Copperfield*. Phonographic
      Edition. London: Edward J. Nankivell, [c. 1885].

Of an intended three volumes, only one volume of this
shorthand edition was published. It is available in the
British Library, London. W.J. Carlton, in "Dickens in
Shorthand," *Dickensian*, 44 (1948), 205-208, mentions
that Nankivell completed only one volume and a small
part of another.

Part II
STUDIES

REVIEWS

173. [Hervey, T.K.]. "*David Copperfield.*" *Athenaeum*, 5 May
     1849, pp. 455-457, 459.

     Appeared after the publication of the first monthly
     number. There is little critical evaluation, but Hervey
     does remark that the autobiographical form made it more
     difficult than usual for readers to speculate about future
     numbers. He notes *Copperfield* as an exception to an un-
     distinguished list of new books. See Chorley (176) for
     the *Athenaeum*'s review of the completed *David Copperfield*.

174. "Schools; or, Teachers and Taught." *Family Herald*, 28
     July 1849, pp. 204-205.

     An early review, which was pained by the third monthly
     number's "revival of that irreverent and persecuting
     spirit for the instructors of youth which formed the
     peculiar feature of one of his earlier productions [*Nicho-
     las Nickleby*]." The reviewer admits the dramatic effect
     of Salem House and Mr. Creakle but doubts that they "can
     have any existence on this side of purgatory" and thinks
     that Dickens should have taken his moral lessons from
     nature and not from the theater, an opinion with which
     Matthew Arnold took issue in an often-quoted comment
     about the novel (185). Murdstone surely would agree with
     this critic's fear that "to teach boys to despise their
     masters, by reviling the masters in books ... is to lead
     boys to be rebels to parents, magistrates, laws, senators,
     and sovereign; for all authority is one and the same,
     and the principle of reverence once broken in youth is
     broken forever, like a porcelain vase which no diamond
     cement can mend without leaving a flaw."

175. "*David Copperfield* and *Con Gregan*." *Rambler*, 4 (Sept.
     1849), 333-337.

     A mixed review of the first four monthly numbers. The
     reviewer finds Dickens "has become the most *mannered* of
     popular writers" in his recent works and suspects that

his present readers are of a lower class than were the
readers of *Pickwick* and *Oliver Twist*. *David Copperfield*,
according to this review, reproduces various portions
of recent Dickens novels and Christmas Books and is "new
in form rather than in idea or in characters." The reviewer is unique in finding David to be a resuscitated
Paul Dombey. The review points to many oddities among
the characters, for nowhere else has Dickens provided
more "strange compounds of ultra-benevolence and queer
personal singularities." Long quotations from David's
first trip to Yarmouth are included as evidence of Dickens's
strong powers of observation. The article does not compare
Copperfield with Charles Lever's *Con Gregan, The Irish
Gil Blas*.

176.   [Chorley, H.F.]. "*David Copperfield*." *Athenaeum*, 23 Nov.
        1850, pp. 1209-1211.

        Regards *Copperfield* as the most beautiful and highly
finished of Dickens's works because of its gentleness
of touch and delicacy of tone. In contrast to many critics
who later found David a pale figure, the reviewer considers him "one of the best heroes ever sketched or
wrought out by Mr. Dickens." The novel, in this reviewer's
opinion, lacks an artistic plot and is marred by such
strained incidents as the exposure of Uriah Heep and the
mystery of Betsey Trotwood's husband. In view of later
disclosures about Dickens's source for Miss Mowcher,
the reviewer's claim that she can have "no natural ante-
type" is interesting. Although many critics object to
Dickens's handling of Rosa Dartle, this reviewer finds
the conception of her "bold, yet not unnatural." He has
high praise for Betsey and the Micawbers. He admits the
wonderful force achieved through accumulation of detail
in the storm scene but claims that it nonetheless gives
the impression of "stage-effect."

177.   "Dickens's *David Copperfield*." *Spectator*. 23 Nov. 1850,
        pp. 1118-1120.

        A generally negative review with objections seldom
sustained by subsequent critics and well answered by the
positive *Examiner* review (178). Although granting an ease
of style resembling Goldsmith's, the reviewer finds *David
Copperfield* more open than Dickens's other novels to un-
favorable criticism. The reviewer finds it lacking a
coherent fable: "So far as *David Copperfield* appears
designed with any other object than as a vehicle for
writing a number of sketches, it would seem to trace the

London career of an inexperienced young man, with infirm-
ity of purpose, a dangerous friend, and no very experienced advisers." The opening numbers, which usually receive high praise, seem "prosy" to this reviewer, and he
finds Salem House an exaggerated repetition of *Nicholas
Nickleby*'s Dotheboys Hall. He finds that there is a less
racy picture of London life than in Dickens's earlier
works, and he thinks the Em'ly-Steerforth story is "too
worn-out" and "as old as tale-telling." He remarks on
the fine natural pathos in the portrayal of David's
mother's death and says that in this incident "we are
called upon ... to attend to the *writing* of Mr. Dickens."

178. [Forster, John]. "*The Personal History of David Copperfield.*" *Examiner*, 14 Dec. 1850, pp. 798-799.

An exceptionally full review that does not follow the
usual nineteenth-century reviewer's practice of including
long quotations. The arguments seem directed against ob-
jections raised by the *Spectator* review (177), although
the earlier review is never mentioned specifically. Forster says that the "alluring" but often "dangerous" autobiographical form works well because Dickens, unlike
William Godwin, exercises "healthy judgment" and avoids
"vague psychological wanderings, overstrained metaphysical
niceties, and mawkish effusions of sentiment." In David,
visionary and real qualities develop to form "the character of the perfect novelist." The review has high praise
for the childhood sections and considers Agnes the novel's
"finishing grace." Forster commends nearly all the characterizations, especially "the felicitious expression of the
loveliness of worth and virtue" in the entire story of
Little Em'ly. He refutes others' notions of a weak fable
by stressing *David Copperfield*'s unity of purpose and
effect. He says the novel has a "profoundly studied aim"
because "every page of the story is a lesson in self-
denial, in the patient endurance of unavoidable ills, in
strenuous effort against such as are remediable, and in
that virtuous aspiration after the pure heart and un-
selfish will which alone give true happiness or lasting
peace."

179. "Charles Dickens and *David Copperfield*." *Fraser's Magazine*,
42 (Dec. 1850), 698-710. Reprinted in Collins's *Dickens:
The Critical Heritage*, pp. 243-248 (189).

Praises Dickens's "all-pervading charity, ... genial
humour, ... deep reverence for the household sanctities."
Copperfield is the best of Dickens's novels for this

reviewer, because it has a well-contrived plot and natural
style. The reviewer praises especially the novel's "epic
unity" but finds fault with the unnaturalness and melodrama of Rosa Dartle. The review also points out the
parallel between Chapter 61 and Carlyle's pamphlet,
"Model Prisons."

180. [Masson, David]. "Pendennis and Copperfield: Thackeray
      and Dickens." *North British Review*, 15 (May 1851),
      57-89. Reprinted in Collins's *Dickens: The Critical
      Heritage*, pp. 249-259 (189).

      Notes essential differences of style and spirit despite
      the external similarity between the two novels. Masson
      lists a number of areas in which Dickens is relatively
      weaker than Thackeray: Dickens is more diffuse with lan-
      guage, more apt also to fall into the commonplace; he
      tends to step beyond the artist's province and function
      as social and moral critic; Dickens does not always pre-
      serve harmony when he uses the extravagant or grotesque,
      but he has more stylistic range than Thackeray. Masson
      grants that Dickens is "the more genial, cheerful, kindly,
      and sentimental, and Thackeray the more harsh, acrid,
      pungent, and satirical writer." Subsequently, in his
      British Novelists and Their Styles (London: Cambridge,
      1859), Masson observes that although there never was a
      Mr. Micawber in nature, "Micawberism pervades nature
      through and through." See also Thackeray's grateful letter
      to Masson in which Thackeray declares Micawber humorous
      but too exaggerated and in which he praises Dickens's
      "wonderful sweetness and freshness." The letter is re-
      printed in Collins's *Dickens: The Critical Heritage* (189).

181. Phillips, Samuel. "David Copperfield and Arthur Pendennis."
      The Times, 11 June 1851, p. 8. Reprinted in Collins's
      Dickens: The Critical Heritage, pp. 261-263 (189).

      Regards Dickens's as the more varied and picturesque
      work. Phillips maintains that Dora is "not a fact" and
      seems an "infliction" and that the Steerforth-Rosa re-
      lationship is overstrained (a frequent complaint of
      readers responding to Dickens's love of melodrama).
      Phillips concludes that the "expressed morality" and
      "exalted teaching" of Dickens's novel gives it an epic
      greatness not present in Thackeray's satire.

182. "*David Copperfield* and *Pendennis*." *Prospective Review*,
      7 (July 1851), 157-191. Reprinted in Collins's *Dickens:
      The Critical Heritage*, pp. 264-268 (189).

Finds the serial form well handled but thinks it pre-
vents *David Copperfield* from becoming a classic. This
reviewer thinks earlier Dickens works were too sentimental,
melodramatic, and quixotic, and he believes *Copperfield*
is relatively free of these flaws. He criticizes Dickens's
portrayal of Rosa Dartle, calling it the novelist's chief
failure in credibility.

183. Richardson, David L. "Dickens's *David Copperfield* and
      Thackeray's *Pendennis*." In *Literary Recreations, or
      Essays, Criticisms, and Poems Chiefly Written in India.*
      London: W. Thacker, 1852, pp. 238-243.

Not usually listed among *David Copperfield* reviews,
Richardson's review probably first appeared in India,
because Richardson says that he had commented on the novel
as it appeared while he was living in India. One of the
first to note the structural demands of the serial format, Richardson thinks the parts of Dickens's novels are
often better than the entirety of other writers' novels.
He locates Dickens's strengths in scenes, incidents, and
portraits; opposing weaknesses include the lack of "breadth
and unity of design" and the failure to concentrate
interest in a hero. Richardson thinks Dickens resembles
but surpasses Leigh Hunt in "catching the literal physiog-
nomy of dead matter, ... giving it a moral tone and sentiment in perfect keeping with the hour and the mind with
which it is associated." Richardson makes no direct comparison of *David Copperfield* and *Pendennis.*

184. "The Collected Works of Charles Dickens." *British Quarter-
      ly Review*, 1 Jan. 1862, pp. 135-159.

Briefly mentions *David Copperfield* in surveying Dickens's
works, observing that the female characters are numerous
and well drawn. This is one of the few commentaries ever
to praise Agnes as Dickens's finest female character. The
review notes that Dickens does surprisingly little with
the life of David as a writer and thinks Charles Kingsley
would have given such a story more attention.

RECEPTION BY
DICKENS'S CONTEMPORARIES

185. Arnold, Matthew. "The Incompatibles." *Nineteenth Century*,
      9 (1881), 1034-1042. Reprinted in part in Collins's
      Dickens: The Critical Heritage, pp. 267-269 (189).

Although this essay is not directly about Dickens, it praises the realism in Dickens's portrayal of Creakle's school. Arnold also remarks that he has not before commented in print about Dickens and is pleased to commend "a work so sound, a work so rich in merits as *David Copperfield*." He finds in it "treasures of gaiety, invention, life" and the "soul of good nature and kindness governing the whole." Creakle's Salem House is, according to Arnold, all too true to life; and in stinging rebuttal to such viewpoints as that of the *Family Herald* reviewer (174), Arnold remarks, "And our middle class ... will not be easily and soon transformed, but while it gets its initiation to life through Salem House and Mr. Creakle, it never will." George Ford in *Dickens and His Readers* (304) notes that Arnold had probably read *Copperfield* in the early 1850's although in a letter of 1880 he stated he was reading it for the first time.

186. Brontë, Charlotte. "To W.S. Williams, September 13, 1849." In *The Brontës: Life and Letters*. By Clement Shorter. London: Hodder and Stoughton, 1908, Vol. II, p. 71.

"I have read *David Copperfield*; it seems to me very good--admirable in some parts. You said it had affinity to *Jane Eyre*. It has, now and then--only what an advantage has Dickens in his varied knowledge of men and things!" If the letter is correctly dated, Brontë would not have been speaking of the completed novel, but in any event her admission of similarities with *Jane Eyre* has encouraged comparison of *David Copperfield* and *Jane Eyre*.

187. Browning, Elizabeth B. *Elizabeth Barrett Browning: Letters to Her Sister, 1846-1859*. Ed. Leonard Huxley. New York: E.P. Dutton, 1930, p. 130.

Writing from Florence on 15 November 1850, Mrs. Browning says that she and Robert "read, and talk, and Robert can't help from letting out the end of *Copperfield*, and I scold him and won't hear a word more."

188. Carlyle, Thomas. *Letter*. In *Thomas Carlyle: A History of His Life in London 1834-1881*. By James A. Froude. New York: Charles Scribner's Sons, 1884, Vol. II, p. 13.

In a letter of 24 September 1849, Carlyle jokingly hopes that his wife has "given up 'thinking of the old 'un,' and much modified the 'Gummidge' view of affairs." More seriously, he goes on to admonish Mrs. Carlyle, "But we can by no means permit ourselves a philosophy à

la Gummidge—not at all, poor lone critturs though we be."
Jane Carlyle, however, grumbled about having "no feeling
but remorse for wasting time on such arrant nonsense" as
David Copperfield. See Lawrence and Elizabeth Hanson in
Necessary Evil: The Life of Jane Welsh Carlyle (London:
Constable, 1952), p. 392.

189. Collins, Philip, ed. "*David Copperfield* (1849-50)." In
      Dickens: The Critical Heritage. London: Routledge and
      Kegan Paul, 1971, pp. 242-271, 617-620.

      Comments briefly on the early critical reception and
      reprints large parts of reviews from *Fraser's Magazine*
      (179), the *North British Review* (180), *The Times* (181),
      the *Prospective Review* (182), a letter from Thackeray
      to Masson (201), Matthew Arnold's comment (185), and
      Thomas Powell's criticism (196). Collins's brief intro-
      duction to his anthology mentions the generally favorable
      reception the novel had, and Collins notes especially the
      praise early readers gave to Dickens's description of the
      storm scene. He observes that despite the novel's hints
      of autobiography, none of the reviews "pursue the specu-
      lation very far." He reprints a number of obituary notices
      which make passing mention of *Copperfield*'s high standing
      among Dickens's works. Appendix I, "The Sale of Dickens's
      Works," by Robert L. Patten, notes that although the
      initial sale was disappointing (nearly 20,000), *Copper-
      field*'s back number sale was the greatest of any Dickens
      work. Reviews: Donald Hawes, *DSN*, 5 (1974), 115-117;
      Irma Rantavaara, *Dickensian*, 67 (1971), 109-111; A.P.
      Robson, *VS*, 15 (1972), 475-480.

190. Eliot, George. "To Mrs. Peter Alfred Taylor, Broadstairs,
      August, 19, 1852." In *The George Eliot Letters*. Ed.
      Gordon S. Haight. New Haven: Yale Univ. Press, 1954,
      Vol. II, p. 52.

      "For the last two months I have been at this pretty,
      quiet place, which 'David Copperfield' has made classic...."

191. Hutton, Laurence. "A Boy I Knew." *St. Nicholas*, 24 (1897),
      412.

      Declares *Copperfield* to have been *the* book of his child-
      hood, a novel from which Hutton "got nothing but what was
      beautiful and helping."

192. James, Henry. *A Small Boy and Others*. London: Macmillan,
      1913, pp. 118, 123-125.

Thinks that "criticism, round about [Dickens] is somehow futile and tasteless." James fondly recalls his childhood reading of Dickens, calling it "a treasure so hoarded
in the dusty chamber of youth." He remembers having been
sent to bed one evening when his family was reading *David
Copperfield*'s first monthly number. James says he lingered
until he broke into tears over the Murdstones. James mentions that "there sprouted in those years no such other
crop of ready references as the golden harvest of *Copperfield*." He also observes that there were frequent stage
adaptations of *David Copperfield*, and they often were
"the roughest theatrical tinkers' work." James recalls
John Brougham (86) as "a monstrous Micawber, the coarse
parody of a charming creation, with the entire baldness
of a huge Easter egg and collar-points like the sails of
Mediterranean feluccas." See also James's remarks about
David Copperfield in *English Hours* (625). For studies of
James's views of Dickens see Ford (304) and H. Blair
Rouse, "Dickens and Henry James," *NCF*, 5 (1950), 151-157.

193.   Lucas, John. "Dickens and Arnold." *Renaissance & Modern
       Studies*, 16 (1972), 96-111.

       Considers Arnold's opinions of Dickens (185). In pass-
       ing, Lucas cites Uriah Heep as an example of the charac-
       ter type Dickens uses to confuse his readers' allegiances.

194.   Mauskopf, Charles. "Thackeray's Attitude Towards Dickens's
       Writing." *NCF*, 21 (1966), 21-33.

       Considers Thackeray's enthusiastic comments in his
       letters and reviews mentioning *David Copperfield* and
       places these remarks in the context of Thackeray's more
       general views of Dickens. Mauskopf notes that the writers
       differed in their conception of the nature of fiction.

195.   Patten, Robert L. "*David Copperfield* and the Cheap Edi-
       tion." In *Charles Dickens and His Publishers*. Oxford:
       The Clarendon Press, 1978, pp. 198-214.

       Authoritative, informative study showing that *Copper-
       field*, for all its continuing popularity, was not one
       of Dickens's greatest commercial successes. Patten de-
       scribes the Bradbury and Evans advertising of the novel
       as a promotional effort less extensive than had been made
       for *Dombey and Son*. As Patten notes, Dickens believed
       the great success of *Dombey* led to a decline in the sales
       of *David Copperfield*. Patten also observes that with the
       exception of the first number, no initial printing order

was exhausted during the serial run. Appendix A provides details of sales and profits for the individual numbers and for Cheap and Library Editions. Appendix B traces the history of the printing of the monthly numbers.

196. Powell, Thomas. "Charles Dickens." In *The Living Authors of England*. New York: D. Appleton, 1849, pp. 153-178.

A largely negative criticism by a man Dickens rightly recognized as a scoundrel—see Nonesuch Letters (1). Powell regards Dickens's imagination as that of "a daguerreotypist, not a great painter," and he especially regrets the reappearance of the tyrannical schoolmaster in *Copperfield*—see also the *Family Herald* attack on Dickens (174). In Powell's view, Dickens as "poet" and "zealot" lacks Thackeray's "*coolness*." Powell comes to the strange conclusion that because Dickens as a dramatic writer failed with a farce acted at the Lyceum, "his want of constructive power should settle the question as to the author of Copperfield being a writer of the first class." Later F.G. Kitton (743) and T.P. Cooper (609) suggest Powell as a prototype for Mr. Micawber. For the background of Powell's connections with Dickens see Wilfred Partington's "Should a Biographer Tell? The Story of Dickens's Denunciation of Thomas Powell's Forgeries," *Dickensian*, 43 (1947), 193-200; 44 (1947), 14-23. The section of Powell's work reprinted by Collins in *Dickens: The Critical Heritage* (189) compares Dickens and Douglas Jerrold and argues that Dickens's humor is more effective than Jerrold's.

197. Ruskin, John. *The Works of John Ruskin*. 39 vols. Eds. E.T. Cook and Alexander Wedderburn. London: George Allen, 1903-1912, passim.

Ruskin's mention of *David Copperfield* is scattered through his writings but is easy to locate in this edition's excellent index. We know that Ruskin had read the novel by 1850, because in the fourteenth chapter of *The Stones of Venice* (1850) he notes the personal appearance of the man who stole Dora's dog. Ruskin had such great respect for Dickens's "Tempest" chapter that he appended a note to *Modern Painters*, remarking that even Turner produced "nothing in sea-description, detailed, like Dickens's storm." In the *Modern Painters* chapter "Of Vulgarity" Ruskin mentions Uriah Heep as an example of the "physical characteristics of vulgarity." In *Fors Clavigera* he speaks of Dickens's concern for morally independent characters such as Peggotty, but it is unclear whether

Ruskin has in mind Clara or Daniel Peggotty. Ruskin
anticipates the more modern interest in Dickens's portrayal of childhood; in *The Art of England*, Ruskin speaks
mainly of Mrs. Allingham and Kate Greenway but traces
"the real beginning of child benediction" in the arts of
England to "the Little Nells and boy David Copperfields."
One of the best summaries of Ruskin's view of Dickens
appears in a letter of 18 January 1863: "I know of no
writer so voluminous and unceasingly entertaining, or
with such a store of laughter ... not at things merely
accidentally ridiculous or at mere indecency ... but at
things inherently grotesque and purely humorous; if he
is ever severe ... as on Heep ... it is always true base-
ness or vice, never mere foibles, which he holds up for
scorn. And as you most rightly say of his caricature, the
fun is always equal to the extravagance." The letter concludes with a repetition of Ruskin's praise for the
description of the storm.

198.   Stephen, Fitzjames. "The Relation of Novels to Life." In
       Cambridge Essays. London: John W. Parker, 1855, pp.
       148-152. Reprinted in *Notorious Literary Attacks*. Ed.
       Albert Mordell. New York: Boni and Liveright, 1926,
       pp. 162-170.

Defines novels as fictitious biographies whose object
is to arouse the readers' curiosity. Stephen discusses
a wide range of authors and issues. He takes Dickens to
task for his sentimentality in treating death, including
Dora's. In contrast to such readers as Ruskin (197), he
finds Dickens's picturesque descriptions of nature offend-
ing "our taste by their obvious effort and elaboration,"
and he is one of few readers not greatly impressed with
the "Tempest" chapter. It, along with the scene on the
Alpine path, he thinks, "would furnish very good drop-
scenes to a theatre; but in the history of a man's life
we can dispense with drop-scenes." Generally favoring
Thackeray's writing, Stephen does grant exquisite play-
fulness and humor to many *Copperfield* incidents, especially
in the surprising recognitions of Micawber. Stephen finds
Copperfield, in contrast to *Robinson Crusoe*, which keeps
personal matters in the background, indiscreetly disclos-
ing "a man's most secret thoughts and most sacred affections, something he would not have done had David been
a real man, though such disclosures are less an offense
in a novel than in real life." Stephen's conclusion not
only is naive about the novel's autobiographical focus
but also is critical of the presence of qualities--"secret

thoughts" and "sacred affections"--which many subsequent
readers appreciate and wish more evident in David's
narration.

199. Taine, H.A. "The Novel--Dickens." In *History of English
      Literature*. London: Chatto and Windus, 1906, Vol. IV,
      pp. 115-164. First published in *Revue des Deux Mondes*,
      1 Feb. 1856. Trans. by H. Van Laun in 1871.

      Remarks that the living Dickens repudiated what con-
      temporary commentators said of him biographically and
      that "what is worse, he claims [in *David Copperfield*]
      to be his own biographer." Taine is the first of many
      commentators to consider the theoretical relationship
      of autobiography and fiction, and he sees Dickens em-
      broidering truth with fiction. Taine says that Dickens's
      is an intense, at times monomaniacal, imagination, and he
      terms *David Copperfield* a masterpiece of the visionary
      imagination--see G.H. Lewes's opinion about the hallucina-
      tory quality of Dickens's imagination (389). Critical
      of the English public's moral repression of authors,
      Taine finds Dickens not venturing "to make us hear the
      ardent, generous, undisciplined blast of the all-powerful
      passion" of love in David's and also in Steerforth's
      stories. Taine's general conclusion echoes the healthy
      morality of a Betsey Trotwood, for he observes, "In
      reality, the novels of Dickens can be reduced to one
      phrase, to wit: Be good, and love; there is genuine joy
      only in the emotions of the heart; sensibility is the
      whole man."

200. Taverner, H.T., pseud. [John C. Hotten]. "*David Copper-
      field*." In *Charles Dickens: The Story of His Life*.
      London: John Camden Hotten, [1873], pp. 186-190.

      The title page states this is "By the author of the
      'Life of Thackeray,'" which purportedly was written by
      "Theodore Taylor," a pseudonym of John Camden Hotten.
      The Catalogue of the Walter Dexter Collection at the
      British Library, therefore, attributes this Dickens book
      to Hotten but notes also that both Joseph Grego and
      Willian M. Thomas have been suggested as its author.
      The author regards *Copperfield* as the happiest of Dickens's
      books and recalls reading it when, like David departing
      from Dover, Taverner had just left the home of a distant
      relative with whom he had lived. He mentions the success
      of the early theatrical adaptations, *Born with a Caul*
      (83) and *The Deal Boatman* (88).

201. Thackeray, William M. *The Letters and Private Papers of
      William Makepeace Thackeray.* Cambridge, Mass.: Harvard
      Univ. Press, 1945, Vol. II, passim.

      Enthusiastic about the first number of *Copperfield*,
      which he read in May 1849, Thackeray wrote Mrs. Brook-
      field and mentioned that the novel had some of Dickens's
      "very prettiest touches." He thought Dickens had taken
      Thackeray's own method of "greatly simplifying his style
      and foregoing the use of fine words." Thackeray repeated
      these views to Lady Blessington two days later, and
      sometime later in May he told Mr. Brookfield that *Copper-
      field* "beats the yellow chap of this month [Thackeray's
      Pendennis] hollow." In September 1849 Thackeray praised
      Dickens's portrayal of Mr. Dick, and in March 1850 he
      found the eleventh number "capital" because Dickens had
      produced "some very neat pretty natural writing indeed--
      better than somebody else again." Writing Mrs. Sartoris
      in late October or early November 1850, Thackeray asked,
      "Have you read *David Copperfield*? the artless rogue! that
      artless dodge makes me laugh (is it only wicked things
      that make one laugh any more?)." In May 1851 Thackeray
      praised Dickens's "wonderful sweetness & freshness" but
      charged him with failing to represent "Nature duly; for
      instance Micawber appears to me an exaggeration of a man,
      as his name is of a name." In a number of his private
      comments Thackeray anticipates the reviewers' comparisons
      of *Copperfield* and *Pendennis*. Thackeray often is generous
      in his praise of Dickens, but comments such as those he
      made in a letter to Lady Blessington on 6 May 1849
      occasionally sound notes of self-deprecation: "My work
      shows my dullness I think--but on the other hand there
      is a fellow by the name of Dickens who is bringing out
      a rival publication and who has written beautifully."
      See also Thackeray's published comments about *David
      Copperfield* (202, 203) and also Mauskopf's study of
      Thackeray's attitude toward Dickens (194).

202. [————]. "Mr. Brown's Letters to a Young Man About Town."
      Punch, 16 (1849), 187.

      Appearing on 5 May 1849, Thackeray's is one of the
      first published notices of *David Copperfield*, which had
      begun its serial run in May 1849. Thackeray's Mr. Brown
      sees that a club member has fallen asleep while reading
      Pendennis, and he turns to ask his nephew if he has read
      David Copperfield. Brown speaks of Dickens's novel as
      "charmingly fresh and simple," and he praises its "ad-
      mirable touches of tender humour." Brown well expresses

Thackeray's high regard for humor as "a mixture of love
and wit," and he goes on to remark that in Dickens "there
are little words and phrases ... which are like personal
benefits to the reader. What a place it is to hold in the
affections of men! What an awful responsibility hanging
over a writer."

203. ————. "Sterne and Goldsmith." In *The English Humourists
of the Eighteenth Century*. New York: Charles Scribner's
Sons, 1904, pp. 374, 414, 420.

Complaining of Sterne's immorality, Thackeray in this
1851 lecture praised Dickens: "I think of these past
writers and of one who lives amongst us now, and am
grateful for the innocent laughter and the sweet and
unsullied page which the author of 'David Copperfield'
gives to my children." In "Charity and Humour," a lecture
Thackeray added in New York to his "The English Humourists"
series in 1852, he remarked: "Popular humour, and especially modern popular humour and the writers, its expo-
nents, are always kind and chivalrous, taking the side
of the weak against the strong." With the language of
another Micawber, Thackeray praises Mr. Micawber: "Who
does not venerate the chief of that illustrious family
who, being stricken with misfortune, wisely and greatly
turned his attention to 'coals'; the accomplished, the
Epicurean, the dirty, the delightful Micawber?" See Mauskopf's study of Thackeray's attitudes toward Dickens
(194).

204. Vann, Jerry D. "*David Copperfield* and the Reviewers."
DA, 28 (1967), 3159A-3160A (Texas Tech., 1967).

Studies the critical reception and suggests that the
high incidence of changes in the serial could have been
prompted by reviewers' opinions.

CRITICISM

205. Adams, Donald K. "Studies in Allegory in the Works of
Charles Dickens." *DA*, 13 (1953), 1190 (Northwestern,
1953).

Identifies in *Copperfield* and later novels "key meta-
phors," which Adams thinks form coherent allegories of
"aspects of Dickens's life and interests." Adams claims

that the moral allegories of earlier novels become "true
poetic allegories" in later works.

206. Adrian, Arthur A. "*David Copperfield*: A Century of Critical
      and Popular Acclaim." *MLQ*, 11 (1950), 325-331.

      Shows that critics and the reading public have steadily
      regarded *Copperfield* as a favorite during the hundred
      years following its publication. Adrian thinks *Copper-
      field* has held up because it is free from earlier Dickensian
      exaggeration, has less melodrama, and represents an
      idealized version of a beloved author's triumph over
      childhood privations.

207. Alain, pseud. [Émile Chartier]. "Imagination in the Novel."
      Revue de Paris, 1 March 1940, pp. 47-52. Reprinted in
      his *En lisant Dickens* (Paris: n.p., 1945); and in English
      in *The Dickens Critics*, ed. George Ford and Lauriat
      Lane, Jr. (Ithaca: Cornell Univ. Press, 1961), pp. 171-
      180.

      Defining imagination as "a sort of *a priori* contempla-
      tion, which consists in viewing my feelings from a distance,
      thereby coloring my contemplation and giving it the sub-
      stance of a world," this important essay pioneers modern
      interest in the relationship of memory and imagination.
      In his commentary on *David Copperfield*, Alain discusses
      imagistic evocations of increasing terror that culminates
      in the storm. He notes small touches, such as the business
      of Mr. Spenlow's silent partner or David's fear of the
      young butcher, which indicate Dickens's psychological
      insight. Alain concludes that Dickens is able to make
      "our own image grimace in the mirror he holds out to us."

208. Allen, Walter. "Charles Dickens." In *Six Great Novelists*.
      London: Hamish Hamilton, 1955, pp. 95-125.

      Very briefly mentions *Copperfield*, finding it to contain
      a mellowness unique among Dickens's works, "probably
      because in it Dickens came to terms with himself and his
      past." The question of how fully Dickens accomplished
      this ideal has been the focus of nearly all the biograph-
      ical and psychological criticism since Allen made this
      observation.

209. ————. *The English Novel: A Short Criticial History*.
      London: E.P. Dutton, 1954, pp. 186-197, 325-326.

      Suggests that Dickens's childlike vision of people
      conditioned his world view and cites the passionate in-

dignation of *Copperfield*'s second chapter as a case in point. Allen sees Uriah Heep as a terrifying example of Dickens's savage comedy, because he represents "the victim of early nineteenth-century good works having his own back on the nineteenth century." As a work of realism the novel fails, according to Allen, because Dickens is primarily a symbolic novelist. Allen also mentions *David Copperfield* as a source for Henry James's interest in a developing consciousness in *What Maisie Knew*.

210. Andersen, Sally S. "Dickens and the Problem of Maturity: *Dombey and Son, David Copperfield, Bleak House, Great Expectations*, and *Our Mutual Friend.*" *DA*, 28 (1967), 3135A (Illinois, 1967).

Sees a clear sense of selfhood, realistic world view, and acceptance of responsibility as signs of the truly mature Dickens character and says that "in *David Copperfield* Dickens fails ... to depict convincingly the growth of his major character." Andersen finds the biographical significance of the novel obvious: the story reflects the inadequacies of Dickens's own parents and the lack of realism in his relationships with women.

211. Archer, William. "Appreciation of *David Copperfield.*" In 1919 Readers' Classic Edition, pp. 15-16 (55).

Archer (himself best known as Ibsen's translator) recognizes Dickens at the summit of his powers in *David Copperfield*, for he had not yet experienced the terror of his greatest rival, whom Archer identifies as Dickens himself. Archer, in his critical judgment that Dickens "was now master of a conscious art which had not yet become self-conscious," is utterly at odds with those critics of the 1970's who were fascinated with David's conscious and unconscious mental processes—see, for example, Gilmour (320), Lougy (391), and Westburg (527). Archer cites a number of characterizations that come across in "psychological shorthand" (Dora, Betsey, Heep, Rosa Dartle, Mr. Dick), and he praises the characterization both of Steerforth and Agnes.

212. Ashby, Ruth. "David Copperfield's Story-Telling in the Dark." *DSN*, 9 (1978), 80-83.

Finds fact and fiction often indistinguishable in David's turning of his life into a book, and sees his final reconciliation as "not worldly or romantic but artistic." For more extensive discussion of the autobiographic see Collins (263) and Cox (269).

213. Augburn, Gerald R. "The Function of Death in the Novels
      of Charles Dickens." *DA*, 29 (1969), 2666A-2667A (Colum-
      bia, 1968).

      Generally argues that Dickens creates atmosphere, re-
      veals character, and carries his themes by his treatment
      of death. *Copperfield*, to Augburn, represents a change
      from the earlier novels, for it shows a hero growing
      out of his innocence and recalling his childhood from an
      adult perspective, thus becoming "vulnerable to the
      corruption which is the inheritance of man in this deathly
      world."

214. Baker, Ernest A. *The Age of Dickens and Thackeray*. Vol.
      8 of *The History of the English Novel*. London: H.F. and
      G. Witherby, 1936, pp. 238-241, 283-292.

      Discusses Forster's use of the autobiographical frag-
      ment (730) and accepts Charles Dickens the Younger's claim
      that his mother had known of it and had urged Dickens not
      to publish it (283). Baker cites *Copperfield* as the best
      novel in which to study the genesis of Dickens's earlier
      books, and he groups it among Dickens's "novels of plot,"
      although the plot is admittedly loose. Some of the episodes
      are as theatrical as any Dickens devised, admits Baker,
      but nowhere else does Dickens "appear so true a realist,"
      especially "in the exactness with which he reproduces the
      intense sensitivity of childhood." Like many earlier
      commentators, Baker realizes that the Dora episodes form
      an enchanting idyll, which Dickens treats with delicate
      humor. He also shares the conventional critical view that
      Steerforth and his mother are the only shallow charac-
      terizations among the minor characters. In a perceptive
      study of Uriah Heep, Baker compares him to the hypocritical
      Pecksniff of *Martin Chuzzlewit* and finds Heep more evil
      because he deliberately adopts his manner and becomes
      "the ugly offspring of hatred, greed, and cunning."
      Histories of the novel seldom give as full attention to
      Dickens's individual works as does Baker, and his com-
      mentary remains one of the better ones before 1940.

215. Bandelin, Carl. "David Copperfield: A Third Interesting
      Penitent." *SEL*, 16 (1976), 601-611.

      Defends the often criticized sixty-first chapter ("I
      Am Shown Two Interesting Penitents") on the grounds that
      in the last half of the novel David himself is penitent.
      This ironic chapter signals the warning of David's "ob-
      sessive self-denial," says Bandelin, and the visit to

Creakle's prison allows David to discover the incomplete-
ness of his repentance. Figuratively, speculates Bandelin,
David has become a "model" penitent, but Heep and Littimer
caricature David's own earlier words. According to this
interpretation, only in the final union with Agnes is
David able to free himself from the self-consciousness
he observes in the other penitents. For the more common
view, that this chapter is not so well integrated with
David's own history, see Monod (425) or Hardy (336), and
for a detailed discussion of Dickens's interests in
prison reform see *Household Words* (35) and Collins's
Dickens and Crime (264).

216. Banta, Martha. "Charles Dickens's Warning to England."
      Dickensian, 63 (1967), 166–175.

      Traces Dickens's recurrent concern for forsaken children,
      noting that the first half of *David Copperfield* provides
      "a litany of the effects upon a child of ... lack of
      encouragement." Banta's article is general in scope and
      does not provide detailed discussion of *Copperfield*.

217. Barickman, Richard. "The Comedy of Survival in Dickens's
      Novels." *Novel*, 11 (1978), 128–143.

      Cites Mr. Micawber's ending as a model colonist as
      fitting perfectly with his own demolition of Heep. Barick-
      man regards Micawber as an instance finally of the "accom-
      modation of the voracious comic imagination to the spare
      diet of ordinary social life, yet another version of
      David Copperfield's own retrenchment from Dora to Agnes."
      Barickman's arguments tend to run counter to Kincaid's
      less orthodox but more persuasive discussion of the book's
      "subversive humor" (374).

218. Barnes, Samuel G. "Dickens and Copperfield: The Hero as
      Man of Letters." In *The Classic British Novel*. Ed.
      Howard M. Harper, Jr. and Charles Edge. Athens: Univ.
      of Georgia Press, 1972, pp. 85–102.

      Sees *David Copperfield* marking "the emergence of Dickens
      as--in Carlyle's terms--the Heroic Man of Letters."
      Barnes's linking of Dickens with Carlyle helps explain
      Copperfield's condemnation of idleness, the national
      aristocracy's lost heroic potential, and cold mechanism.
      Barnes finds the novel stressing Carlylean notions of
      personal reform. He thinks Carlyle's ideas also shaped
      Dickens's portrayal of the Peggotty group as ideal workers.
      According to Barnes, Dickens's positive program of per-

sonal reform transmutes "Carlyle's hero-worship into a
code of conduct," though Carlyle himself did not see the
resemblance. For other studies of Carlylean elements in
the novel see Dunn (656) and Oddie (684).

219.   Barter, A.A. "Introduction." In 1903 School Edition, pp.
       v-xxiv (48).

       Gives a short sketch of the history of the English novel
       and discusses *David Copperfield*'s autobiographical elements.
       Barter notes that although Dickens is known as a social
       reformer, social reform is not prominent in *David Copper-
       field* because of the focus on his own life. Barter finds
       that first-person narration inhibits the naturalness of
       David's self-revelation. He comments upon Dickens's skill-
       ful characterizations and is one of the earliest commenta-
       tors to grant that Agnes is more an influence on David
       than a credible character in her own right. Also, Barter
       is one of the first to suggest Mary Hogarth as a possible
       model for Agnes.

220.   Basch, Françoise. "The Myth in the Novel," "Charles
       Dickens's Anti-Women," and "Dickens's Sinners." In
       *Relative Creatures: Victorian Women in Society and the
       Novel 1837-67*. Trans. Anthony Rudolf. London: Allen
       Lane, 1974, pp. 53-74, 141-151, 210-228.

       Ranges widely through Dickens's novels to discuss what
       Basch considers his intentions with conventional and un-
       conventional female characters. Concerning *Copperfield*'s
       heroine, Agnes, Basch notes uncertainties in Dickens's
       manuscript revisions. The uncertainty seems to have been
       created by Dickens's reluctance to have Dora die even
       though he seems to have been clearly committed to the
       idea of Agnes as guardian angel. Basch points out simi-
       larities between Dora and David's mother and also notes
       that David's great concern is whether Dora conforms to
       the Victorian ideal of a middle-class wife. Among Dickens's
       less conventional females mentioned by Basch, Betsey
       Trotwood remains one of Dickens's most complete charac-
       ters, at once independent and motherly. Rosa Dartle, the
       most enigmatic woman to many readers over the years, does
       not receive much attention from Basch, who regards her
       as too theatrical, "a monstrous puppet." Basch discusses
       Em'ly in the chapter on "Dickens's Sinners," and hers is
       one of the best treatments of Dickens's portrayal of
       fallen women, because Basch is sensitive to Dickens's
       mixture of melodrama and sympathetic social commentary
       in the Little Em'ly story. She realizes that he heightened

the melodramatic effect by comparing Em'ly with Martha
Endell, but Basch also remarks how he muted his stage
effects because he wanted to present a contemporary social
problem without offense.

221. Bayne, Peter. "*David Copperfield.*" *Literary World*, 9 May
1879, pp. 296-298; 16 May 1879, pp. 312-314.

Claims the public has accepted Dickens's personal
preference for *Copperfield*, which Bayne labels as a combination of Oliver Goldsmith's ease and Charlotte Brontë's
"burnished brilliancy." Bayne, like many more recent
commentators, resists the idea that Steerforth is shallow
and stagey and calls him "one of Dickens's most careful
portraits." Also Bayne praises Agnes and Dora and finds
Betsey a triumph: "No one but Dickens would have dared
to unite eccentricity so wild with ability so high."

222. Beach, Joseph W. *The Technique of Thomas Hardy.* New York:
Russell and Russell, 1962, pp. 86-87.

Argues that generally the cultivation of form in the
novel is "the cultivation of the dramatic idea" and that
David Copperfield stands as an exception because its
first third seems to lack plot and theme. Dickens, argues
Beach, takes every occasion to divert attention to minor
and intrusive figures, "to the infinite petty happenings
that lead from nowhere to nowhere.... It is a moving picture without plot and without subject." Beach finds
Dickens's presentation of Little Em'ly (we are never given
her version of her love affair) contrasting markedly with
Hardy's portrayal of Tess of the D'Urbervilles' sufferings.

223. Beebe, Maurice. *Ivory Towers and Sacred Founts: The
Artist as Hero in Fiction from Goethe to Joyce.* New
York: New York Univ. Press, 1964, pp. 88-97.

Finds David possessing most of the traditional characteristics of the artistic temperament and shows that his
development as an artist follows a familiar pattern (he
is a close observer and can abstract himself from his
surroundings), but he seems to lack an artist's egoism.
Beebe argues that Dickens does not "write a portrait-of-
the-artist novel until ... he discovers that his hero,
like himself, has become an artist unaware." David is
capable of a triple point of view—the view of the David
of the past, and of the David of the present, and also
of the omniscient artist who can see through both selves.

Beebe thus makes an important contribution to the con-
siderable debate about David as professional writer which
has extended from early reviews through more recent
psychological character study.

224. Bell, Vereen M. "The Emotional Matrix of *David Copperfield*."
      SEL, 8 (1968), 633-649.

      Applies Freud's notion of fiction-making as wish-ful-
      fillment to *Copperfield* and finds the novel culminating
      in the hero distancing himself from his childhood inno-
      cence. Bell sees David settling for a mature Agnes and
      completing a growth Dickens himself did not attain be-
      cause he moved perpetually between real and ideal worlds.
      Bell also notes that the young heroines are very conspic-
      uous features in a complicated imaginary landscape popu-
      lated by a variety of innocents "menaced by time and by
      the encroachment of the world outside."

225. Berndt, David E. "'This Hard, Real Life': Self and Society
      in Five Mid-Victorian *Bildungsromane*." *DAI*, 33 (1973),
      5713A-5714A (Cornell, 1972).

      Links *Jane Eyre* and *David Copperfield* as fictional
      "models of self-integration" and of "a deeply satisfying
      reconciliation between self and society." Berndt thinks
      that marriage affirms each character's ethical ideals,
      and the use of "retrospective autobiographical narrative
      perspective reflects ... [a] deep sense of personal co-
      herence between present and past selves."

226. Black, Michael. "*David Copperfield*: Self, Childhood, and
      Growth." In *The Literature of Fidelity*. London: Chatto
      and Windus, 1975, pp. 82-102.

      Sees Dickens, unlike Flaubert in *Madame Bovary*, main-
      taining a mature balance of involvement and judgment.
      Copperfield's most vital parts for Black are its searing
      account of dereliction in childhood and its picture of
      David's first marriage. One of Black's most original
      points is his observation that the Murdstone brand of
      Puritanism is a temptation "David finds in himself, and
      shrinks from, in relation to Dora."

227. Blount, Trevor. *Charles Dickens: The Early Novels*. London:
      Longmans, Green, 1968, pp. 29-33.

      Brief mention of *Copperfield*, placing it at a crucial
      point in Dickens's career. Despite Blount's reservations
      about making too much of the autobiographical elements

(see Forster, 730), he describes the book as a partial
fictionalizing of experience, "both exploratory and therapeutic."

228. ———. "Introduction." In 1966 Penguin Edition, pp.
13-37 (69).

Useful introduction both for first readers and those
more familiar with the novel. Blount discusses the scale
of Dickens's endeavor and the deliberate control he exer-
cised over his abundant imagination. The autobiographical
elements are strong, but Blount cautions against over-
playing the obsessional quality of the childhood experience. "It is essential ... to stop thinking for a while
of the transmuted autobiography and to start giving due
weight to Dickens's skill in fashioning a work of independent artistic identity." Blount argues that serial
publication was not a great artistic liability, and that
the form "is far from being shapeless innovation." To
Needham's study of control over head and heart as a
dominant theme (433), Blount adds two noteworthy points.
He sees the skeletons on Traddles's slate as "an emblem
of the self-knowledge and control David has yet to learn,"
and he compares David with Thackeray's Henry Esmond. He
finds the novel mingling many moods and presenting them
with "cinematic visualness." His introduction attends to
many topographical, dialectical, and documentary details
and sensibly concludes with the reminder that "splendid
though the individual ingredients are, the novel compre-
hended as a totality is infinitely richer than its separate parts."

229. Bodenheimer, Rosemarie. "Dickens and the Art of the
Pastoral." *Centennial Review*, 23 (1979), 452-467.

Examines the self-conscious literary quality of Dickens's
nature rhetoric and traces a general development in his
use of "landscape as a metaphor for psychological con-
figurations and their changes." Bodenheimer finds nature
descriptions surprisingly rare in *David Copperfield* (one
of Dickens's most pastoral works), where they are dependent on conventional literary images. She sees the
remembering mind employing Edenic imagery and the storm
signaling "a general psychic upheaval, an apocalyptic
change." Not until *Great Expectations*, does Dickens,
according to Bodenheimer, create a "fully resonant con-
junction of landscape and point of view."

230. Boege, Fred W. "Point of View in Dickens." *PMLA*, 65
      (1950), 90-105.

      Disputes the frequent pre-1950 assumption that Dickens
      was simply another pre-Jamesean novelist with little
      technical skill. By treating all the characters in *Copper-
      field* except David objectively, Dickens avoided what
      Boege terms the "pitfalls of psychological analysis"
      at this stage of his career. Ranging more broadly through
      Dickens's works, Boege also suggests that later, with
      more objective points of view than David's, Dickens could
      manifest interest in more than surface life.

231. Bort, Barry D. "A Study of Dickens's Heroes from Oliver
      Twist to John Jasper." *DA*, 23 (1962), 1696A-1697A (Brown,
      1960).

      Treats *Oliver*, *Nickleby*, *Chuzzlewit*, *Copperfield*, and
      Great Expectations as a cycle about the initiation of
      young men into the world with the last novel as "a summing
      up and criticism of all that has gone before."

232. Brown, Arthur W. "*David Copperfield*." In *Sexual Analysis
      of Dickens' Props*. New York: Emerson, 1971, pp. 232-
      236 and passim.

      No separate treatment of *Copperfield* but frequent men-
      tion of it in a psychoanalytic discussion intended to
      reveal meaning "which one might not ordinarily know was
      there" in Dickens. Brown includes such speculations as
      Dickens associating his own "feelings about blacking with
      David's feelings about wine" and Mr. Mell's flute being
      a sexually symbolic object. Brown's is one of the most
      reductive and least critically incisive comments on
      Dickens. Reviews: Martin Dodsworth, *Dickensian*, 68 (1972),
      191-193; Susan Horton, *VS*, 16 (1972), 251-252; Laurence
      Senelick, *DSN*, 4 (1973), 50-52; Deborah A. Thomas, *L&P*,
      23, iii (1973), 129-131.

233. Brown, Earl B., Jr. "The Rhetoric of Charles Dickens:
      A Study of *David Copperfield*." *DAI*, 32 (1972), 6367A
      (Emory, 1971).

      Argues that Dickens uses the form of fictional auto-
      biography "to undercut other fictional autobiographies
      which either fail to find order in their world or see
      order as contingent on determination (*Tristram Shandy*),
      which believe order is divinely imposed (*Jane Eyre*) or
      that ... a new order is dependent on the creation of a
      new religion or philosophy (*Sartor Resartus*)."

234. Brown, E.K. *"David Copperfield." YR*, 37 (1948), 651-666.
     Reprinted as introduction to 1950 Modern Library Edi-
     tion, pp. v-xii (61).

     Regards Dickens as less ideologically grandiose than
     Balzac and more technically masterful than Scott. Brown
     is one of the first modern critics to defend the novel's
     artistry, insisting that the rambling plot and many subtle
     contrasts are necessary and effective. Brown finds a more
     dramatic center of David's life in personal relationships
     than in his life as a writer. For Brown, Dickens's final
     treatment of Agnes is inadequate; the ending is twisted
     by Dickens's evident repression in characterizing her.
     This introduction compactly summarizes the main resem-
     blances between the autobiographical fragment published
     by Forster (730) and the novel.

235. Brown, Janet A. "The Narrator's Role in *David Copper-
     field." DSA*, 2 (1972), 197-207.

     Considers the relationship between narrator and his
     story and believes David is a reliable narrator: "The
     action of his memory somehow bears as much meaning as the
     memories themselves." Brown finds David's memory ultimately
     redemptive, because David never renounces his past.

236. Browne, Gerald D. "The Significance of Time in the Novels
     of Charles Dickens." *DAI*, 31 (1971), 6541A-6542A (Wis-
     consin, 1971).

     Devotes a chapter to *Copperfield*, considering it another
     effort to escape time through the manipulation of history.
     Browne says that David in effect creates his past and so
     gains mastery over time, but Copperfield's mastery is
     qualified by his "subjective posture in an objective con-
     text that indicates time's dominion over him."

237. Brunetière, Ferdinand. "Comment on *David Copperfield*."
     In 1919 Readers' Classic Edition, p. 56 (55).

     Reprints 1889 *Revue des Deux Mondes* comment in praise
     of Dickens's "swarming imagination" as his most "English"
     characteristic.

238. Buck, Philo M., Jr. "Introduction." In 1910 Ginn Edition,
     pp. xi-xxxv (51).

     Explains for readers as young as twelve that *David
     Copperfield* is an autobiographical novel. Buck claims
     that all Dickens's works are autobiographical in the sense

that they record his impressions and show that he was
by nature an optimist. Buck defends Dickens's loose plot
structure as the consequence of his stress on character
rather than on ordered events. Buck thus resists the
Jamesean fictional theories that were growing increasingly
intolerant of Dickens at the time this introduction was
written. Following Charles Dickens the Younger's practice
(283), Buck closes with Thackeray's and Arnold's praise
of *David Copperfield*.

239. Buckley, Jerome H. "Autobiography in the English *Bildungs-
      roman*." In *The Interpretation of Narrative: Theory and
      Practice*. Ed. Morton W. Bloomfield. Cambridge, Mass.:
      Harvard Univ. Press, 1970, pp. 93-104.

      Finds the *The Prelude* foreshadowing the development of
      a significant narrative form and argues that Dickens went
      on to combine "the subjective impulse and the dispassionate
      vision of the dramatist." Buckley expands this discussion
      in *Season of Youth* (240).

240. ————. "Dickens, David and Pip." In *Season of Youth:
      The Bildungsroman from Dickens to Golding*. Cambridge,
      Mass.: Harvard Univ. Press, 1974, pp. 28-62.

      One of the few thoughtful comparative considerations
      of the two Dickens novels written entirely from the first-
      person point of view. Buckley notes that although *Pendennis*
      has often been compared with *Copperfield*, Thackeray's novel
      is too constrained by convention to be a *Bildungsroman*.
      Buckley views David as more Dickens's counterpart than
      double and believes the novel reads as David's, not
      Dickens's, autobiography. He compares the function of
      David's memory with Wordsworth's and Proust's, noting that
      the novel "describes the education, through time remem-
      bered, of the affections." In David's dark night of despair
      and discovery of purpose Buckley ascertains a pattern
      evident in Carlyle, Tennyson, Mill, and Newman. In Buck-
      ley's analysis, the bland David of the final chapters
      does not become an adequate surrogate for the tempestuous
      Dickens, but ten years later in *Great Expectations* Dickens
      no longer dealt "in wish-fulfillment but in forces pre-
      cluding a tranquil resolution." Reviews: George Goodin,
      DSN, 6 (1975), 95-96; B[ryan] H[ulse], *Dickensian*, 71
      (1975), 54-55.

241. ————. *The Triumph of Time: A Study of the Victorian
      Concepts of Time, History, Progress, and Decadence*.
      Cambridge, Mass.: Harvard Univ. Press, 1966, pp. 108-
      109.

Notes that although David is self-conscious of déjà vu, he does not attach metaphysical importance to the experience. According to Buckley, David effortlessly "achieves the sort of recovery of the past that Proust's hero seeks with great deliberation."

242. Butt, John. "*David Copperfield* Month by Month." In *Dickens at Work*. By John Butt and Kathleen Tillotson. London: Methuen, 1957, pp. 114-176.

Of primary interest for textual study, but this study of Dickens's serial practices does touch on a variety of topics such as characterization, structure, and thematic patterning. No reader interested in Dickens as serial writer and topical novelist should neglect Butt's work. See Butt (8) for fuller annotation.

243. Caine, Hall. "Introduction to *David Copperfield*." In the 1912 Waverly Edition, pp. v-xii (53).

Realizes literary men seldom ponder the question of which is their favorite work, but Dickens in declaring *David Copperfield* his favorite child is an exception. Caine believes that through the first third of the book both David the character and the novel itself stand "absolutely at the head of all fiction." In delineating the "child-heart" Dickens ranks high with Caine as a storyteller, showing a talent Caine finds lacking in Charlotte Brontë.

244. Calder, Jenni. *Women and Marriage in Victorian Fiction.* New York: Oxford Univ. Press, 1976, pp. 100-102.

Briefly mentions Dora and Agnes as examples of the problem Dickens had presenting images of domestic normality when "the whole tendency of his fiction questions whether normality exists."

245. Calder-Marshall, Arthur. "Introduction." In the 1967 Pan Edition, pp. v-xviii (70).

Summarizes biographical background under such subheadings as "The First Betrayal" (the blacking factory), "The Second Betrayal" (Maria Beadnell), "The Unhealing Marriage." In these experiences Calder-Marshall finds the roots of what he regards as Dickens's manic-depressive temperament. Critically, this introduction is original in recognizing the varied theme of "the second chance" as it applies to many characters (the Micawbers, Betsey, David's mother), but Calder-Marshall overextends the argument by

applying it also to Heep, Littimer, Creakle, and even
Steerforth in Italy. Calder-Marshall thinks there is unity
in the David and Steerforth stories because in paralleling David's and Em'ly's personal histories Dickens shows
them both victims of Steerforth's charms. Calder-Marshall
does not regard Georgina Hogarth as the model for Agnes—
contrast Adrian (710)—but he suggests that under Dickens's
influence Georgina later came to resemble the idealized
Agnes.

246. Canning, Albert S. "*David Copperfield.*" In *Philosophy of
      Charles Dickens*. London: Smith, Elder, 1880, pp. 234–
      260. Reprinted in *Dickens Studied in Six Novels*. London:
      T. Fisher Unwin, 1912, pp. 125–151.

      More summary than critical commentary. Canning describes
      David's experiences as commonplace. He comments on many
      of the characters, describing Uriah Heep as "one of
      Dickens's most carefully drawn rogues" and Steerforth as
      the chief villain about whom readers are for some time
      left in doubt. Canning sees David as a successful man of
      the world, achieving "all the success which a man in his
      position ... could reasonably desire." Despite many simply
      appreciative statements, Canning is one of the few earlier
      commentators to mention the general melancholy that comes
      through despite the novel's many amusing characters.

247. Carabine, Keith. "Reading *David Copperfield.*" In *Reading
      the Victorian Novel: Detail into Form*. Ed. Ian Gregor.
      London: Vision Press, 1980, pp. 150–167.

      Finds at least three quarters of the novel "extraordi-
      narily plural and unsettling" largely because of David's
      equivocal responses to much of his experience. Carabine
      thinks that critics too often praise the first fourteen
      chapters without noticing how David's childhood is para-
      digmatic. On the other hand, Carabine notes how the
      strange experiences and sordidness embodied in the eccen-
      trics alert readers to "mysterious, ambivalent and disturb-
      ing forces at work in the fiction," for the careers of
      these people often contrast those of both David and Agnes.
      Carabine looks closely at Heep's role and Dora's death
      "in order to capture how elusive, uncertain and surpris-
      ing these middle chapters are." Also he shows that as
      the Heep-Agnes and David-Dora courtships proceed, both
      Heep and Dora pose threats to David's integrity. Like a
      number of recent critics interested in the role of memory
      and in Mr. Dick particularly, Carabine finds that just as
      Mr. Dick banishes King Charles from his thoughts, so

also must David deny some of his earlier imaginative experience.

248. Carey, John. *The Violent Effigy: A Study of Dickens'
      Imagination*. London: Faber and Faber, 1973, passim.

      Published in New York as *Here Comes Dickens: The Imagina-
      tion of a Novelist* (Schocken Books, 1973). Carey does not
      separate his discussion of various works but mentions
      Copperfield in his chapters on "Dickens and Order,"
      "Dickens' Humour," "Dickens' Children," and "Dickens and
      Sex." Throughout this thought-provoking book Carey deals
      with the paradoxes of Dickens's art--his love of order
      yet his descriptions which reveal his fascination with
      chaos, his humor which has a "double effect of smirking
      at the viewer and despising the viewed," his sympathy for
      children yet his honesty about the "child's desperate
      selfishness and ... hunger for prestige." The chapter on
      children is one of the best discussions of the childhood
      imagination in Dickens's fiction. Carey believes that
      Dickens went on writing the "fragment of his autobiography
      in novel after novel" and returned frequently to the
      image of "the bright, pure child in the mouldering house."
      Examining Dickens's portrayal of sexuality, Carey argues
      that the adult David "is unable to associate maturity
      with sex." Carey therefore thinks that the sexual evasive-
      ness of the final chapters of *Copperfield* concerns
      Dickens's portrayal of David as much as of Agnes. Carey's
      argument is that sex in Dickens's books "is not banished
      but driven underground, to emerge in perverted and in-
      hibited forms." Reviews: Richard Dunn, *SNNTS*, 8 (1976),
      223-233; K.J. Fielding, *RES*, NS 26 (1975), 235-237; Robert
      Giddings, *DSN*, 6 (1975), 115-119; Michael Goldberg, *NCF*,
      29 (1974), 354-357; Barbara Hardy, *Dickensian*, 71 (1975),
      49-51.

249. Carmichael, Thomas A. "Self and Society: Marriage in the
      Novels of Charles Dickens." *DAI*, 38 (1977), 3511A-3512A
      (Illinois, 1977).

      Treats *Copperfield* as transitional in Dickens's por-
      trayal of marriage because earlier he had "relied on
      marriage as ... a means to round out a plot or to high-
      light the folly of his characters. But as he matured ...
      marriage [became] a means of externalizing the internal
      conflict between concepts basic to his fiction."

250. Cary, Joyce. "Including Mr. Micawber." *New York Times
      Book Review*, 15 April 1951, pp. 4, 21. Reprinted in

Selected Essays. Ed. A.G. Bishop. London: Michael
Joseph, 1976, pp. 172-175.

Defends Dickens's exaggeration in characterizing Micawber.
Cary puts Micawber in the curious company of Sancho Panza,
Raskolnikov, and the Red Queen, as particular examples of
the paradoxical effectiveness of "unreal" characters in
fiction.

251. Cecil, David. "Charles Dickens." In *Victorian Novelists:
      Essays in Revaluation*. Chicago: Univ. of Chicago Press,
      1958, pp. 50-53.

Revision of work published first as *Early Victorian
Novelists* (New York: Bobbs-Merrill, 1935). Cecil regards
the first hundred and sixty pages of *David Copperfield*
as the best Dickens ever wrote, "for though the world
that he reveals is more exaggerated ... than that of most
grown-up people, it is exactly the world as it is seen
through the eyes of a child." Cecil thinks the certainty
of this vision is absent later in the novel, "where acute
observation and brilliant fantasy and unctuous sentimentality and preposterous improbability tread on one another's
heels."

252. Chapman, Raymond. "Dickens." In *The Victorian Debate:
      English Literature and Society 1832-1901*. London:
      Weidenfield and Nicolson, 1968, pp. 111-114.

Discusses *Copperfield* only in passing, but notes Micawber's triumph over Malthusian theory, and mentions Steerforth's "Shelleyan fate" as "a judgement for offence not
only against the morality of sex but also against that
of class."

253. Chesterton, G.K. *Charles Dickens*. London: Methuen, 1906,
      pp. 192-199. Republished as *Charles Dickens: A Critical
      Study*. London: Dodd, Mead, 1913. Reissued as *Charles
      Dickens: The Last of the Great Men*. New York: The Readers
      Club, 1942.

Treats *David Copperfield* as the transitional novel in
Dickens's career. Exaggeration of the personalities comes
not from the author, says Chesterton, but from the views
of the characters' friends and enemies as Dickens takes
into account illusion as a fact of life. Unlike other
Dickens novels, *Copperfield* is concerned "with quite
common actualities," although with typical love of paradox
Chesterton describes the novel as "realistic because it
is romantic." He calls Mr. Micawber "an immense assertion

of the truth that the way to live is to exaggerate everything," and he thinks Mrs. Micawber ranks as nearly the
best thing in Dickens, as someone we should consider as
"an unconscious satire on the logical view of life."
Chesterton's influential discussion centers on minor
characters and favors the earlier parts of the novel.
For a less enthusiastic but more comprehensive study
see his introduction to the Everyman Edition (255).

254. ———. "Charles Dickens." In *Charles Dickens. Bookman
Extra Number.* London: Hodder and Stoughton, 1914, pp.
7-11.

Praises Dora as a "more personal character than all
Dickens's waxworks heroines," but sees Dickens "follow-
ing his evil genius" when he has Dora commend David to
Agnes.

255. ———. "*David Copperfield.*" In 1907 Everyman Edition,
pp. v-xiv (50). Reprinted in *Appreciations and Criticisms of the Works of Charles Dickens.* London: J.M.
Dent, 1911, pp. 129-139.

Sees *Copperfield* as Dickens's deliberate break from
limiting conventions, his "romantic attempt to be realistic" (cf. 253). Chesterton thinks signs of fatigue, such
as the tone of false optimism in later parts, mar the
book. He considers the ending's despotic dismissal of
characters as all wrong; Micawber's Australian success
is an instance of hazy optimism, and David's marriage
to Agnes seems "a middle-aged compromise." With a critically despotic tone of his own, Chesterton declares Dora
a nuisance whom Dickens condemns to death. But, he admits,
in spite of these flaws, *Copperfield* contains a number
of unforgettable characters, "more actual than the man
who made them." George Ford, in *Dickens and His Readers*
(304), states that in this introduction Chesterton's
"Little Englandism and his theories of marriage are ob-
trusively aired at the expense of any profitable discussion of the novel or the author."

256. ———. "The Great Victorian Novelists." In *The Victorian
Age in Literature.* London: Home University Library,
1913. Reprinted, London: Oxford Univ. Press, 1966, p.
54.

Cites Betsey Trotwood as an example of Dickens's use
of "realism in order to make the incredible credible."
Chesterton notes the comparisons of Dickens and Thackeray
that had been made by some of the early reviewers.

257. Churchill, R.C. "Charles Dickens." In *From Dickens to*
      Hardy. Ed. Boris Ford. Harmondsworth: Penguin, 1958,
      pp. 119-123.

      Surveys Dickens's works with the general view that
      "genius and rubbish exist side by side in the same novels."
      David is, for Churchill, the most credible of Dickens's
      heroes, but he does not think the credibility extends
      to Dora.

258. Claretie, Jules. "Appreciation of *David Copperfield*."
      In 1919 Readers' Classic Edition, pp. 20-21 (55).

      Recalls first reading the novel in translation with the
      title *Le Neveu de ma Tante* and declares it to be "auto-
      biography where one may find the heart-throbs of the
      author."

259. Clayborough, Arthur. "Dickens: A Circle of Stage Fire."
      In *The Grotesque in English Literature*. Oxford: The
      Clarendon Press, 1965, pp. 201-255.

      Classifies the many uses Dickens made of the grotesque
      throughout his career and notes the two-sided grotesque-
      ness of Mr. Micawber. Like a number of comic characters
      Clayborough mentions, Micawber evokes both sympathy and
      censure from readers aware of the social conditions which
      distress the character. Clayborough includes Mr. Dick and
      Betsey Trotwood in a group of sentimentally portrayed
      eccentrics, and he places Uriah Heep among distinctly
      villainous characters with grotesquely inhuman features.
      Clayborough does not discuss any of Dickens's novels
      individually.

260. Cockshut, A.O.J. "*David Copperfield*." In *The Imagination*
      of Charles Dickens. London: Collins, 1961, pp. 114-126.

      Considers this a difficult book to assess critically
      because of opposing qualities--the clarity of its nostal-
      gic pictures and the marked tendency toward fantasy.
      Cockshut sees the novel evading "the consequences of its
      own assumptions" and thereby lacking inner logic. The
      autobiographical issue, Cockshut thinks, is a question
      of how extensively Dickens exorcised his early fantasies
      through mature examination and how far he created new
      ones "by adding fuel to the fire of his self-pity." With
      brief but incisive discussion, Cockshut notes the com-
      plexity of David's repulsion for Heep and his admiration
      for Steerforth. He also notes that fairy-tale tradition
      is often evident; at first it is appropriate, but the

effect is "bound to be spoilt" in the later "deliberately
'mature' passages." Concluding on a negative note, Cockshut thinks *Copperfield* goes bad at the point where retrospective reverie merges into disingenuous self-justifica-
tion, thirsting for vengeance. Reviews: K.J. Fielding,
Dickensian, 58 (1962), 21-22; Steven Marcus, *NSN*, 62
(1961), 278-279; Harry Stone, *NCF*, 17 (1962), 89-91.

261. Collins, Norman. "Introduction." In 1952 Collins Edition,
      pp. 9-12, (62).

      Comments upon Dickens's statement that *Copperfield* was
      his favorite work, noting that he had already termed
      Martin Chuzzlewit the best of his stories. Collins
      examines the *Copperfield* preface's phrasing closely be-
      cause he thinks it reveals the essence of Dickens, "a
      natural actor and therefore fascinated by himself but,
      even more like an actor," worried "that his audience
      should fail to be fascinated, too." In the remainder of
      his short introduction Collins discusses the novel's
      autobiographical sources, especially the women in Dickens's
      life who affected the novel's recurrent "image of young,
      innocent, prematurely-extinguished womanhood." Collins
      also provides a few short quotations to demonstrate that
      Dickens was "an incomparable stylist" with a sense for
      the right word and an ear for prose rhythm.

262. Collins, Philip. *Charles Dickens: David Copperfield*. Lon-
      don: Edward Arnold, 1977. 63 pp.

      Part of a series of studies in English literature
      designed to stimulate students' critical insights, but
      not a study guide with a summary of the novel. The first
      chapter considers "The Author, the Hero, and the Narrative"
      and argues that David lacks spiritual, moral, and ideo-
      logical perplexity. The second and third chapters discuss
      David the child and David the adult, noting that "the
      re-creation of childhood joys is unfailingly felicitous."
      Collins takes a traditional position in holding to the
      opinion that, in this first Dickens novel to present the
      hero fully both as child and man, Dickens does not sustain
      the brilliance of the book's first half. He also thinks
      it a mistake for Dickens to have made his hero a novelist--
      contrast Beebe (223). Includes brief selected bibliog-
      raphy. Reviews: Edwin M. Eigner, *MLR*, 74 (1979), 920-921;
      Sylvère Monod, *EA*, 31 (1978), 403.

263. ————. "*David Copperfield*: 'A Very Complicated Inter-
      weaving of Truth and Fiction.'" *E&S*, NS 23 (1970), 71-86.

Discusses many of the familiar autobiographical details
and shows that many of the differences between the novel
and the author's personal story can be accounted for by
the fact that Dickens was writing a novel with its own
demands of "consequentiality and credibility." Many of
the book's triumphs, Collins argues, are where Dickens
created purely fictional material; some weakness comes
through his blending of fiction and fact and through the
dream solutions he offered for real problems.

264.   ———. *Dickens and Crime*. London: Macmillan, 1962,
         pp. 113–115, 157–163.

Shows Dickens's philanthropic work at Urania Cottage
as running counter to the optimism in *Copperfield* concerning emigration as a possibility for fallen women.
Collins discusses Dickens, Carlyle, and the "Interesting
Penitents" chapter (Chapter 61). He grants that this chapter is comic though confused in its penology, and it does
provide a final view of Littimer and Heep. Collins incorporates material from his 1961 note about the Middlesex
Magistrate (606). Reviews: John E. Butt, *Dickensian*, 59
(1963), 44–45; Monroe Engel, *VS*, 7 (1963), 105–106; K.J.
Fielding, *RES*, NS 14 (1963), 308–309.

265.   ———. "The Popularity of Dickens." *Dickensian*, 70
         (1974), 5–20.

General essay including the observation that the
characterization of David, like many of Dickens's self-
descriptions, stresses popular, workaday virtues.

266.   Coolidge, Archibald C., Jr. *Charles Dickens as Serial
         Novelist*. Ames: Iowa State Univ. Press, 1967, pp. 109–
         111, 162–172, 183–209.

Shows that even in the middle of his career Dickens
followed "the simple idea of incidents arranged like beads
on a string" to advance one or more parts of the plot
in each installment. Coolidge provides a detailed chart
of the thirteenth part of *David Copperfield* to show
Dickens's technique for arousing curiosity. He discusses
Dickens's growing interest in creating plots around a
passive protagonist and considers *Copperfield* instrumental
in presenting the kind of psychological reformation in
the hero which would later distinguish *Great Expectations*.
Coolidge thinks that by use of the child-hero and the
child-viewer in *Copperfield* Dickens maintains a precise
and constant relationship between his emotional and

philosophical postures and those of his hero. Appendices
chart the novel's part divisions and describe stock
characters, incidents, and motifs. Reviews: K.J. Fielding,
Dickensian, 63 (1967), 156–157; George H. Ford, *Novel*, 2
(1969), 184–185; J.A. Sutherland, *DiS*, 4 (1968), 95–98.

267.   Corthell, Roland. "The Transformation of Mrs. Gummidge."
         Dickensian, 16 (1920), 189.

Can recall no other Dickens character so splendidly
regenerated from whining selfishness.

268.   Coveney, Peter. "The Child in Dickens." In *Image of
         Childhood: The Individual and Society: A Study of the
         Theme in English Literature*. Baltimore: Penguin, 1966,
         pp. 111–161. Revision of *Poor Monkey: The Child in
         Literature*. London: Rockliff, 1957.

Shows that Dickens's awareness of childhood experience
was the basis of a fundamental criticism of life in his
fiction. This is a general essay with only passing attention to *David Copperfield*, a novel Coveney considers
flawed by "conscious self-identity."

269.   Cox, C.B. "Realism and Fantasy in *David Copperfield*."
         BJRL, 52 (1970), 267–283.

Contends that *Copperfield*'s mixture of realism and
fantasy is not solely the projection of childhood anguish
but is deeply involved with Dickens's "characteristic
adult vision of life." Cox thinks Dickens plays with
words to control the darker side of his imagination and
uses bizarre comparisons to individualize his people. He
discusses how objects and landscapes in *David Copperfield*
partake of both the real and the subjective as memory
becomes the novel's controlling medium.

270.   Crotch, W. Walter. *The Pageant of Dickens*. London: Chap-
         man and Hall, 1915, passim.

A more descriptive than critical survey of Dickens's
memorable characters, but it contains a few interesting
observations about a few *Copperfield* characters. Crotch
thinks it all too easy to enjoy Dickens's eccentrics and
not understand the high moral purpose he sometimes expresses through them. Mr. Dick is an instance Crotch
cites of "childishness" rightly and wisely controlled in
an eccentric character. Mr. Dick thus is an effective
moral agent, and so, in Crotch's view, is Betsey ("auster-
ities and angularities" of her character soften as she

continues to care for other people). Crotch, however,
seems determined to exercise moral judgments of his own
concerning Rosa Dartle, a character he includes with Heep
in a gallery of Dickens's hypocrites. Dartle, says Crotch,
symbolizes "all the women, who, hugging their wrongs to
their hearts, have blistered their lips with lying words
and seared their souls with cruel acts."

271. Cruse, Amy. *"David Copperfield."* In *Famous English Books
      and Their Stories.* New York: Thomas Y. Crowell, 1926,
      pp. 241-251.

      Places the novel in the Dickens canon and points out
      factual differences between David's and Dickens's boy-
      hoods but notes the general similarity of their child-
      hood pleasures. Cruse discusses familiar prototypes for
      characters but stresses Dickens's general sympathy for
      the poor as his impetus for the hearty Yarmouth group.
      She concludes with the curious observation that Dickens's
      subsequent life "was an uneventful one."

272. Dabney, Ross H. *"David Copperfield* and *Bleak House."* In
      Love and Property in the Novels of Dickens. Berkeley:
      Univ. of California Press, 1967, pp. 66-92.

      Finds *David Copperfield* shifting from the sense that
      other Dickens novels have of the need for radical social
      reformation. Dabney thinks most of the book's bad marriages
      are disinterested, innocent, impulsive, and its good ones
      passionless. The Heep and Murdstone stories are excep-
      tions, he finds, for they follow Dickens's more customary
      interest in forced and mercenary marriages. Dabney men-
      tions similarities between Mr. Murdstone and David, for
      David's success is "explained by the qualities of energy
      and steely determination" that typify Murdstone. He finds
      no Dickens characters after David Copperfield surviving
      mistakes in love so undamaged, and he views this novel
      as a holiday from Dickens's "usual moral insistences."
      Reviews: George H. Ford, *MP*, 66 (1969), 381-383; Robert
      Hamilton, *Dickensian*, 63 (1967), 110; Arnold Kettle, *VS*,
      11 (1967), 249; Lauriat Lane, Jr., *DiS*, 3 (1967), 170-175.

273. Dark, Sidney. *"David Copperfield."* In *Charles Dickens.*
      London: T. Nelson, 1919, pp. 83-90.

      Attends to Dickens's remark that in finishing *Copper-
      field* he seemed to be sending some part of himself into
      the shadowy world, but Dark finds less of the essential
      Dickens in David than in lesser characters from other

novels. Dark argues that although Dickens tried to be
realistic, he in fact produced another fairy tale: "*David
Copperfield* is above all things the complete assertion
that Everyman's life is a romantic adventure." Dark
thinks Dora is a successful creation up to the point of
Dickens's decision to have her endorse Agnes as David's
second wife. Generally this essay echoes G.K. Chesterton's
ideas of the realism of the novel's romance (253).

274.   Darroll, G.M.H. "A Note on Dickens and Maria Beadnell,
       and Dickens's Comic Genius." *ESA*, 7 (1964), 81-87.

       Applies George Meredith's definition of the comic
       spirit to the portrayal of Dickens's love for Maria as
       it appears in David and Dora. Darroll notes that when
       Dickens returned to the subject in *Little Dorrit*, he had
       Flora Finching comment more comically than Dora on young
       love.

275.   Darwin, Bernard. *Dickens*. London: Duckworth, 1933, pp.
       91-96.

       Notes that the initial sales figures of *David Copper-
       field* were surprisingly low compared to *Dombey and Son*.
       Darwin considers David an admirable hero but cannot defend
       Agnes as heroine.

276.   ————. "In Defense of Dora." *Dickensian*, 45 (1949), 91-
       96.

       Finds "something beautifully sincere and simple" about
       the David-Dora love story and thus repeats the frequent
       appreciative defence of Dickens's portrayal of Dora.

277.   D'Avanzo, Mario L. "Mr. Creakle and His Prison: A Note
       on Craft and Meaning." *Dickensian*, 64 (1968), 50-52.

       Rebuts A.O.J. Cockshut's argument that Creakle's
       reappearance as magistrate was a mistake (260) and finds
       subtle irony in the presentation of Creakle as a charac-
       ter who undergoes apparent transformation. D'Avanzo be-
       lieves Creakle finally demonstrates the wrongness of a
       penal system designed to re-educate men. He argues that
       Creakle is dangerous and consistent in both of his jobs
       because he lacks love.

278.   Davis, Earle. "The Creation of Dickens's *David Copper-
       field*: A Study in Narrative Craft." *Bulletin: Municipal
       University of Wichita*, 16 (April 1941), 2-30.

Summarizes Forster's advisory role, describes the novel's
autobiographical elements, and discusses the picaresque
and epic principles *David Copperfield* shares with eighteenth-century fiction, finding David as a hero similar
to Tom Jones. Davis thinks *Roderick Random* may have suggested to Dickens ways to avoid direct confession of his
actual family history. Davis is alone in suggesting the
bombast of Dr. Johnson and Bulwer-Lytton as well as that
of John Dickens as prototypic of Mr. Micawber's grandiloquence. Davis argues that the final three quarters of the
novel reveal a conflict between the first-person narration and Dickens's broadly panoramic plan. He also thinks
the novel is weakened by Rosa Dartle's story, Dickens's
evident shift of intent with the Strongs, and the whitewashing of Miss Mowcher. But the book remains for Davis
great "because of its accomplishments in first person
narration and its distinctive combination of panoramic
viewpoint with the biographical method."

279.   ————. "First Person—*David Copperfield*." In *The Flint
       and the Flame: The Artistry of Charles Dickens.* Columbia:
       Univ. of Missouri Press, 1963, pp. 157-182.

Expands the discussion in his 1941 article (278) concerning Dickens's eighteenth-century literary models and
the novel's plot conflicts between panoramic and first-
person perspectives. Reviews: John E. Butt, *NCF*, 19 (1964),
88-91; J. Hillis Miller, *JEGP*, 63 (1964), 534-536; N.C.
Peyrouton, *Dickensian*, 60 (1964), 40-42.

280.   Dawson, Carl. "'The Lamp of Memory': Wordsworth and
       Dickens." In *Victorian Noon: English Literature in
       1850.* Baltimore: The Johns Hopkins Univ. Press, 1979,
       pp. 123-152.

Significant study of how *The Prelude* and *David Copperfield* rely on memory as "a way of imagination that is at
once retrospective and self-assertive." Dawson notes that,
like Wordsworth, Dickens records the disciplining of
the self and less explicitly the disciplining of the
life of the imagination. Dawson admits some basic difference in the portrayal but shows noticeable similarity
between Wordsworth's and Dickens's descriptions of Alpine
spiritual awakenings. Dawson is convincing in his discussion of how a compounding of past and present memories
works in *Copperfield*, as it often does in Wordsworth,
to make descriptions vivid and to transform the banal
into the extraordinary. Also this discussion compares
both authors' innocent characters, citing Mr. Peggotty
as, "in Wordsworth's terms, one of those silent poets"

and Mr. Micawber, in contrast, as "without a memory, at
least without a memory for suffering." Dawson's reference
to Ruskin in his chapter title somewhat complicates his
Dickens-Wordsworth comparison, but the point is that in
Seven Lamps of Architecture Ruskin categorized values
Dawson shows to have been held by Wordsworth and Dickens.
Reviews: Patrick Brantlinger, *NCF*, 34 (1980), 468-470.

281. Dent, H.C. "Chapter X [*David Copperfield*]." In *The Life
     and Characters of Charles Dickens*. London: Odham's
     Press, [1933], pp. 343-362.

An often overlooked but sensible discussion about the
problems of writing a genuinely autobiographical novel.
Dent remarks that never did a novelist so effectively
present "a vividly accurate picture by the conscious use
of inaccurate detail." He likens Dickens's novels (and
letters) to Turner paintings. Also he notes the sadness
and suffering touching many of the characters' lives:
"Even Mr. Micawber is no mere figure of fun," though his
Australian success could have been conceivable. Dent finds
"more than a hint of Forster" in Traddles and considers
this character one of Dickens's "neglected heroes"--see
Clark (605). He finds many of Steerforth's characteristics
in Dickens himself. Because Dickens was forced to show
him growing up, Uriah Heep is, for Dent, the least satisfactory major charcter. Dent regards Agnes as necessary
to the story but thinks her not well portrayed. He thinks
Dickens's problems with Agnes arose because she "lay
nearly as close to his heart as David Copperfield."

282. De Wyzewa, Theodor. "Appreciation of *David Copperfield*."
     In 1919 Readers' Classic Edition, pp. 23-25 (55).

Considers the autobiographical basis as the source of
the novel's "vigorous life and truth." This commentator
defends the Steerforth and Little Em'ly story against
the usual charges of sentimentality, for the character
of Steerforth, though spoiled a little near the end, is
"very truly 'English.'" De Wyzewa regrets that Dickens
had not used Dora in another novel where he "would have
been more at liberty to turn her to better account."

283. Dickens, Charles, the Younger. "Introduction." In 1892
     Macmillan Edition, pp. xix-xxv (44).

Most important for his efforts to establish that Dickens
had shared his fragmentary autobiography with his wife
before the novel was published. According to Dickens's

son, Mrs. Dickens counseled her husband against publication of it. Unsurprisingly, this introduction resists the
idea that the Micawbers are largely based on Dickens's
parents.

284. Dobrin, David N. "'Veels Vithin Veels': The Secret Self
      and the World in the Novels of Charles Dickens." *DAI*,
      38 (1978), 6740A (San Diego, 1977).

      Asserts that in *David Copperfield* the secret self "is
      manifested in visible tags, the central technique of the
      novel." Dobrin says that, unlike autobiography, *Copper-
      field* is compartmentalized, but comic elements are the-
      matically connected, and the sentimental parts are tied
      together by such symbols as the sea. In a typically modern
      assessment of David as writer, Dobrin thinks that David's
      written memory defines the boundary of his secret self,
      protecting "his present happiness from the malign mem-
      ories of the past."

285. Donovan, Frank. "Dickens' Favorite Child." In *Dickens and
      Youth*. New York: Dodd, Mead, 1968, pp. 24-60. Published
      in England as *The Children of Charles Dickens*. London:
      Leslie Frewin, 1969.

      Shows Dickens to have been the first English novelist
      to give children and young people central parts in stories.
      Donovan acknowledges that autobiographical details of
      remembered incidents appear, but he thinks the emotional
      reality of the novel goes deeper. Donovan's discussion
      is disappointing because he does not consider in detail
      the important topics of memory and the lasting psycho-
      logical effects of childhood. He summarizes David's
      earlier experiences, drawing on both Forster (730) and
      Edgar Johnson (738). Donovan placidly agrees with earlier
      popular assessments favoring the early parts of the novel
      and extends some praise to Dickens's treatment of David
      and Dora. He concludes by reiterating Chesterton's re-
      gard for the book's "romantic realism" (253).

286. Dunn, Albert A. "Time and Design in *David Copperfield*."
      ES, 59 (1978), 225-236.

      Takes issue with Monod (425) and argues that David's
      self-justifications are as much those of any young man
      as of Dickens in particular. Dunn is right in insisting
      that purely autobiographical reading limits understand-
      ing of the book's use of Victorian social myths, and he
      is convincing in arguing that structured comparison be-

tween David's and his mother's marriages helps us to
"perceive the representative nature of failed romantic
expectations." Dunn's is a useful essay to be considered
with Easson (291), Gilmour (320), and others who, like
Dunn, realize that in the process of David's history, "the
past is recreated to effect a reinterpretation of that
past."

287. Dunn, Richard J. "*David Copperfield*: All Dickens Is
      There." *English Journal*, 54 (1965), 789-794.

      General discussion of Dickens's strengths and weak-
      nesses evident in a novel retaining many elements of
      his earliest successes. Dunn discusses how David deflects
      attention from himself as he gets older, especially by
      narrating Micawber's denunciation of Heep and by pro-
      jecting his own mental turmoil into the characterization
      of Steerforth and into the description of the great storm.
      This discussion is directed primarily toward secondary
      teachers using *Copperfield* as a representative Dickens
      work.

288. ———. "Far, Far Better Things: Dickens' Later Endings."
      DSA, 7 (1978), 221-236.

      Uses the conclusion of *David Copperfield* as a starting
      point to discuss how Dickens found ways to preserve some
      comic resolutions in novels that were not primarily comic.
      Dunn admits that *Copperfield* especially reflects a con-
      sciousness of separation and death, but he shows that
      David finds some vicarious joy with the married Traddles,
      whose domestic life seems a fictional version of Dickens's
      happy days with Mary Hogarth. Dunn claims that many de-
      tails of the final number make this novel's conclusion
      Dickens's "most comprehensive effort to perpetuate
      pleasant memories while exorcising unpleasant ones."

289. Du Pontavice, R. "Comment on *David Copperfield*." In 1919
      Readers' Classic Edition, pp. 56-57 (55).

      A selection from his *The Inimitable Boy* (1889), men-
      tioning *David Copperfield* as the best written of Dickens's
      novels. Du Pontavice makes the observation that Betsey
      Trotwood is "abrupt, angular, eccentric," but she is
      "kindness and uprightness itself."

290. Dyson, A.E. "*David Copperfield*: The Favourite Child."
      In *The Inimitable Dickens: A Reading of the Novels*.
      London: Macmillan, 1970, pp. 119-153.

Notes the infrequency with which David is addressed or
thought of by his own name. Dyson discusses a pattern of
images growing from David's various names. He also suggests that Dickens makes his characterization vivid by
converging speech rhythms, underlying archetypes, and
images. "The obsessions of his people are always congruent
with the many other detailed perceptions through which
he creates them, and contribute to our sense of depth and
roundness behind the stylized facade." Dyson gives extensive consideration to the book's treatment of sex,
observing that the David who passionately sought a lost
childhood is "devitalized by his second marriage." But
though he shares a number of Dickens's traumas, David
"is very little like Dickens." Although he presents a
broad discussion of the novel, Dyson is most informative
in his reading of such details as David's names and nick-
names. Reviews: Anthony Burton, *Dickensian*, 66 (1970),
244; Bert G. Hornback, *DSN*, 1 (1970), 11-13; *TLS*, 4 June
1970, pp. 597-598.

291.   Easson, Angus. "The Mythic Sorrows of Charles Dickens."
       Literature and History, 1 (1975), 49-61.

       Centers on Dickens's understanding of his childhood
and considers how his concepts of narration and his handling of emotion and recollection changed after he transformed his private sorrows into the fiction of *David
Copperfield*. Easson suggests that Dickens's bitterness
over the sense of young talent unrecognized permeates the
autobiographical fragment. Easson parallels *Copperfield*
and *The Prelude*, saying that in the novel "experience is
controlled by an understanding of feeling and a stress
upon those moments that seem particularly significant
in retrospect." Also he finds kinship between the novel
and Carlyle's sense of history as "the first distinct
product of man's spiritual nature." One of few critics
to grant the necessary ongoing quality of David's thinking as a writer with works before him, Easson ponders
what the ending's mention of David's child may imply
about David's future.

292.   Eigner, Edwin M. *The Metaphysical Novel in England and
       America: Dickens, Melville, and Hawthorne*. Berkeley:
       Univ. of California Press, 1978, passim.

       Attending to David's function as character, hero, and
autobiographer, Eigner notes that sub-characters provide
a number of unsatisfactory careers to which David responds
strongly beacuse he recognizes their lives as potentially

his own. He therefore insists that it is inadequate to
read the novel as psychological autobiography and not
attend to the minor characters and subplots. He thinks
it especially necessary to notice both the realistic and
the allegorical aspects of the central character, for it
is the allegorical idealization that distinguishes *David
Copperfield* as a metaphysical novel. Eigner sees this
novel as less obviously a religious allegory than *A Tale
of Two Cities*, but he grants that Agnes Wickfield is one
of Dickens's most clear images of the Virgin. By regarding this novel as a mixture of *Bildungsbiographie* and
English novel of development, Eigner shows that the metaphysical novel is essentially a mixed form. This sophisticated study may be most useful to those widely read in
English and American fiction.

293. Elton, Oliver. "Charles Dickens." In *Dickens and Thackeray*. London: Edward Arnold, 1924, pp. 7-49. Revision
of chapter in *Survey of English Literature*. London:
Edward Arnold, 1912, Vol. I, pp. 195-221.

In a brief discussion of *David Copperfield* Elton notes
the frequent concern in nineteenth-century fiction for
educating the heart and the conscience and for allowing
reason to look after itself. Elton mentions *Pendennis*,
Jane Eyre, *Villette*, and *Tom Brown's Schooldays* as other
examples. He speaks of "wonderful harmony of tone in most
of *David Copperfield*; it is attained by the art which has
released the writer from his own remembered troubles."
Elton challenges the frequently voiced notion that
Dickens's powers were in decline in *Copperfield* and in
later novels.

294. Engel, Monroe. "*David Copperfield*." In *The Maturity of
Dickens*. Cambridge, Mass.: Harvard Univ. Press, 1959,
pp. 148-156.

Generally regards Dickens as a realistic novelist and
considers both *David Copperfield* and *Great Expectations*
in his fifth chapter, "The Sense of Self." Engel, following a frequent course of modern criticism, argues that
the novel is primarily about the hero's need to develop
prudence but finds the book's power coming from a "render-
ing of the beauty of incaution and the poignancy of
limitation and defeat." Engel anticipates Kincaid (374)
by finding a subversive quality in the humor. Reviews:
John E. Butt, *RES*, NS 11 (1960), 440-443; Edgar Johnson,
NCF, 14 (1959), 182-184; Ada Nisbet, *VS*, 3 (1960), 311-
313; N.C. Peyrouton, *Dickensian*, 55 (1959), 155-156.

295. Eoff, Sherman H. "A Fatherly World According to Design."
      In *The Modern Spanish Novel: Comparative Essays Examin-
      ing the Philosophical Impact of Science on Fiction*.
      New York: New York Univ. Press, 1961, pp. 21-50.

      A frequently overlooked discussion, arguing that Dickens
      generally and *Copperfield* particularly represent a peace-
      ful coexistence of science and religion. Eoff traces the
      philosophic roots of the novel's optimism to a broad
      prescientific sense Dickens shared with many contemporaries
      of "a systematical universe under divine interest." The
      novel's narrator, according to Eoff, occupies a dual role,
      shifting his attention between that of a spectator in
      "a world of classifiable beings created by a wise God"
      and that of someone reflecting on the problem of finding
      his place in his world. Although few would call the novel
      picaresque, Eoff states that in the character development
      of the hero and in the authorial outlook, *David Copper-
      field* is antipicaresque. Less convincingly he makes a
      case for Dickens's method of characterization as being
      similar to the biological sciences' methods of classifica-
      tion during the later eighteenth and early nineteenth
      centuries, because the characters are "generic representa-
      tions of the human species" and more abstract than those
      of most of Dickens's contemporaries. In a related dis-
      cussion of José María de Pereda's *Sotileza* (1884), Eoff
      finds the Spanish novel resembling *David Copperfield* in
      subject matter and in comprehensive narrative development.
      He does not make a case for direct influence but contrasts
      both of these writers with later naturalists. Most
      readers will not think of *Copperfield* in Eoff's terms,
      and many will find his arguments most applicable to his
      broadly comparative investigations.

296. Fadiman, Clifton. "Afterword." In 1962 Macmillan Classics
      Edition, pp. 849-850 (66).

      Considers this as one of those few novels "that we *live*
      inside of," because it is the kind of story that causes
      readers to think they are remembering their own lives.
      Characters, especially Micawber, are, for this editor
      of many classics, "fantastic and real at the same time."

297. Fairley, Edwin. "Introduction." In 1911 Macmillan Edition,
      pp. xv-xxiv (52).

      Introduction designed for American public school use
      with a biographical sketch comprising most of the intro-
      duction and with a brief discussion of *Copperfield*,

describing it as "idealized autobiography." Fairley
praises the characterization of Dora but regards Rosa
Dartle as unbelievable in her monstrous cruelty.

298.   Ferris, Norren. "Circumlocution in *David Copperfield*."
       DSN, 9 (1978), 43-46.

       Discovers that David, like Micawber, resorts to circum-
       locution before he comes to understand how words may
       both reflect and distort. Ferris's article is a good start-
       ing point for any reader concerned with Dickens's verbal
       dynamics.

299.   Fido, Martin. "*David Copperfield*, Ch. 61." In *Charles
       Dickens*. London: Routledge and Kegan Paul, 1968, pp.
       58-62.

       One of a "Profiles in Literature" series, this book
       excerpts *Copperfield* passages, which Fido closely studies.
       Calling attention to a number of "curiosities and anom-
       alies" arising from Chapter 61 ("I Am Shown Two Interest-
       ing Penitents"), he argues that the visit to the new prison
       demonstrates Dickens's skill in introducing extraneous
       material on contemporary problems of immediate concern
       to him.

300.   Fielding, K.J. "Actor, Editor, and Author: *David Copper-
       field*." In *Charles Dickens: A Critical Introduction*.
       London: Longmans, Green, 1965, pp. 124-143.

       Expanded version of his 1958 edition. Fielding takes
       into account the ways Dickens's many activities while
       writing *David Copperfield* affected the novel's mix of
       fiction and autobiography. He finds unity in the book
       and stresses the thematic control with which Dickens
       treats his concern for the disciplined heart--see Needham
       (433). Fielding thinks Dickens is successful with comic
       characters because they live so completely in their
       dialogue, but his serious characters are often shadowy
       and conventional. He sees Agnes, one of the least con-
       vincing of these serious characters, standing "as a
       symbol of how love can lead a man's life to be fulfilled."
       Copperfield is "the central novel of Dickens's develop-
       ment" according to Fielding. His lucid discussion well
       supports his stress on *Copperfield*'s centrality.

301.   ————. "Dickens and the Past: The Novelist of Memory."
       In *Experience in the Novel*. Ed. Roy H. Pearce. New
       York: Columbia Univ. Press, 1968, pp. 107-131.

Argues that, dogged by his past, Dickens tried to re-
make it. Fielding thinks *Copperfield* is a less confined
work than *Little Dorrit*, for *Copperfield* moves toward a
sense of fulfillment absent in *Little Dorrit*. The essay
is concerned primarily with *Little Dorrit*.

302.   Fleishman, Avrom. "The Fictions of Autobiographical
       Fiction." *Genre*, 9 (1976), 73-86.

Theorizes that success in fiction is measurable by the
degree a writer resists self-magnification. According
to Fleishman, the fictional center of an autobiographical
novel must be "a freshly discovered man or image of the
man"; Dickens sees the hero's identity as that of a child
passing through life and "continually repeating his
moments of birth and renewal." The article also discusses
The Mill on the Floss and *Sons and Lovers*.

303.   Flower, Linda S. "Fantasy Perception and the Myth of
       Innocence in Dickens." *DAI*, 34 (1973), 3340A-3341A
       (Rutgers, 1973).

Sees alternation of satiric omniscient narrator and
personal, intrusive perspective in Dickens's novels. For
Flower "*David Copperfield* is an anthology of inadequate
innocents in which both innocence and pastoral retreat
are no longer identified with sentimental character types
but with a quality of the imagination and a state of mind
rooted in the saving detachment of the romantic child and
the visionary powers of fantasy."

304.   Ford, George H. *Dickens and His Readers: Aspects of
       Novel-Criticism Since 1836*. Princeton: Princeton Univ.
       Press, 1955; New York: W.W. Norton, 1965, pp. 119-228
       et passim.

Definitive study of Dickens's reputation among English
readers and critics and a necessary work for any readers
interested in Dickens generally. Ford mentions *David
Copperfield* frequently in his discussion of Dickens the
artist and in his consideration of Dickens's reputed
failure to provide sophisticated readers with psychological
insight. He provides also an excellent survey of the
reactions of contemporaries (Carlyle, Thackeray, the
Brownings, Arnold) to *David Copperfield*. Ford states that
Dickens the developing artist was becoming increasingly
versatile "in a prose style which flows almost effortlessly in *Copperfield*" and that early reviews, like
Dickens himself, were attentive to "the techniques of

novel writing." Excellent index. Reviews: Edgar Johnson,
VQR, 31 (1955), 644–648; Franklin P. Rolfe, *NCF*, 10
(1955), 242–245; Geoffrey Tillotson, *Sewanee Review*, 64
(1956), 671–673; *TLS*, 6 Jan. 1956, p. 3; Angus Wilson,
Encounter, 6 (Apr. 1956), 75–77.

305. ———. "Dickens and the Voices of Time." *NCF*, 24 (1970),
      428–448.

Traces the development of a private prose style, a
"music of memory," that counterbalances a more confident
public voice. Ford discusses a number of works, finding
pertinent examples in *Copperfield*'s "Retrospect" chapters.

306. ———. "Introduction." In 1958 Riverside Edition, pp.
      x–xv, (63).

One of the most incisive short introductions, noting
that adult reading brings impressions different from
those formed in childhood acquaintance with *Copperfield*.
Much humor remains for older readers, says Ford, but it
may seem a sadder book to adults. Ford believes that
Freud's admiration of the novel may have been because of
"its brilliant symbolic expression of themes he himself
was to explore," especially the relation of children to
parents. Although one of many children himself, Dickens
focused on the plight of the orphan, a focus which Ford
takes as the sign possibly of an "undersurface of uncertainty" in Dickens's mind. Although Ford admits evident
autobiographical elements, he finds the novel's transformation "extraordinarily complex." Ford discusses
structural implications of the first-person narration
and of the book's dramatic elements ("dramatist and
choreographer" combine in its temporal and spatial movements). He notes also that in this novel Dickens is less
concerned than usual with the plight of the poor, and it
lacks the savage invective with which he usually attacked
social abuses.

307. Forster, E.M. *Aspects of the Novel*. New York: Harcourt,
      Brace, and World, 1927, pp. 65–82.

Frequent mention of Dickens and of *Copperfield* characters in his famous distinction between "flat" and "round"
types. Readers should not stress qualitative differences
between the artistry essential for both types; Forster
notes how remarkably Dickens portrays flat characters,
avoiding mechanical effects and shallow visions of humanity. As he says of Mrs. Micawber, "There is Mrs. Micawber––

she says she won't desert Mr. Micawber, she doesn't, and
there she is." Forster finds David, like Pip in *Great
Expectations*, representing Dickens's attempt at a more
rounded character, but he thinks both heroes are presented
"so diffidently that they seem more like bubbles than
solids."

308.   Forster, John. "*David Copperfield* and *Bleak House*." In
       The Life of Charles Dickens. London: Chapman and Hall,
       1874, Vol. III, pp. 21-50.

Originally published in three volumes between 1872 and
1874, Forster's work is now available in 2 vols., edited
by A.J. Hoppé (London: Dent, 1966). Forster's views of
Copperfield and his accounts of its sources and history
of composition are frequently repeated by other early
biographers and critics. Forster regarded the novel as
the high point of Dickens's career. He begins with a
general discussion of the frequency of veiled autobiography in fiction, citing instances from Smollett and
Scott. He discusses Dickens's embarrassment when Miss
Mowcher's prototype confronted him and his subsequent
change of plan for the character. Forster defends Dickens's
portrayal of traits of his father in Micawber, insisting,
"Nobody likes Micawber less for his follies: and Dickens
liked his father more, the more he recalled his whimsical
qualities." All in all, claims Forster, not too much
should be made of the autobiographical quality, because
there is not a complete identification between David and
Dickens. Unsurprisingly this friend of Dickens believes
that powers of "healthy judgement and sleepless creative
fancy" control Dickens's "imaginative growths." Because
humor for Forster does not weaken "enchanting sentiment,"
the novel, for him, "is the perfection of English mirth."
Contrary to some twentieth-century critics, Forster finds
Dickens avoiding "the indulgence of mental analysis,
metaphysics, and sentiment." He speaks of the storm scene
as one of the most impressive descriptions in the English
language. Well aware of the tensions of Dickens's private
life, Forster recognizes strains of disillusioned love
in the portrayal of the heroines, but he finds "the spoilt
foolishness and tenderness of the loving little child-
wife, Dora, is more attractive than the too unfailing
wisdom and self-sacrificing goodness of the angel-wife,
Agnes." This biography remains useful to modern readers,
because its critical judgments well exemplify the tradition of respect for Dickens's characterization, humor,
and storytelling. See also Forster's biographical discussion (730).

309.   France, Anatole. "Comment on *David Copperfield*." In 1919
       Readers' Classic Edition, p. 55 (55).

       Excerpted from France's *On Life and Letters*, first
       published in English in 1909. France mentions Dickens's
       liking for madmen and commends the tender grace of his
       description of Mr. Dick. France calls Mr. Dick "a sensible
       madman, for the only reason left him is the reason of the
       heart, and that is hardly ever deceived." Thus, to France,
       Mr. Dick's madness seems "a sort of mental originality."

310.   Frank, Lawrence D. "The Enigmatic Hero: Atonement and
       the Urban Man in the Later Novels of Charles Dickens."
       DA, 29 (1969), 2259A (Minnesota, 1969).

       Discusses protagonists caught between a desire for
       permanent innocence and a need to abandon it for the
       sake of psychic survival. In *David Copperfield* Frank
       finds an apparent tension between the optimism of secu-
       larized Christian vision and Dickens's intuitive pessi-
       mism about the reconciliation between the individual and
       society. Frank describes a "series of vicarious atone-
       ments in which diseased sensibilities, like those of
       David Copperfield, ... are cured through the sacrificial
       acts of a Steerforth."

311.   Franklin, Stephen L. "Dickens and Time: The Clock Without
       Hands." *DSA*, 4 (1975), 1-35.

       Discusses a number of Dickens's works and suggests that
       Dickens's attitude toward time was firmly imbedded in
       his essential Christianity. In a short section on *Copper-
       field* Franklin notes that in attending to the passing of
       time Dickens asserts the primacy of external over internal
       realities, even in such moments of internal stress as
       David's experiences during the great storm. Franklin
       mentions Mr. Dick's "Memorial" as the novel's most inter-
       esting example of Dickens's reinforcing of his ideas
       about time through a character's own narrative approach
       to personal recollection. Thus Franklin, like Tick (509),
       parallels Mr. Dick's writings and those of Dickens him-
       self, and Franklin observes that where Dickens (and
       also David) successfully includes past traumatic experi-
       ences in his writing, Mr. Dick does not. But the basic
       question that the novel's attention to time poses for
       Franklin is larger than that of Mr. Dick's failure or
       success; Franklin finds *David Copperfield* asking, "What
       good, then, is the past?" Franklin places Betsey Trotwood
       at the book's moral center, because she provides an an-

swer to this key question, declaring that it is vain to
recall the past unless the recollection works influen-
tially upon the present.

312. Freeman, Janet H. "Story, Teller, and Listener: A Study
      of Six Victorian Novels." *DAI*, 36 (1976), 5315A (Iowa,
      1975).

      Opposes the idea that "narrators of Victorian fiction
      represent a generalized omniscience" and argues that the
      relation of story to teller to listener is a particular
      strength of the Victorian novel. *Copperfield* is narrated,
      says Freeman, "with the joy of absolute self-realization:
      its teller finds in his fulsome memory an identity he
      accepts as perfectly understood."

313. Friedman, Stanley. "Dickens' Mid-Victorian Theodicy:
      David Copperfield." *DSA*, 7 (1978), 128-150.

      Considers Dickens's complex religious and philosophic
      attitudes and views the novel as Dickens's "attempt to
      determine whether effort or providence or chance is the
      decisive factor in this world, whether suffering can be
      redeemed, whether belief in divine justice can be reaf-
      firmed." In pursuit of this ambitious thesis, Friedman
      argues that David is both attracted and repelled by death
      and can face it only by confirming a religious faith
      evoked by Agnes. Friedman links *Copperfield* with a tradi-
      tion of spiritual autobiography and also with such eigh-
      teenth-century fiction as *Robinson Crusoe* and *The Vicar
      of Wakefield*, and he concludes with the arguable notion
      that David is an Everyman whose autobiography is "a
      theodicy asserting eternal providence."

314. G., St. J.O.B. "Literary Allusions in Dickens: *David
      Copperfield*." *N&Q*, NS 12 (1923), 155-156.

      Brief notice of literature read or alluded to by David,
      Barkis, Clara Peggotty, Uriah Heep, Steerforth, Miss
      Mowcher, Mrs. Markleham, and Mr. Micawber.

315. Ganz, Margaret. "The Vulnerable Ego: Dickens' Humor
      in Decline." *DSA*, 1 (1970), 23-40.

      General study which finds an alteration in Dickens's
      humorous style in *David Copperfield*, a loss of "distinc-
      tive creativity" as he tends "to substitute one particu-
      lar expression for a general eccentricity of expression."
      Ganz compares *Martin Chuzzlewit*'s Mrs. Gamp, who is "in-
      toxicated with imagination," to Mr. Micawber, who simply

is "intoxicated with words" and is a more stylized character. Her critical evaluation of *Copperfield*'s humor is
less convincingly iconoclastic than James Kincaid's
studies (373, 374).

316. Gard, Roger. "*David Copperfield*." *EIC*, 15 (1965), 313-325.

Impressed by the detachment of the narrator's observation and by the "aura of sexual implication, often of a
corrupt or distorted kind," in his vision, Gard praises
the clarity of vision Dickens maintains through the eyes
of a child. But when Dickens attempts to handle adult
problems "his famous lack of 'intellectual distinction'
becomes evident" to Gard.

317. Garis, Robert E. *The Dickens Theatre: A Reassessment of
the Novels*. Oxford: The Clarendon Press, 1965, pp. 94-95.

This controversial study gives little direct attention
to *David Copperfield*, but it does go against the grain
of much modern criticism by arguing that "the fact that
Dickens never really developed a fictional mode suitable
for self-examination suggests that what took place within
him was really not self-examination at all." In taking
this position, Garis finds the writing of *David Copperfield* "a disappointing mimicry" of Dickens's own experience, although the book brings some of his "most vivid
performing characters" to its stage. Reviews: William
Burgan, *VS*, 9 (1966), 208-210; George H. Ford, *DiS*, 2
(1966), 96-101; Edgar Johnson, *NCF*, 20 (1966), 395-402;
Martin Price, *YR*, 55 (1965), 291-296; *TLS*, 10 Feb. 1965,
p. 104.

318. Gibson, Frank A. "Was Dickens Tired? or the Poem of
Memory." *Dickensian*, 45 (1949), 157-159.

Disputes Chesterton's sense that there is an air of
fatigue in *David Copperfield* (253) by citing Dickens's
enthusiasm while at work on the novel and by finding true
optimism in his portrayal of Micawber's success. Gibson
thinks Alain is surely correct in regarding the book as
"the poem of memory" (207).

319. Gibson, Katherine M. "The Changing Function of the
Characters' Memories in the Fiction of Charles Dickens."
DAI, 39 (1978), 2288A-2289A (Drew, 1978).

Finds memory playing no consistent role in early novels,
but "by the time of *David Copperfield* ... memory functions
in the individual struggle to master ... pride, selfishness, loneliness, love, disappointment."

320.   Gilmour, Robin. "Memory in *David Copperfield.*" *Dickensian*,
        71 (1975), 30–42.

        One of the most intelligent discussions of this fre-
        quently treated topic. Gilmour argues that the narrator's
        remembering consciousness is a unifying factor and gives
        readers a sense of subtle and ambivalent effects. Gilmour
        acknowledge the novel's awareness of intractable tragic
        elements in life which counterbalance the prudential
        morality of the disciplined heart. The rhythm of memory
        imaginatively mediates between what Gilmour terms "differ-
        ent states of being." Gilmour believes that David's
        diminishing capacity for intense feeling in his mature
        attraction to Agnes remains the central ambiguity because
        David retains his intense recollective powers.

321.   Gissing, George. *Charles Dickens: A Critical Study.* Re-
            vised Edition. London: Gresham, 1903, pp. 59–60, 93–95,
            123–125.

        First published in 1898 (London: Blackie) and revised
        considerably in 1903, Gissing's is one of the first
        lengthy critical evaluations of Dickens that have remained
        influential. His study centers on the form of *David Copper-
        field*, noting the frankness with which Dickens accepts
        the conventionalities of first-person narration. The
        Little Em'ly story is "unhappily conceived," writes
        Gissing, who handled such material differently in his
        own fiction; and Uriah Heep's knavery has "no claim on
        our belief." Especially for a serious novelist, Gissing
        responds positively to Dickens's comic conclusion, for
        he thinks that the final triumphs of Micawber, Mr. Mell,
        and Mrs. Gummidge signal Dickens's mission of embodying
        "the better dreams of ordinary men" in conclusions that
        ignore "cold fact." Thus, for Gissing, Dickens is at
        his best when dealing with an "amiable weakness," and
        Micawber remains his greatest success, though his Aus-
        tralian conversion to practicality lacks credibility.
        Gissing anticipates much later interest in Mr. Dick:
        "The craze about King Charles's head has been, and is
        likely to be, a great resource to literary persons in
        search of a familiar allusion." The wooing of Dora re-
        mains for Gissing "one of the sweetest dreams of humour
        and tenderness ever translated into language."

322.   ————. "Introduction." Written in 1898 for the Rochester
            Edition. The *Copperfield* volumes for that edition were
            never published, but the introduction, edited by Richard
            J. Dunn, appears in the *Dickensian*, 77 (1981), 3–11.

Although this introduction is missing from the Gissing
Dickens introductions that were collected in the 1920's,
page proofs survive among the F.G. Kitton papers at the
Dickens House, London. Gissing starts by considering what
the terms "best" and "author's favorite" connote for
readers attempting critical evaluation. He calls the
book's vision "more simply human" than that of Dickens's
other novels and recognizes the peculiar irony--see Kincaid (373) and Sucksmith (500)--with which Dickens regarded "human weaknesses, even the exasperating and the
harmful, with a gently forbearing smile." Gissing thinks
that the autobiographical form, very successful early in
the novel, burdened Dickens little with plot contrivance.
As he does in his other writings on *Copperfield*, Gissing
calls the Steerforth-Em'ly story the work of an "unskil-
ful, but eager, melodramatist," but Dickens's fine render-
ing of the David-Dora relationship largely atones for the
other's melodrama. Gissing does not find David to be a
convincing study of a literary man, but he terms Micawber an immortal character, one who "walks beside us,
sits at our tables." Shrewdly, Gissing recognizes Betsey
Trotwood to be "a happy medium between Dickens's women
who have no sex at all, and those in whom we see only the
most irritating of feminine characteristics." Uriah Heep
"illustrates the evil of exaggerating and perverting one
of the laws of social equilibrium." Gissing concludes that
Dickens's conservatism and obvious moral sympathies along
with the novel's incorporation of every element of imaginative interest beloved by average readers make *Copperfield* "the typical English novel."

323. ———. "Introduction." In 1903 Autograph Edition, pp.
      xiii-xxv (47).

This introduction to the 1903 limited edition is different from Gissing's 1898 work for the Rochester Edition (322). Gissing argues that David ends not as the
hero of his own life and that finally David hints only
remotely at "the life and personality of Dickens as man
and author" (just as Traddles only slightly resembles
Dickens's friend John Forster). Although many of Dickens's
characters seem to live in a radically different world
than the one Gissing portrayed in his own novels, Gissing
grants that such characters as Mr. Micawber illustrate
a "law of natural idealism," for to Dickens's thinking
"there *is* a law of nature which renders it impossible
that such a man should wax old amid squalid circumstance,
and still retain the virtues of his weaknesses." Gissing

regrets Dickens's "weakness for very crude melodrama" in
the Steerforth-Little Em'ly story but finds the novel
always providing a compensating truthfulness that "triumphs over his conventionalities or fantastic freakings."
For a thorough study of Gissing's writings on Dickens,
see Pierre Coustillas, "Gissing's Writings on Dickens,"
Dickensian, 61 (1965), 168-179.

324.   Gold, Joseph. "'The Disciplined Heart': *David Copperfield*."
        In *Charles Dickens: Radical Moralist*. Minneapolis:
        Univ. of Minnesota Press, 1972, pp. 175-184.

        Discusses David's principal narrative effort of realiz-
        ing "ways in which the self can develop" autonomously.
        Gold notes a similar moral purpose in the novel and in
        The Prelude and says *Copperfield* is an "exemplary tale
        of how art is made." He discusses drowning as the novel's
        main metaphor; for such characters as Mr. Peggotty
        "water ... comes nat'ral," but for other characters sur-
        vival depends on drowning others. When David returns home
        to Agnes he discovers himself, says Gold, who finds that
        the book concludes with an endorsement of stoic values.
        Reviews: Angus Easson, *Dickensian*, 69 (1973), 190-191;
        Avrom Fleishman, *MLQ*, 34 (1973), 191-199; Bert G. Horn-
        back, *DSN*, 4 (1973), 56-58; Robert L. Patten, *NCF*, 28
        (1973), 103-107; Alexander Welsh, *YR*, 62 (1973), 281-287.

325.   Goldfarb, Russell M. "Charles Dickens: Orphans, Incest,
        and Repression." In *Sexual Repression and Victorian
        Literature*. Lewisburg: Bucknell Univ. Press, 1970, pp.
        114-178.

        Ranges widely through Dickens but has bearing on topics
        central to *Copperfield*. Goldfarb calls attention to the
        extraordinary number of orphans in Dickens's novels and
        stresses the incest theme, which he thinks has been too
        often overlooked. He shows David repeatedly falling in
        love with mother figures. Goldfarb thinks Dickens often
        writes about the extremes of love, the "centripetal ex-
        periences of incest opposed by centrifugal experiences
        of his orphans."

326.   Gomme, A.H. *Dickens*. London: Evans Brothers, 1971, pp.
        174-176.

        Contrasts *David Copperfield* briefly with *Great Expec-
        tations*, noting that the former lacks any guiding theme.
        David functions as "universal moral recorder," says
        Gomme, who finds David's repulsion for Heep tinged with
        special pleading.

327. Graves, Robert. "Foreword." In *The Real David Copper-*
      field, pp. 4-9 (167).

      Graves's foreword is in part his self-justification
      for a controversial abridgment and in part brief commen-
      tary on Dickens's work. Graves thinks Dickens lacked
      straightforwardness: the chief impediment for modern
      readers is that "at least a quarter-million of the half-
      million words in *David Copperfield* add nothing to the
      story." Graves also thinks that Dickens was too indirect
      in presenting his "gentleman-obsession," a topic Graves
      decides to stress.

328. Grayson, Nancy J. "The Mentor Figure in Selected Novels
      by Thackeray, Dickens, and Meredith." *DA*, 29 (1968),
      1511A (Texas, 1968).

      Discusses Micawber with *Bleak House*'s Jarndyce and
      Great Expectations's Herbert Pocket and Wemmick as mentors
      expressing a double theme: "At some time all indicate
      through example that various types of cruelty can only
      be overcome by humanitarianism. Through precept and
      example, they present the second theme, that only disci-
      plined emotions produce a balanced, pleasant existence."

329. Grob, Shirley. "Dickens and Some Motifs of the Fairy
      Tale." *TSLL*, 5 (1964), 567-579.

      Suggests that the fairy godmother figure is a good in-
      dex to Dickens's changing use of fairy-tale motifs. Like
      Harry Stone, who more recently has given lengthy attention
      to the subject (496), Grob shows that Dickens in *David
      Copperfield* begins to exploit the fairy tale, and the
      novel is "more closely related to the fairy tale than to
      the usual *Bildungsroman*." Grob thinks that except for
      some skepticism by Miss Mowcher, there is none of the
      ironic play on fairy-tale convention which occurs in
      later Dickens novels.

330. Grundy, Dominick E. "Growing Up Dickensian." *L&P*, 22
      (1972), 99-106.

      General discussion showing Dickens preoccupied with
      childhood because it provides a perspective on adult-
      hood. In *Copperfield*, *Bleak House*, and *Great Expectations*,
      Grundy finds questions of identity and development to
      be paramount. He argues that Dickens defines maturity
      as a loss of integrity and that the few "whole people"
      stay the most childlike. Betsey and Mr. Micawber are for
      Grundy "split" people whose fostering of David seems un-

related to their functions in the adult world. This critic
points to the child's "interior, sensitive, and constantly
developing" world as opposing a finished and repetitive
adult world.

331. Guerard, Albert J. *The Triumph of the Novel: Dickens,
      Dostoevsky, Faulkner*. New York: Oxford Univ. Press,
      1976, pp. 75-76, 139-145.

      Far ranging and often original in interpretation, this
      book gives no detailed study of *Copperfield* but does find
      it indulging "various forbidden wishes in remarkable un-
      censored forms." The most serious game Guerard finds is
      David's marriage to "bodiless angelic Agnes," who has
      strong connections with Mary Hogarth. Guerard thinks
      Copperfield a sombre book, often sounding Dickens's
      "grave interior voice." As part of a detailed discussion
      of Dickens's authorial voice in a number of works, Guerard
      notes that *Copperfield*'s personal prose "invites the
      pleasing rhythms of a calm speaking voice." Guerard sug-
      gests that the double vision of the "Retrospect" chapters
      anticipates Conrad's impressionism. Reviews: Richard J.
      Dunn, *Review*, 1 (1979), 91-104; Joseph H. Gardner, *DSN*,
      9 (1978), 55-58; Barbara Hardy, *Novel*, 11 (1977), 77-79;
      James M. Holquist, *CL*, 31 (1979), 185-187; Michael Mill-
      gate, *NCF*, 32 (1977), 255-258; Robert L. Patten, *Dickensian*,
      75 (1979), 39-41.

332. Hamada, Kōichi. "The Style and Theme of Dickens's Later
      Novels: *David Copperfield*, *Bleak House* and *Great Expec-
      tations*." *Doshisha Studies in English*, 21 (1979), 34-60.

      Written in English and concentrating on early and late
      retrospective paragraphs to demonstrate the serenity and
      clarity of the narrator's "apologetic and regretful tone."
      Hamada concludes that "what we can say about *David Copper-
      field* is that it is a series of confessions of a man who
      has become a renowned writer by sacrificing other people."

333. Hamilton, Robert. "Dickens and Boz." *Dickensian*, 36
      (1940), 242-244.

      Finds contrasts between *Pickwick* and *Copperfield* re-
      vealing a distinction between Boz and Dickens, for the
      novelist of the later book was able to produce moving
      retrospects. This essay is too general and too brief to
      be of much critical value.

334. ————. "Dickens in His Characters." *Nineteenth Century*, 142 (1947), 40-49.

   Views Dickens primarily as a novelist of character but also as capable of more complex characterization than is usually recognized. Though Hamilton thinks *Pickwick* and *Copperfield* are Dickens's masterpieces, he makes only passing mention of characters in *David Copperfield*. Hamilton asserts that "Dickens was more than any of his great characters," and he thinks Dickens least successful with figures far from his own experience.

335. ————. "Dickens's Favourite Child." *Dickensian*, 45 (1949), 141-143.

   Finds David one of Dickens's least personal creations and thereby a symbol of normal childhood. With Hamilton taking such a curious view of Dickens's hero-narrator it is hardly surprising that he finds the early chapters remarkable for their "monumental serenity." He states, in a more orthodox view, that the "Retrospect" chapters move readers with their Wordsworthian sadness and calm happiness in accepting the past as past.

336. Hardy, Barbara. "The Change of Heart in Dickens' Novels." *VS*, 5 (1961), 49-67.

   Notes the familiar "disciplined heart" theme in *Copperfield*, and points out some discrepancy between the narrative action and the hero's moral development because David finally is blind to his dependence on Agnes "rather than to a weakness which his life harshly corrects." This article examines patterns of moral conversion in a number of Dickens's novels.

337. ————. "Dickens's Storytellers." *Dickensian*, 69 (1973), 71-78. Incorporated in *Tellers and Listeners: The Narrative Imagination*. London: Athlone Press, 1975, pp. 165-174.

   Briefly mentions David in a general discussion of the many functions of Dickens's storytellers, who "possess understandable, common, human needs." One of Hardy's points bears upon the issue of David's passivity, for she thinks that David's education concerns his "learning to listen before he can truly tell."

338. Harris, Wendell V. "Of Time and the Novel." *Bucknell Review*, 16 (1968), 114-129.

Examines *David Copperfield*, *Nostromo*, and *The Sound and the Fury* to show time as a frequent subject of fiction. Harris argues that "the sufficiency or insufficiency of David's values is demonstrated in time," as Dickens avoids irony in insisting on the importance of individual views of life. Harris's essay is useful for readers interested in the function of memory in *Copperfield*.

339. Harrison, Frederic. "Charles Dickens." In *Studies in Early Victorian Literature*. London: Edward Arnold, 1895, pp. 128-144.

Sees Dickens as a great humorist, citing the likening of Dora to a lap dog as an instance of his humor's "exact truth to nature." This survey of Dickens's works mentions *Copperfield* frequently, for Harrison considers it, *Pickwick*, and *Nickleby* as Dickens's masterpieces.

340. Hennelly, Mark M., Jr. "*David Copperfield*: 'The Theme of This Incomprehensible Conundrum Was the Moon.'" *SNNTS*, 10 (1978), 375-396.

From the title, the substance of this essay might seem restricted, but the study is well grounded in Hennelly's reading of the Romantics. He sees the romantic riddle of solar and lunar contraries of permanence and change as one of Dickens's interests in *David Copperfield*, and he suggests thirty-one lines from *The Prelude*, Book XIII, as an outline of the novel's major nuances. The essay is valuable for readers interested in the book's thematic complexity, narrative technique, fairy-tale and romance structure, and various image patterns. David himself finally embodies for Hennelly the union of reconciled romantic contraries as the narrating man and the growing child unite.

341. Hennequin, Émile. "Comment on *David Copperfield*." In 1919 Readers' Classic Edition, pp. 57-59 (55).

Originally written for *Écrivains Françaises* (1889), this article finds David less alive than the secondary characters. Also, Hennequin makes what must be for twentieth-century readers an unusual claim, that Dickens was not skillful at description because of his inclination toward the fantastic and the grotesque.

342. Hirsch, Gordon D. "Hero and Villain in the Novels of Charles Dickens: A Psychoanalytic Study." *DAI*, 32 (1972), 4612A (California, 1971).

Does not treat *David Copperfield* separately but has
general bearing on its portrayal of heroism and villainy.
Hirsch argues that the novels are "elaborations of fantasies concerned with paternal oppression and filial
rebellion ... characteristically manifested in the relationships between the hero or heroine and the villain."
Eventually, for Hirsch, "the villain is no longer seen
solely as an oppressive 'father' to the hero, but is also
his double."

343.   Hornback, Bert G. "Dickens's Language of Gesture: Creating
        Character." *DSN*, 9 (1978), 100–106.

        Focuses on Jane Murdstone and Uriah Heep as examples
        of richly developed gesture-characters. Language of
        gesture represents for Hornback a cause or source of a
        character's identity, and with both Jane Murdstone and
        Uriah Heep, Dickens proceeds from description to metaphor
        to symbol or metaphysical identification.

344.   ———. "Frustration and Resolution in *David Copperfield*."
        SEL, 8 (1968), 651–667. Revised and incorporated in
        Noah's Arkitecture: A Study of Dickens's Mythology.
        Athens: Ohio Univ. Press, 1972, pp. 63–82.

        Sees *David Copperfield* as Dickens's most positive effort
        to deal with the problem, "both real and mythic, of order-
        ing a disordered world." Hornback discusses the novel's
        attention to the disintegrating order of natural family
        units (the Micawbers are an ironic exception), which are
        replaced by the ordering of art as exemplified by David's
        vocation as a novelist. Hornback finds David engaged in
        the blending of experience and imagination to recreate
        his past. Taking a slightly different view than that
        usually held by commentators on the novel's romanticism,
        Hornback argues that David as novelist avoids the roman-
        tic falsification that at times affects Dickens's own
        view of reality. Reviews: Avrom Fleishman, *MLQ*, 34 (1973),
        191–199; Joseph Gold, *DSN*, 4 (1973), 58–60; B[ryan]
        H[ulse], *Dickensian*, 69 (1973), 129–130; R.D. McMaster,
        NCF, 28 (1973), 107–110; George J. Worth, *JEGP*, 72 (1973),
        246–249.

345.   ———. "The Hero Self." *DSA*, 7 (1978), 151–162.

        Ponders the vocal implications of *Copperfield*'s opening
        sentence "as a reflective, recollective, observing con-
        sciousness." Hornback's lively essay claims that the
        narrative voice is so special that *it* becomes the book's

central character. The question of heroism for Hornback
is one of whether "the imagination can become substantial
and heroic, and the pages can prove it by demanding the
imagination's comprehension of a real phenomenal world."
Hornback thinks that although not a Raskolnikov, David
has a need "to understand it all," and he remains a model
no one lives up to, for he attains through conversion "a
pleasure of the soul." Hornback challenges readers to
hear the voice of the retrospective chapters as "an
appeal from mind to mind" and to accept it as the same
voice that speaks the opening sentence, making meaning
and pleasure from the process of recollection.

346. House, Humphry. *The Dickens World*. Oxford: Oxford Univ.
      Press, 1941, passim.

      Takes issue with Chesterton's doubting of Micawber's
      Australian success (255), for the moral of Micawber con-
      cerns the "secret possibility of success." House observes
      how surprisingly little is said about the Murdstones'
      religion; bullying temperament, more than religious
      doctrine, is the object of Dickens's scorn. House's use-
      ful study of the world in and around Dickens's novels
      accepts David himself as a spokesman for Dickens's posi-
      tion on social issues, revealing especially his horror
      of manual work. The class problem is most acute, says
      House, when sexual love attempts to cross class barriers
      as in the Little Em'ly story.

347. Howells, William D. "Heroines of Dickens's Middle Period"
      and "Dickens's Later Heroines." In *Heroines of Fiction*.
      New York: Harper and Brothers, 1901, Vol. I, pp. 136-
      160.

      Discusses various *David Copperfield* women as less mon-
      strous characters than Dickens's earlier female charac-
      ters. Howells praises the treatment of David's and Dora's
      young love. The Little Em'ly and Agnes stories are to
      this eminent American realist "further from nature," but
      Rosa Dartle's characterization represents more true art.
      Howells thus is one of the relatively few earlier commen-
      tators to find Rosa convincing. He links her with Edith
      Dombey and Lady Dedlock as a "deadly-haughty heroine."

348. Hueffer, Ford Madox. "Appreciation of *David Copperfield*."
      In 1919 Readers' Classic Edition, pp. 17-18 (55).

      Sees David as less vital than Dickens because in the
      characterization Dickens was justifying his own actions.

Hueffer thinks David "is anaemic because of his ideals: of women, of virtue, of comfort." This novelist-critic thinks the dénouement arouses suspicions because it is a quixotic falsification of the dénouement of Dickens's own career.

349. Hughes, Felicity. "Narrative Complexity in *David Copper-field*." *ELH*, 41 (1974), 89-105.

Important essay distinguishing three interpretations of people and events in the novel's varied perspectives—the points of view of young David as protagonist, of the narrator, and of Dickens himself. Hughes suggests that the perspectives tend to qualify one another, and the divergent "views of the efficacy of the agents of good and evil" taken by David the fictional novelist and Dickens the actual novelist are often disquieting. Hughes notes that David's views of evil figures (Heep, Murdstone, Steerforth) progress from fairy tale through realism toward higher allegory. But she finds Dickens viewing the evil figures differently; insisting on the reality of their evil, he draws on mesmerism to apply the most scientific psychology he knew—see Kaplan (363).

350. Hurley, Edward. "Dickens' Portrait of the Artist." *VN*, (Fall, 1970), 1-5.

Examines the novel's attention to various uses and abuses of verbal communication. Hurley thinks David's sensitivity to communication problems may explain his hesitancy to present directly the history of his development as a novelist. For Hurley, "David the writer exists in the matrix of verbal concerns demonstrated in other characters and events"; Micawber, Heep, and Mr. Dick are cases in point. Covering much critical ground in a brief space, Hurley also extends Spilka's (486), Lindsay's (390), and Manheim's (406) discussions of David's Oedipal struggles.

351. Hursey, Richard C. "The Elusive Angel: The Development of the Orphan Theme in the Early Novels of Charles Dickens." *DA*, 28 (1967), 3144A (Ohio Univ., 1967).

Finds Dickens coming to a mature concept of "the meaning of orphanhood in relation to his own life and to his age" in *David Copperfield*. According to Hursey, the novel's resolution "shows that the source of identity is in the recognition by another of the orphan's true self—the self behind the social mask."

352. Jackson, Holbrook. "Appreciation of *David Copperfield*."
      In 1919 Readers' Classic Edition, pp. 25-31 (55).

      More a discussion of Dickens generally than a commentary
      on *David Copperfield*. Jackson sees Dickens as the first
      writer to interpret the moods and sentiments of urban,
      industrial people. He claims that Dickens's successful
      female characterizations are eccentric and peculiar
      characters and that "his failures fail in realities, be-
      cause they are not real women, but personifications of
      the popular conception of what a woman should or should
      not be." Agnes is one of Jackson's examples of an un-
      realistic female character.

353. Jackson, T.A. "David Copperfield." In *Charles Dickens:*
      The Progress of a Radical. New York: International
      Publishers, 1938, pp. 119-128.

      Notes the influence of Defoe as *David Copperfield*
      traces "one man's journey through ... a many-faceted
      picture of life-as-it-is." Jackson finds good and evil
      balanced throughout this meliorist book, whose moral
      is that people must bear evil in common--an elusive moral
      best expressed through Betsey Trotwood's admonitions.
      Jackson claims that politically and socially *Copperfield*
      shares the *Dombey and Son* view of the world as a muddle,
      but that *Copperfield* shows a change in Dickens's class
      orientation because lower-middle-class and proletarian
      characters (Mr. Micawber, Traddles, the Peggotty group)
      "reap all the laurels." It is obvious that *David Copper-
      field* is not the strongest support for Jackson's inter-
      pretations of Dickens's social and political arguments;
      Oliver Twist, *Bleak House*, or *Little Dorrit*, to name
      three, are more applicable.

354. Janowitz, Katherine E. "Inviolable Goodness: The Idyllic
      Mode in the Novels of Charles Dickens." *DAI*, 39 (1979),
      6776A (Columbia, 1976).

      Shows the novels after *Barnaby Rudge* giving "gradually
      increasing emphasis to the aspect of the idyllic....
      The idyllic, the vision of the 'privileged' sanctuary,
      emerges, finally, as willed counterreality, a 'fiction
      of innocence' juxtaposed against the broader context of
      experience in the narrative."

355. Jarmuth, Sylvia L. "An Outstanding Achievement: *David
      Copperfield*." In *Dickens' Use of Women in His Novels*.
      New York: Excelsior, 1967, pp. 97-111.

Lacking the critical acuity of Basch (220) and relying
heavily on secondary sources, Jarmuth believes that in
portraying female characters Dickens successfully plumbed
the depths of his emotional life. This chapter is a survey of the novel's women. It repeats other writers' earlier comments, summarizes various attitudes toward Dora
and Agnes, and notes that in contrast especially with
Brontë characters Em'ly "remains a figure of paste-board."
For an abstract of Jarmuth's work see "Dickens' Use of
Women in His Novels," *DA*, 29 (1968), 568A-569A (New York
Univ., 1966).

356.   Johnson, Edgar. "Afterword." In 1962 Signet Edition, pp.
        871-879 (67).

Cites the penultimate episodes of Uriah Heep's downfall
and the storm at Yarmouth as instances of Dickens's com-
mand over "opposing emotional tones of triumph and grief."
Johnson resists any notion that the novel is an improvisa-
tion, for it carefully works out its related themes. The
primary theme concerns the disciplining of the heart, and
Johnson says there are nearly two hundred and fifty
occurences of the heart image to reinforce this dominant
theme. In Johnson's opinion, David, as first-person
narrator, achieves "a kind of lucid double exposure shad-
ing [his recollection] with the hidden future." Johnson
divides the novel into three major movements, culminating
with the maturing of David.

357.   ————. "His Favorite Child." In *Charles Dickens: His
        Tragedy and Triumph*. New York: Simon and Schuster,
        1952, pp. 677-700. (Omitted from Johnson's revised and
        abridged edition in 1977.)

A critical chapter discussing ways in which Dickens
disguised the most painful truths of his past through
portrayal of a series of surrogate parents and through
various suppressions and fantasies. Johnson notes the
paradox of a dearth of happy homes and good parents "in
a writer whose warm celebration of family life and fire-
side has created a glow in which readers overlook how
relatively seldom he portrays what he praises." Johnson
finds the book's mixture of fact and fiction remaining
"undeviatingly true to the emotional reality" of Dickens's
life, even if *Copperfield* does not reveal the whole truth
about Dickens's temperament. Johnson praises the portrayal
of David and Dora and acknowledges the centrality of the
"disciplined heart" theme—see Needham (433). As a study
of childhood he thinks the novel surpasses *Alice in*

Wonderland, most of *A Portrait of the Artist as a Young
Man*, and *Tom Sawyer* and *Huckleberry Finn*; "no other boy
has known exactly the same circumstances as David Copperfield, and yet all childhood is there." The childhood
perspective toward the Murdstones is very effective, says
Johnson, for it helps establish the sense of a "struggle
in the world between simple goodness and cruel cunning."
Although it is natural that we see Steerforth through
David's admiring eyes and come to regard his charm as
"a refinement of egoism," Johnson agrees with many earlier critics who observe that Dickens never reveals the
character from within. Surveying a number of the novel's
strengths and weaknesses, Johnson says that the Little
Em'ly story is not handled well. Uriah Heep, however,
is a success; he is "at once comic, revolting, and fright-
ening." Flexible in structure, the plot fuses autobiographic content and "admits all that crowding world of
accident and contingency which characterizes the multi-
plicity of life it seeks to mirror." Johnson provides
an excellent overview for readers interested in the
novel's autobiographical elements and in its place in
Dickens's autobiographical elements and in its place in
Dickens's total career.

358.   Johnson, E.D.H. *Charles Dickens: An Introduction to His
       Novels*. New York: Random House, 1969, pp. 97-99.

       Johnson's direct discussion of *David Copperfield* is
brief, but as he combines biographical information with
a general survey of Dickens's works, he focuses on the
novel's autobiographical content. He suggests that
Dickens's choice of first-person narration may have been
influenced by the recent success of *Jane Eyre*. Johnson
believes that the first-person narration provides psychological continuity within the book's picaresque structure,
and he says that a fusion of personal experience with
imagination promotes a comprehensive mythic unity. As
part of this unity, Steerforth's death comes as what
Johnson calls "the terminal link in a predestined chain
of cause and effect."

359.   Johnson, Pamela H. "The Betrayal of Self in Fiction."
       Listener, 41 (1949), 367-368.

       Brief but incisive study showing in the fiction of
Dickens, George Eliot, and Proust autobiographical
revelation ranging from repressed to overt. Johnson takes
issue with Edmund Wilson's view (536) that *Copperfield*
"is not one of Dickens's deepest books," for she argues

that the inner life of childhood comes through and so
does the tormented life of Dickens's maturity. Steerforth,
Dickens's most profound creation, for Johnson, expresses
the nature of Dickens's own struggles. Without pursuing
the point, Johnson notes that "instead of writing of one
falling man ... he wrote of three fallen women," possibly
to release in disguise his own frustrations. Littimer, as
proud underling, shows Johnson the depths to which Dickens
could reach even with a minor character, because his
criticisms of David's high-handedness may point as much
at Dickens as at David. Nonetheless, in Johnson's opinion,
Dickens was not "a manic-depressive Santa Claus," and his
most wonderful characters are drawn from the most public
part of his own nature.

360. Jones, Howard M. "On Rereading *Great Expectations*." *South-
west Review*, 39 (1954), 328-335.

Thinks that comparison of the later novel, *Great Expectations*, with *David Copperfield* best shows Dickens's
artistry. Jones sees in *Copperfield* a superiority of
parts but thinks Dickens was unable in that novel to move
from the child's into the man's universe. For more detailed comparison of the novels see Buckley (240).

361. Jones, John. "*David Copperfield*." In *Dickens and the
Twentieth Century*. Ed. John Gross and Gabriel Pearson.
London: Routledge and Kegan Paul, 1962, pp. 133-144.

Argues that in liking it best Dickens believed *Copperfield* to be his best book according to the serial writer's
measure of "Make 'em laugh. Make 'em cry. Make 'em wait."
Jones thinks that in early chapters Dickens's lack of
spirituality, education, and intellect is unimportant;
later in the book readers well may wonder what Dostoevsky,
Tolstoy, or George Eliot might have made of the same
material. Jones sees two links--the Peggotty group (including Steerforth) and Mr. Micawber--binding the "Trials
of David" to the "Portrait of the Artist." He thinks the
novel's "closing serenities offend" modern readers and
represent a failure of the conventional happy ending in
Victorian fiction. Holding generally to a traditional
view of the novel, Jones finally does not locate any
truly convincing central theme in *David Copperfield*.

362. Jump, John D. "Dickens and His Readers." *BJRL*, 54 (1972),
384-397.

This essay ranges broadly through Dickens. Jump uses
Miss Murdstone as an example of how Dickens maintains
humorous methods even when most in earnest.

363.   Kaplan, Fred. *Dickens and Mesmerism: The Hidden Springs*
       of Fiction. Princeton: Princeton Univ. Press, 1975,
       passim.

       Contains no separate discussion of *David Copperfield*
       but is of particular interest because it discusses para-
       doxes of personal power and human attraction in Dickens's
       novels. Kaplan mentions the mesmeric force of Rosa Dartle
       and says that Steerforth's imperviousness to her may
       signal his "rejection of belief in a vital power in the
       universe." Kaplan also observes that David's relationships
       with Uriah Heep show how a person with concentrated
       strength of will may temporarily dominate the weak hero.
       Avoiding simplistic conclusions about the novel's message,
       Kaplan says that David himself resists the conclusion
       that nature's energies may be employed for good or ill
       according to individual will but that subsequent Dickens
       novels evince this point. Reviews: Richard J. Dunn,
       SNNTS, 8 (1976), 223-233; Thomas McFarland, *SEL*, 16
       (1976), 722-723; Michael Steig, *NCF*, 33 (1979), 505-508;
       Garrett Stewart, *DSN*, 7 (1976), 117-120.

364.   Karl, Frederick R. "Charles Dickens: The Victorian Quixote."
       In *A Reader's Guide to the Nineteenth-Century British*
       Novel. New York: Farrar, Straus, and Giroux, 1972,
       pp. 105-175. First published in 1964 as *An Age of Fic-*
       tion: The Nineteenth Century British Novel.

       Without treating *David Copperfield* separately, Karl
       describes it as a "kind of cathartic" for Dickens, bring-
       ing to an end his comic works. But contrasted with *Great*
       Expectations, it lacks a theme, says Karl, and presents
       "the shifting fortunes of a pleasant but superficial
       protagonist." Karl mentions Steerforth with Orlick of
       Great Expectations and Headstone of *Our Mutual Friend*
       as self-destructive characters who may disturb the com-
       placent world.

365.   Kearney, Anthony. "The Storm Scene in *David Copperfield*."
       Ariel, 9 (1978), 19-30.

       Shows that in contrast to other storm descriptions in
       Dickens, the "Tempest" chapter is written with "real
       descriptive power" and thematic control. Kearney argues
       that its imagery is relevant to the entire novel; "sym-
       bolism of sea, sky and storm is successfully integrated
       to achieve what amounts to a mystical dimension in the
       novel." Although a number of commentators mention this
       chapter, few before Kearney so concentrate on it.

366. Kelty, Jean M. "The Modern Tone of Charles Dickens."
      Dickensian, 57 (1961), 160-165.

      Cites three instances of interior monologue in *David
      Copperfield* (from Chapters 17, 24, 43) in her general
      demonstration of how Dickens employed stylistic devices
      later claimed as the innovations of twentieth-century
      writers.

367. Kennedy, George E., II. "Women Redeemed: Dickens's Fallen
      Women." *Dickensian*, 74 (1978), 42-47.

      Shows that the characterization of Martha and of Little
      Em'ly gave Dickens a chance to combine the ideals of a
      redemptive formula with his first-hand knowledge of fallen
      women at Urania Cottage. Kennedy compares the fate of
      these characters with fallen women in other Dickens novels.

368. Kennedy, G.W. "Dickens's Endings." *SNNTS*, 6 (1974), 280-
      287.

      Wide-ranging survey of the types of Dickens's endings,
      describing that of *David Copperfield* as "marked by cele-
      bration and near-agelessness rather than by the grinding
      destruction of ordinary time."

369. Kettle, Arnold. "Life and Pattern." In *An Introduction
      to the English Novel*. London: Hutchinson, 1951, Vol. I,
      pp. 15-17.

      Notes that *David Copperfield*'s vitality is "limited by
      Dickens's failure to master and organise significantly
      the raw material of his novel." Kettle thinks the last
      half, especially, lacks conflict or a pattern of moral
      significance. Kettle's stringent assessment treats the
      novel as an example of a work possessing more vividness
      than wisdom.

370. ―――――. "Thoughts on *David Copperfield*." *RES*, 2 (1961),
      65-74.

      In a more detailed and positive assessment than his
      earlier book (369), Kettle places the novel in a context
      of romantic self-discovery and shows it as a necessary
      phase in Dickens's artistic development. Kettle upholds
      the often maligned chapters following David's flight
      to Dover, because much of the novel centers on David's
      misjudgments of Steerforth and of Dora. David finally
      attains a genuine self-reliance, Kettle thinks, but the
      problem both for David and for Dickens is essentially that

of "how to advance to a more complete, more morally
responsible, realism."

371. Kibblewhite, E. "Editor's Introduction." In 1916 Oxford
      Edition, pp. 1-12 (54).

      Discusses Dickens's attitudes toward his favorite work,
      notes its autobiographical nature, but thinks the latter
      part probably owes no more or less to Dickens's life
      than do any of his other novels. Although Kibblewhite
      thinks *Copperfield* has much of Dickens's best writing,
      he says it also exhibits "traces of a fatigue which had
      not appeared in his earlier novels." Distant enough from
      the nineteenth century to criticize Dickens's sentimen-
      tality, Kibblewhite nonetheless grants a genuine pathos
      achieved with Dickens's humor. In addition to his criti-
      cally lucid introduction, Kibblewhite provides extensive
      explanatory notes, including even the score for the
      twelfth chapter's college hornpipe. There is a useful
      index to the notes.

372. Kincaid, James R. "The Darkness of *David Copperfield*."
      DiS, 1 (1965), 65-75.

      Describes the narrator's progress as a turning toward
      a dream world ruled by Agnes as the "specter of a fan-
      tastic, sexless, vague benevolence." Kincaid thinks
      David rejects any heroic role, but the novel is about
      the forces combating him. Goodness is embodied in "a
      legion of weakness," says Kincaid, and David himself
      remains ineffectual in dealing with forces of evil.

373. ————. "*David Copperfield*: Laughter and Point of View."
      In *Dickens and the Rhetoric of Laughter*. Oxford: The
      Clarendon Press, 1971, pp. 162-191.

      Extends the study begun in his earlier articles con-
      cerned with subversive humor and the novel's darkness
      to show "the relation of the novel's established values
      to those generally accepted by David and the control of
      our attitude toward both sets of values." Kincaid sees
      David as neither the voice of Dickens nor the voice of
      the novel, and he outlines three phases of David's chang-
      ing life matched by changing rhetorical techniques. First,
      the childhood Eden of the opening three chapters fosters
      a rhetoric for the comic values of happy childhood. Second,
      in chapters four through thirteen, laughter becomes "a
      rhetoric of attack" to build sympathy for David's boy-
      hood suffering. Third, in the remainder of the book

there is a rhetorical split between the comic value sys-
tem and that of the hero, who depends upon fantasy even
as he drifts ironically "towards Murdstonean firmness."
Kincaid vigorously opposes readings which stress the
successful disciplining of David's heart, especially
Needham's (433), and finds *David Copperfield* "a reluctant
farewell to comedy," with David a representative nineteenth-century man who divorces the ideal from the prag-
matic. The Micawbers "climax a great line of Dickens's
comic characters," writes Kincaid, and they, along with
other misfits, comprise half of the conflicting forces,
"the approved but impossible life of the imagination."
Kincaid concludes that although there is no ultimate moral
judgment against David, he is suspended "between alternate
values, which, ironically, he calls 'the secret of my
success.'" Kincaid's discussion remains one of the most
thoughtful and provocative modern critical evaluations.
For an earlier version of his argument see his "A Critical
Study of *David Copperfield*," *DA*, 27 (1966), 478A (Western
Reserve, 1965). Reviews: K.J. Fielding, *RES*, NS 24 (1973),
100-102; Margaret Ganz, *DSN*, 4 (1973), 89-93; Harvey
Peter Sucksmith, *YES*, 4 (1974), 323-325; G.B. Tennyson,
NCF, 27 (1973), 369-375; Alexander Welsh, *YR*, 62 (1973),
281-287.

374.   ————. "Dickens's Subversive Humor: *David Copperfield*."
       NCF, 22 (1968), 313-329.

Starts with a thorough review of traditional views of
David Copperfield's humor and proceeds to his own interpretation to show that Dickens used humor as a "founda-
tion out of which serious and tragic incidents grow."
Kincaid submits that much of *Copperfield*'s humor is
deliberately ironic and that Dickens subverts normally
comic situations and expands comic characters beyond
their limited traditional roles. Kincaid finds examples
of varied situation comedy in the descriptions of David's
and Dora's marriage, in the account of Mr. Omer's business,
and in the portrayal of Betsey Trotwood's confrontation
with the Murdstones. His examples of expanded comic characterization include Julia Mills, Miss Mowcher, Tommy
Traddles, and Doctor Strong. Kincaid finds Dickens's
treatment of the Micawbers "the most subtle and most
ultimately deceptive" comedy in the novel. Kincaid also
calls attention to a dark side of Mr. Micawber, regarding him as "a curious mixture of attraction and repulsion,
of open honesty and ugly selfishness."

375. ————. "The Structure of *David Copperfield*." *DiS*, 2
      (1966), 74-95.

      Providing one of the most detailed analyses of the
      novel's plot and subplots, Kincaid traces a central pat-
      tern balanced by two major subplots. He divides the book
      according to a four-part division of tragedy to stress
      David Copperfield's ironic and tragic implications. He
      sees irony and tragedy giving spatial solidity to the
      book's structures. Like much of Kincaid's work on Dickens,
      this article displays an informed and stimulating icono-
      clasm.

376. ————. "Symbol and Subversion in *David Copperfield*."
      SNNTS, 1 (1969), 196-206.

      Refutes the notion that the disciplining of the heart—
      see Needham (433)—or the attainment of security with
      Agnes is the novel's central concern. Kincaid suggests
      that a pattern of sea, dream, prison, and animal imagery
      works against the novel's comic surface to cast doubt
      on David's rehabilitation.

377. Korg, Jacob. "Society and Community in Dickens." In
      Politics in Literature in the Nineteenth Century. Ed.
      Pierre Coustillas. Lille: Univ. de Lille III, 1974,
      pp. 85-109.

      General discussion of Dickens, noting that David
      searches for another community like the initial one he
      finds at the Peggotty home. Korg says that their resi-
      dence in a beached ship symbolizes communal security
      and fits into a "pattern of safety in a context of danger."
      He cites Betsey Trotwood's cottage as another idealized
      Dickensian community.

378. Kotzin, Michael C. *Dickens and the Fairy Tale*. Bowling
      Green: Bowling Green Univ. Popular Press, 1972, passim.

      A disappointing study, which has been superseded by
      Stone (496). Kotzin observes that although David several
      times identifies with fairy-tale heroes, he ultimately
      applies himself to diligent work. Thus Kotzin thinks the
      novel reflects Dickens's understanding that his own life
      was not one of fairy-tale happiness. Less speculatively,
      Kotzin observes that Peggotty's house offers a fairyland
      escape from "the urban forest," and he notes that in this
      novel Dickens often uses metamorphosis and animism to
      describe people from the child's viewpoint.

379. Krugman, Laura. "The Child in the Novels of Charles
      Dickens." *DAI*, 32 (1972), 7001A (Yale, 1971).

      States that from *David Copperfield* through *Little Dorrit*
      "Dickens elaborated a system of child psychology in which
      emotional deprivations are more significant than physical
      needs." Krugman says *Copperfield* "recognizes the hero's
      claim to a private vision as a basic right of childhood"
      and establishes "the positive value of the child's in-
      sight and imagination in defending his world from adult
      evil."

380. Lane, Lauriat, Jr. "Dickens' Archetypal Jew." *PMLA*, 73
      (1958), 94-100.

      Contains little directly concerning *David Copperfield*
      but does suggest racial implications in David's responses
      to Uriah Heep, for David's anger toward him "has the
      pathological intensity of much racial prejudice," and
      Micawber makes a possible allusion to Heep's "Jewishness."

381. Lang, Andrew. "Introduction." In the 1897 Gadshill Edi-
      tion, pp. x-xiv (45).

      Thinks Dickens was wise in terming this novel his
      favorite child, although readers might value *Pickwick*
      more highly. Lang compares the strength of memory in
      Dickens's *Copperfield* and in George Sand's autobiography,
      seeing childhood memory as the "indispensable basis of
      poetry and mythology." Lang also notes "the associated
      difficulty of discerning between dreams and realities."
      He is one of the first commentators to identify the child
      voyant as an element common to Dickens's and Wordsworth's
      imaginations. Like Gissing (321), he finds the Steerforth
      story melodramatic and is not surprised that it became
      a favorite on the nineteenth-century stage. Lang notes
      that in *Copperfield*, as in *Great Expectations*, first-
      person narration replaces an "irresponsible third person"
      in which Dickens too freely indulged his sense of the
      grotesque or the didactic.

382. Langley-Levy, Doris. "The Fascination of Steerforth."
      Dickensian, 18 (1922), 191-193.

      A weak analysis of the artistry Dickens employed in
      making "Steerforth say and do the most abominable things."

383. Lankford, William T. "'The Deep of Time': Narrative Order
      in *David Copperfield*." *ELH*, 46 (1979), 452-467.

Discusses the form the novel takes as David's attempts
to articulate and thus master the conflicting and irrational impulses in his experience. Lankford argues that
in David's novel of memory he moralizes memory "because
it makes him a child again." In the process, however,
Lankford thinks David advances in experience beyond a
simple world, departing from his past in the act of narration. Thus in form and rhythm the book is "shaped by its
dominant thematic concern with time." A serious rhetorical
barrier remains, says Lankford, because as Dickens himself told Forster, David's experience is "the so happy
and yet so unhappy existence which seeks realities in
unrealities, and finds dangerous comfort in a perpetual
escape from the disappointment of heart around it."
Lankford concludes that David's voice finally shows "that
neither discipline nor memory alone can comprehend the
'deep of Time.'" Lankford attempts to mediate between
critics who regard the adult David as a shallow character
and those who see more resolution of his conflicts than
Lankford can grant.

384. ———. "Prisoners and Children: Forms of Growth in
      Dickens' Novels." *DAI*, 36 (1976), 4512A–4513A (Emory,
      1975).

      Observes that the "disciplined heart" metaphor works
      in *Copperfield* "to assimilate the virtues of childhood
      into a maturity which can endure as experience." Lankford
      also notes that "David's sentimental reliance on memory
      as re-enactment negates the value of time and experience."

385. Leacock, Stephen. *Charles Dickens: His Life and Work.*
      London: Peter Davies, 1933, pp. 118–128.

      Ranks *David Copperfield* with *Pickwick* as Dickens's most
      popular and greatest book. Leacock acknowledges the novel's
      gallery of memorable characters, but he thinks David him-
      self one of the strangest things in the novel. Leacock
      calls him the looking-glass in which we see the other
      characters. In a critical stance recalling Chesterton's,
      Leacock says that Mr. Micawber and other characters with
      discovered prototypes "represent the art of genius to
      seize the deceiving aspects of real people and turn them
      into the realities of imaginary ones."

386. Leavis, Q.D. "Dickens and Tolstoy: The Case for a Serious
      View of *David Copperfield*." In *Dickens the Novelist*.
      By F.R. Leavis and Q.D. Leavis. London: Chatto and
      Windus, 1970, pp. 34–117.

A major study in which Leavis uses Tolstoy's high regard for *David Copperfield* as fuel for her fiery opposition to certain critics, primarily Garis (317) and Edmund
Wilson (536), who she thinks have not seemed to grant the
novel's seriousness. Leavis reports that Tolstoy found
in the novel "an immediate relevance to his own creating
problems, in helping him to formulate what he, through
Dickens's eyes, saw as the essential difficulties of
living that pressed on him." She makes specific comparisons with *War and Peace*, especially between the married
life of Prince Andrew and that of David and Dora. Just
as Levin isn't Tolstoy, David is not Dickens, and Tolstoy
evidently realized that *David Copperfield*'s real issues
were not simply personal to Dickens. Through extensive
discussion of the women in David's life, Leavis traces
the novel's theme of increasing uneasiness with an idealized domestic bliss. She says that the book's varied
images of marriage do not enable Dickens "to provide an
adequate answer to the question of Victorian man's happiness that he set out to tackle." But Leavis thinks Dickens
shows the complexities involved and does not simplify
the issues. For her Tolstoy is the novelist who "incar-
nates the Victorian ideal of woman, the Victorian ideal
of marriage." Another major theme Leavis finds in *Copperfield* concerns the value of moral simplicity, shown in
Daniel Peggotty's compulsive fantasizing. Leavis acknowledges Dickens's interests in "morbid states and in the
strange self-deceptions of human nature" that complicate
his visions of innocence. Leavis cites Steerforth and
Rosa Dartle as Dickens's pioneering studies in the psychology of passion. Micawber, whom she regards as an
affectionate version of John Dickens, "bears witness to
a pre-Victorian enjoyment of living." Useful appendices
to the chapter include notes on "Dora 'from a woman's
point of view'" (various women writers' presentations
of David-Dora type marriages), "*Oliver Twist*, *Jane Eyre*,
and *David Copperfield*" (variations of the orphan myth),
and "Dickens's exposure scenes" (including Micawber's
denunciation of Heep). For additional annotation, see
Leavis (678). Reviews: K.J. Fielding, *DSN*, 2 (1971), 37-
39; George H. Ford, *NCF*, 26 (1971), 95-113; Lauriat Lane,
Jr., *SNNTS*, 5 (1973), 125-138; W.W. Robson, *Dickensian*,
67 (1971), 99-104.

387. Legouis, Émile. "Appreciation of *David Copperfield*." In
     1919 Readers' Classic Edition, pp. 21-23 (55).

     Considers Dickens's own preference for *Copperfield* and
     finds it the "best proportioned of his novels," with a

balance of sentiment and humor, sublimity and the grotesque. Legouis cites other novels with similar features--
Oliver Twist, *The Old Curiosity Ship*, *Nicholas Nickleby*,
and *Dombey and Son*--but thinks none possesses *Copperfield*'s
continuity of interest in a central, autobiographical
character.

388. Lehr, Dolores. "Charles Dickens and the Arts." *DAI*, 39
     (1979), 6778A (Temple, 1979).

     Surveys Dickens's response to theater, music, archi-
     tecture, painting, and literature and claims that David
     embodied Dickens's dedication to art. Compare with Beebe
     (223).

389. Lewes, George H. "Dickens in Relation to Criticism."
     Fortnightly Review, 17 (1872), 141-154.

     One of the first serious critical considerations of
     Dickens's art. Lewes's is a general essay, but his point
     that Dickens portrayed character and events with "mingled
     verisimilitude and falsity" applies readily to *David
     Copperfield*. Lewes complains that in some instances--in-
     cluding Mr. Dick and Rosa Dartle--Dickens substitutes
     "mechanisms for minds." He takes exception even to Micaw-
     ber, who may remind us "of the frogs whose brains have
     been taken out for physiological purposes." Despite these
     strictures, Lewes yet notes that criticism should not
     overvalue technical skill and should admit the delight
     Dickens produces even though he fails to conceive much
     complexity. In defending Dickens's "overflowing fun,"
     Lewes, like the early French critic, Taine (199), notes
     "the action of the imagination in hallucination" through-
     out Dickens's works.

390. Lindsay, Jack. "The Bleak House." In *Charles Dickens:
     A Biographical and Critical Study*. London: Andrew
     Dakers, 1950, pp. 285-292.

     Struggles to discuss *David Copperfield* primarily in
     terms of Dickens's social and political ideas. Most
     biographical critics point more to Dickens's personal
     life than does Lindsay in explaining the "deep pivotal
     changes in his life and work," changes which Lindsay in
     part attributes to the effects of 1848 political revolu-
     tions upon Dickens. Neglecting the novel's structural
     tension between realism and fantasy, Lindsay places
     David Copperfield in a tradition of critical realism.
     He thus finds the book's social views relatively simple

and its portrayal of most class conflicts explicit. He
does not, however, think the social distinction between
David and Steerforth is fully worked out. For a more
balanced view of Dickens's social and political views
at the time of *David Copperfield* see House (346) and
Edgar Johnson (738).

391. Lougy, Robert E. "Remembrances of Death Past and Future:
     A Reading of *David Copperfield*." *DSA*, 6 (1977), 72-101.

     Described by the *DSA* editor as "a phenomenological
     meditation ... deriving primarily from Heidegger, Barthes,
     and Laing, ... a combination of Romanticism, philosophy,
     psychology, and Marxist theory, none of which overwhelms
     [Lougy's] personal reaction to the subject." This is one
     of the more controversial essays concerning David's
     memory and the novel's thematic structure. Lougy finds
     Dickens experiencing the terror of discontinuity and
     separation and sees the novel struggling with formal tra-
     dition. Lougy describes multiple possibilities for self-
     deception and illusion because he finds *David Copperfield*
     to be a book both of remembering and forgetting, "en-
     couraged by the very structures that the narrator's
     memory clings to." The ending is troublesome to Lougy,
     but a "haunting and compelling beauty" comes from the
     effort to procrastinate as far as possible the final
     stasis. Lougy well states his position: "If *David Copper-
     field* fails to find a world that can adequately reflect
     its hero's depths, Dickens' struggle to envision such a
     world makes his novel a magnificent work, one whose power
     is evidenced in that at times faltering, at times pro-
     phetic, structure into which his vision unfolds." See
     also McGowan (397) and Westburg (527).

392. Lubbock, Percy. *The Craft of Fiction*. New York: Charles
     Scribner's Sons, [1921], pp. 128-134, 151.

     Cites *David Copperfield* as a work in which first-person
     narration favors a "far stretch of the past" over present
     intrigue. Contrary to many readers, Lubbock thinks it
     matters little how David's mind works, for the sole need
     is for the reader to see what he sees. Lubbock's point
     is that had Dickens taken the next (Jamesean) step and
     treated the story from David's perspective but not used
     him as narrator, he might have better shown the operation
     of the hero's mind.

393. Lucas, Audrey. "Some Dickens Women." *YR*, 29 (1940), 706-
     728.

Appreciates Dickens's success with conventional women
characters. Mentioning characters from a number of the
novels, Lucas defends the portrayal of Dora as a "wistful
study of young love" which "ends just in time." Lucas
thinks that "until his turgid ending," Dickens in his
portrayal of Little Em'ly makes the oldest story read
like a new one.

394. Lucas, John. "David Copperfield." In *The Melancholy Man:
A Study of Dickens's Novels*. London: Methuen, 1970,
pp. 166-201.

One of the more thorough social and psychological
readings finding thematic unity and character growth
in *David Copperfield*. Lucas shows that the Christmas
Book, *The Haunted Man*, contains germs for *David Copperfield*'s interest in the personal past. He finds the
inevitability "of temporal rhythms that cumulatively
establish a human life" giving the novel structural unity.
Like a number of modern critics, he notes the similarity
between Wordsworth's *Prelude* and the Alpine scene in the
fifty-eighth chapter. He thinks the novel is about
growth, not just childhood, and it should not be thought
of in two parts. Steerforth's power and vitality are convincing to Lucas because Steerforth objectifies "an
element of snobbishness in the young David." (The moral
design of the David-Steerforth relationship is to establish "David's identity out of lost worlds and attained
insights.") Rather than accept the Steerforth-Em'ly story
as crude melodrama, Lucas says we should take it as an instance of a person corrupted through co-opting the in-
equities of class distinctions, a story further "elaborated
in the Heeps and their humility." Reviews: K.J. Fielding,
Dickensian, 67 (1971), 115-116; Margaret Ganz, *VS*, 15
(1971), 234-236; Jerome Meckier, *DSN*, 2 (1971), 100-102.

395. Lyons, John O. *The Invention of the Self: The Hinge of
Consciousness in the Eighteenth Century*. Carbondale:
Southern Illinois Univ. Press, 1978, pp. 223-224.

Briefly contrasts the authors' attitudes toward the
heroes of *David Copperfield* and *Tom Jones*. Lyons contends that Fielding works with the facility of a comic
playwright dealing with stereotypes, but that Dickens
works with an idealized memory of his youthful martyrdom.
Lyons points out a basic difference between the writers
by stating that Fielding does not create any complexity
between the hero and his society while Dickens uses in-
direction and symbolic action to show the complicity of
his heroes in the vices of the age.

396. McCullough, Bruce. "The Comedy of Character: *David Copper-
      field*." In *Representative British Novelists: Defoe to
      Conrad*. New York: Harper and Brothers, 1946, pp. 136-
      151.

      Asserts that *David Copperfield*'s "comparative simplicity
      may be attributed to the fact that it was written ...
      out of boyhood memories." More modern critical discussion
      frequently bases arguments for the book's structural com-
      plexity on the very grounds on which McCullough argues
      its simplicity. McCullough seems similarly out of touch
      with modern evaluations in his view that the book's mean-
      ing resides more in Dickens's general philosophy, a "gospel
      of kindness," than in any specific theme. In his generally
      negative assessment, McCullough makes the curious obser-
      vation that David's world lacks "definiteness of outline.
      It has no true center." McCullough thinks Dickens most
      praiseworthy for his command of laughter, and Micawber an
      example of Henri Bergson's comic automaton.

397. McGowan, John P. "*David Copperfield*: The Trial of Realism."
      NCF, 34 (1979), 1-19.

      Applies the theoretical terms of Jacques Derrida to
      this study of Dickens's ambivalent attitudes toward realism.
      McGowan thinks David's narrative strives for immediate
      perception and develops its own style as it "fluctuates
      between accepting the difference inherent in writing and
      its repetition and struggling to overcome that difference
      to 'see' his past as if it were present." McGowan differs
      from Lougy (391) by arguing that language while bearing
      warning of death also offers compensation for the con-
      sciousness of loss. McGowan's is one of the more original
      and challenging theoretical discussions of the novel.

398. ————. "Dickens' Comic Vision of History." *DAI*, 39
      (1978), 1595A-1596A (Buffalo, 1978).

      Discusses the action of language designating "who
      enjoys comedy's happy ending and who is excluded from
      it" in *David Copperfield*. McGowan thinks various struc-
      tural contradictions "can be attributed to the attempt to
      evade recognition of language's aggressive 'plot.'"

399. McNulty, J.H. "The Position and Influence of *David Copper-
      field*." *Dickensian*, 27 (1931), 273-282.

      Compares *David Copperfield*, as the author's preeminent
      work, with *Hamlet* because, like Shakespeare's play, it
      is a popular and "perfectly balanced production." McNulty

sees Dickens's Micawber as a possible influence on George
Meredith's Ray Richmond (in *Harry Richmond*) and believes
other minor Dickens characters could step right into
Walter de la Mare's books. McNulty's comparative linkages
remain speculative. The Dickens-Shakespeare connection
receives later attention from Fleissner (659) and Harbage
(666).

400.   Malden, R.H. "Introduction." In 1948 New Oxford Illustrated
       Dickens Edition, pp. v-xi (60).

       Accepts Dickens's own verdict that this was his best
       work. Malden thinks the plot weak, and he notes separate
       components, each of which night have provided material for
       a moderate-length novel. The strength he finds is in the
       observation and delineation of character, especially in
       Micawber and Heep. He comes to a number of familiar crit-
       ical conclusions: Dora is admittedly tiresome; Agnes
       made David a fine wife. He speaks of the portrayal of
       Steerforth as a convincing account of "admiration born
       at school for an older boy, who seems then to be more than
       everything which we ourselves could ever hope to become."
       Malden is one of few commentators to find the "I Am Shown
       Two Interesting Penitents" chapter germane to the story,
       and he also accepts the fiction of Micawber's Australian
       success. Readers using the Oxford Edition may wish to
       turn to Blount (229) or Ford (306) for more far-reaching
       introductions to the novel.

401.   Manheim, Leonard F. "The Dickens Hero as Child." *SNNTS*,
       1 (1969), 189-195.

       Argues that although Dickens may have often "falsified
       his conscious observation in his direct portrayal of
       children, there is a rich mine of insight into uncon-
       scious character" in his presentation of them. Manheim
       discusses child characters from a number of Dickens's
       novels and in *David Copperfield* identifies "a whole
       panoply of figures [Ham, Traddles, Steerforth, Heep] ...
       embodying aspects of the hero." As in his other essays
       on *Copperfield*, Manheim applies Otto Rank's definitions
       of the mythic hero.

402.   ————. "The Dickens Pattern—A Study in Psychoanalytic
       Criticism." *Microfilm Abstracts*. 10, No. 4 (1950),
       218-219 (Columbia, 1950).

       Although the abstract does not make specific mention
       of *Copperfield*, the thesis subject and Manheim's subse-

quent work make this dissertation relevant to the novel.
Manheim considers "literary-psychological patterns underlying the novels." He divides his study into a five-fold
discussion of "The Father, The Mother, The Hero, Ill-
ness, ... and Death."

403. ———. "Dickens' Fools and Madmen." *DSA*, 2 (1971),
      69-97.

Discusses the many Dickens characters who, "like
Shakespeare's fools and madmen, are great literary creations" and "recognizable clinical pictures." Manheim
supposes that for Mr. Dick the diagnosis would be schizo-
phrenia with paranoid traits.

404. ———. "Dickens's HEROES, *heroes*, and heroids." *DSA*,
      5 (1976), 1-22.

Applies psychoanalytic theory to a study of how Dickens
incorporated his personal fantasies into his fiction.
Considering a number of Dickens's novels, Manheim applies
Otto Rank's hero myth (the hero as a product of a writer's
unconscious; the hero as a fantasy compensating for an
author's mundane life). Manheim repeats much of his earlier essay on *David Copperfield* (406). This article strives
to place *Copperfield* with *Dombey and Son* and *Bleak House*
as one of Dickens's three attempts "at self-analysis and
therapy." Manheim remarks, "In *Dombey* the aim was to come
to terms with ... the Father; in *Copperfield* the analytic
process concerned ... the Hero, and in *Bleak House* the
analytic aim concerned ... the heroine."

405. ———. "Floras and Doras: The Women in Dickens' Novels."
      TSLL, 7 (1965), 181-200.

Finds Dickens generally limited by patterned portrayals
of women, but argues that in *Copperfield* and the novels
immediately surrounding it Dickens attempted to come to
terms creatively with the figures of the Mother and the
Virgin. Manheim says there is no real analysis of David's
life with Agnes, because "Dickens simply cannot see the
inexorable round in which he re-creates the same fantasy-
image."

406. ———. "The Personal History of David Copperfield: A
      Study in Psychoanalytic Criticism." *AI*, 9 (1952), 21-43.

Considers *David Copperfield* as an effort at self-
analysis resulting in "a queer sort of confession." Manheim argues that because David encounters a number of

father surrogates while meeting many odd mother figures
he follows a mythological pattern described by Otto Rank
(who does not himself mention David). David remains, for
Manheim, a more mythological than modern hero, because
Dickens could not come to grips with parts of himself
"he would not and could not bear to meet." Nonetheless,
Manheim respects the book as a titanic effort of frustrated
self-analysis, with an impressive "grasping at literary
and artistic realism." Manheim's is one of the pioneering psychoanalytic studies of *David Copperfield*.

407. Mankowitz, Wolf. "Perfect Possession." In *Dickens of
      London*. New York: Macmillan, 1976, pp. 160-166.

      Drawing heavily upon standard sources for its familiar
      biographical material and critical opinions, this book
      stresses the dream quality of *Copperfield* and insists
      that the novel works "by dislocation, symbol, reversal,
      compression." Academic readers need more support than
      Mankowitz gives for his critical summations, and general
      readers may be mystified.

408. Manning, Sylvia. "Dickens, January, and May." *Dickensian*,
      71 (1975), 67-75.

      Discusses a number of female characters from *David
      Copperfield* as part of her larger argument that as Dickens
      changed his characters' views of the January-May relation-
      ship from fascination to rejection, he became more able
      "to conceive of women as women."

409. ————. "Masking and Self-Revelation: Dickens's Three
      Autobiographies." *DSN*, 7 (1976), 69-74.

      Shows that Dickens's treatment of his characters'
      progress from suffering to security becomes more compli-
      cated as his career advances: in *Oliver Twist* it takes
      a fantasy form; it appears as a realistic success story
      in *David Copperfield*; and it is inverted finally in *Great
      Expectations*. Manning thinks *Copperfield* unique because
      the question of criminality is absent from its "rational,
      ostensibly confessional" mode.

410. ————. "A Note on *David Copperfield*." In *Dickens the
      Satirist*. New Haven: Yale Univ. Press, 1971, pp. 96-98.

      Manning excludes *David Copperfield* from the main part
      of her study because she finds it only incidentally
      satiric, but she mentions Dora and Agnes as contrasting
      concepts of womanhood (types which change in later Dickens
      novels).

411. Marlow, James E. "Memory, Romance, and the Expressive Symbol in Dickens." *NCF*, 30 (1975), 20-32.

Ranges widely through Dickens's works and uses examples from *David Copperfield* to show that he struggled in his art to reconcile his conflicting instincts--to accommodate mankind to the world and to find escape from it. Marlow says that like Wordsworth, Dickens found nature spiritually beneficial, and through memory-bound romance he fused his impulses of acceptance and escape.

412. Marshall, William H. "The Image of Steerforth and the Structure of *David Copperfield.*" *Tennessee Studies in Literature*, 5 (1960), 57-65.

Regards the novel as David's private effort to understand himself through the narrative method of dramatic monologue. Marshall finds David's mental image of Steerforth crucial throughout because it is an index to "David's emotional development, both at the time of the experiences recalled and at the time of their recollection." Marshall's is an important essay both for its recognition of Steerforth's significance and for its insights about the operation of David's memory.

413. ————. "The Myth of the Self." In *The World of the Victorian Novel.* New York: A.S. Barnes, 1967, pp. 169-185.

Studies *David Copperfield* with *Jane Eyre*, *Henry Esmond*, and *Great Expectations*. *Copperfield* is most concerned with the "problem of disorientation, the disturbance of values which have been firmly established." As in his earlier article (412), Marshall stresses David's function as writer beginning privately to understand himself. The key character relationship for Marshall is between David and Steerforth; "the structural function of Steerforth" and the novel's method are necessarily related. Marshall's point is that "the quality of David's feeling for Steerforth, implicit in the boy's every act, becomes explicit in the recollections of the man." Marshall extends this argument to his commentary on the conclusion, which has provoked much critical debate. According to Marshall, David's recognition of his love for Agnes after David tells of Steerforth's death is not an anticlimax but "the full resolution" of his private record.

414. Maugham, W. Somerset. "Charles Dickens." *Atlantic Monthly*, 182 (July 1948), 50-56. Reprinted as the preface to his

1948 abridged edition of *David Copperfield* (59) and expanded as "Charles Dickens and *David Copperfield*," in
Ten Novels and Their Authors (London: Heinemann, 1954),
pp. 135-161.

Although he says *Copperfield* is not an autobiography,
Maugham provides a biographical sketch so that readers
may be more interested in the novel. He notes the advantages of the first-person narrator (those of a clear
story line and verisimilitude). The disadvantage for
Maugham is that the hero-narrator may be pallid as a
character. Maugham does not believe David is himself a
successful novelist, for he lacks Dickens's "drive,
vitality, and exuberance." He concludes that the book is
a delightful "fantastication" to be read in the same
spirit as *As You Like It*.

415.   Maurois, André. *Dickens*. Trans. Hamish Miles. New York:
       Harper and Brothers, 1935, pp. 69-77.

       Defends the autobiographical method and claims that
       "for the first time Dickens had been freed from his need
       for far-fetched inventions." Maurois finds the portrayal
       of Dora delicate and indulgent and remarks that, in pre-
       senting Agnes as a perfect woman, Dickens may have "fic-
       titiously allied himself to his sister-in-law, Mary
       Hogarth, of whom he had been deprived." Maurois is one
       of the first commentators to suggest Mary as a source for
       Agnes.

416.   Mersand, Joseph. "Introduction." In 1958 Pocket Books
       Edition, pp. v-xi (64).

       Recapitulates numberous critics' praise for the novel,
       citing in particular a 1958 television showing of the
       1935 film version as evidence of Dickens's continuing
       popularity. Mersand says the novel's main appeal is as
       a study of childhood and first love and as a psychologi-
       cally revealing autobiography. He reminds us that the
       book's characterization is its principal strength; its
       plot lacks unity. This introduction seems designed par-
       ticularly for adolescent readers.

417.   Meynell, Alice. "Appreciation of *David Copperfield*." In
       1919 Readers' Classic Edition, pp. 18-19 (55).

       Claims that readers prize *Copperfield* chiefly for the
       sake of Mr. Micawber and notes that Mr. Micawber, along
       with a number of elderly men ranging from Falstaff to
       Major Pendennis, proves the character of the humorist to
       be "a matter of custom and years."

418.   Michasiw, Barbara L. "The Heroines of Charles Dickens:
        Their Meaning and Function." *DAI*, 37 (1977), 6505A
        (Toronto, 1974).

        Asserts that "the pattern of development expressed
        through his heroines from simple to complex, unequiv-
        ocal to ambiguous, belies the general criticism of them
        as insipid stereotypes." Her chapter on *David Copperfield*
        "shows how ... Dickens minimizes the contribution of the
        will to David's success, concentrating instead on his
        growth in experience through the women whose lives are
        bound up with his and the dimensions of love they reveal
        to him."

419.   Miller, J. Hillis. "*David Copperfield*." In *Charles Dickens:
        The World of His Novels*. Cambridge, Mass.: Harvard
        Univ. Press, 1958, pp. 150-159.

        Miller's book is a keystone in modern Dickens criticism,
        and many subsequent studies acknowledge their indebtedness.
        He finds *Copperfield* organized around the complexities
        of romantic love. Miller accepts Micawber as a great comic
        character, one who can always completely spiritualize
        his situation and thus escape it, "effecting a transcen-
        dence through language." Miller finds that David's narra-
        tive links the alienated child's point of view with the
        gift of creative imagination. Like many subsequent critics
        Miller regards the novel as one primarily of memory; "any
        one point radiates backward and forward in a multitudinous
        web connecting it to past and future." Miller explains the
        compulsion, if not the success, with which David idealizes
        Agnes, for he finds the hero transposing "religious lan-
        guage into the realm of romantic love" and at once work-
        ing out his own destiny and accepting the secret workings
        of Providence. Miller concludes that "David, then, has
        both made himself and escaped the guilt which always
        hovers, for Dickens, over the man who takes matters into
        his own hands." Reviews: Bradford A. Booth, *MP*, 57 (1959),
        69-71; Barbara Hardy, *MLR*, 55 (1960), 433-436; Sylvère
        Monod, *NCF*, 13 (1959), 360-363; N.C. Peyrouton, *Dickensian*,
        55 (1959), 32-33; Kathleen Tillotson, *MLN*, 75 (1960), 439-
        442.

420.   ————. *The Form of Victorian Fiction*. Notre Dame: Univ.
        of Notre Dame Press, 1968. 151 pp.

        No separate discussion of *David Copperfield*, but the
        entire book is of value because of Miller's discussion of
        "intersubjective" and ontological fictional structures

in which narrators function as voices for a general consciousness. Miller notes that losing the happy intimacy
of childhood, Dickens gains a desolate identity that
"remains all his life with him as his deepest sense of
himself, something he wanders back to in his dreams, even
when he is famous and caressed and happy."

421.   ————. "Three Problems of Fictional Form: First-Person
        Narration in *David Copperfield* and *Huckleberry Finn*."
        In *Experience in the Novel*. Ed. Roy H. Pearce. New
        York: Columbia Univ. Press, 1968, pp. 21-48.

An important discussion of narrative technique most
useful to readers familiar with Miller's theories of novels
as intersubjective structures expressing forms of lived
human time. There is for Miller a paradoxical realism in
fiction because, although based on reality, a novel is a
verbally subjective construct. First-person novels offer
Miller particularly good examples of the interaction of
these formal issues. He thinks English fiction tends
toward discovery of the narrator's place within the
community, but American fiction maintains the narrator's
individuality. In *David Copperfield*, writes Miller, "personal memory within is matched by a cosmic memory without,"
and Agnes is the mediator of these organizing powers.

422.   Miller, Michael G. "Dickens and the Law." *DAI*, 36 (1976),
        6708A-6709A (Kentucky, 1975).

Considers *David Copperfield* as the only Dickens novel
"whose characters or structure can be better understood
through a realization of the origin of his legal figures."
Miller notes that Murdstone is linked to the law often,
and so is Uriah Heep.

423.   ————. "Murdstone, Heep, and the Structure of *David
        Copperfield*." *DSN*, 11 (1980), 65-70.

Argues that Dickens links David's antagonists, Murdstone
and Heep, through parallel scenes, similarities in their
relationship to David, "and through the empowering of
David to join the two men by psychological transference."
Miller finds that this "unobstrusive but unmistakable"
paralleling gives the novel unity and also reveals David
as "an active if unconscious fashioner of his own narrative." He reminds us of Freud's "hypothesis that legal
institutions are one social counterpart of the father
figure in individual psyches." With this in mind as he
notes the connections of both Heep and Murdstone with
the law, Miller suggests that "when Micawber triumphs

over Heep, who is an extension of the tyrannical Murdstone,
clearly the good father casts out the bad."

424. Moers, Ellen. "Charles Dickens, Gentleman." In *The Dandy:*
      Brummell to Beerbohm. New York: Viking, 1960, pp. 228-
      234.

      Notes that with Steerforth, Dickens for the first time
      gives a major role to a character with aristocratic atti-
      tudes. Moers says that like the "grey men" in later Dic-
      kens novels, Steerforth foreshadows the late nineteenth-
      century connection between decadence and dandyism.

425. Monod, Sylvère. "At the Top." In *Dickens the Novelist*.
      Norman: Univ. of Oklahoma Press, 1968, pp. 275-369.
      Expanded translation of his *Dickens Romancier* (Paris,
      1953).

      This chapter is one of the most extensive and thoroughly
      intelligent modern discussions of *David Copperfield* and
      provides the focus for the rest of Monod's book. Monod's
      thorough study attends to nearly every critically sig-
      nificant aspect of *David Copperfield*, and it is impossible
      to here summarize *all* of the critical insights he provides.
      In a chapter-by-chapter analysis of the novel, Monod makes
      careful use of the number plans and Dickens's correspon-
      dence concerning the book in progress. He finds Dickens
      more technically competent than in earlier books but
      also records traces of old weaknesses--abused coincidence,
      a few mistakes and inconsistencies. Monod shows Dickens
      to be innovative in his use of names, especially in giving
      various forms to the same name to emphasize "differences
      in the nature of the relationships involved." On the
      question of "autobiographical reality and invention"
      Monod examines biographical facts to discuss the relative
      force of memory and imagination. Observing that emotions
      are often of greater value than facts in autobiographical
      literature, Monod argues that David himself is not the
      dim, slightly incoherent figure some critics have thought
      him. Besides finding David possessed of a rich emotional
      life, Monod finds him growing both as a character and as
      a novelist. His education is dominated by a notion of
      firmness, but, as Monod shows, it is not the heartless
      firmness of Murdstone that finally prevails. Monod terms
      Copperfield "a study in psychological autobiography in
      which Dickens has not spared himself." Among the many
      parent figures Monod mentions, Betsey Trotwood is the
      most significant, because she is both ideal parent and
      educator. As an entirely imaginary creation she "is the

supreme achievement of Dickens' art in his autobiographical
novel." In his detailed study of the novel's language and
style, Monod points out recurrent words ("little," "own,"
"old") which carry much of Dickens's sentimentality. He
thinks that the vocabulary reveals Dickens's intensity,
although elaborate verbal structures may sometimes under-
mine his purpose. Dickens presents many original images,
and Monod argues that in *Copperfield*'s best passages
Dickens resists "his natural tendency toward overemphasis
and his permanent temptation of cumulative effects and
exalted writing"--contrast Robert Graves (167). Generally,
Monod finds the style more sober than in earlier Dickens
novels. He regards Dickens's handling of psychology and
morality as an artistic advance and considers his characterization of Rosa Dartle to be bold. The pathos and comedy
are under control, he asserts, and for the first time in
Dickens "humor and serious psychology seem to go hand in
hand." Monod, like most of the more recent commentators,
realizes that the novel exhibits the part played by unconscious sensory associations in human memory. He sees
Dickens's advance in artistry being evident in his treatment of the themes of love and friendship; to Monod this
is *the* novel of married life, presenting the beautiful
idyll of David and Agnes to emphasize the value of per-
severance. As Monod's title, "At the Top," indicates, he
regards this novel as the summit of Dickens's career, for
after *Copperfield* "novel-writing ceased to be the single
focal point of Dickens's life." Reviews: K.J. Fielding,
Dickensian, 65 (1969), 49-51; R.D. McMaster, *NCF*, 23
(1968), 359-361; Michael Slater, *EA*, 33 (1970), 212-214;
Taylor Stoehr, *Novel*, 2 (1968), 81-82.

426. Morris, Mowbray. "Charles Dickens." *Fortnightly Review*,
      38 (1882), 762-779. Reprinted in *Littell's Living Age*,
      155 (1882), 793-803; *Eclectic Magazine*, 100 (1883),
      182-194; *Manhattan*, 1 (1883), 296-309.

      General discussion of Dickens's reputation with fre-
      quent notice of his faults. Morris thinks *David Copper-
      field* less defective than Dickens's other works; "in this
      alone ... his imagination prevails over his fancy."

427. Morris, Patricia. "Some Notes on the Women in *David
      Copperfield*: Eleven Crude Categories and a Case for
      Miss Mowcher." *ESA*, 21 (1978), 17-21.

      Categorizes the women according to their roles and
      morality, with the basic division between the saintly
      and the fallen. Clara Peggotty and Betsey Trotwood are

the most realistic women for Morris, but Miss Mowcher is
"the most interesting, humorous and endearing," because
she comes the closest to being an independent modern
heroine. Morris's essay would profit from expansion of
her observations; it is less useful than a number of other
modern studies.

428. Morton, Thomas L. "Language and Reality in Dickens's Later
      Novels." *DAI*, 38 (1978), 5500A (Toronto, 1975).

      Approaches the novel as an account of David's struggle
      to express himself. Morton notes that David "is a post-
      humous child, and many characters seem to be 'ghosts'
      who come, symbolically, from his father's grave, either
      to embody or enforce his sentence or to relieve it....
      The father's silence is never ended, but David learns to
      fill it by his writing."

429. Mulvey, Christopher E. "*David Copperfield*: The Folk-Story
      Structure." *DSA*, 5 (1976), 74-94.

      Mulvey discusses elements that should interest readers
      concerned with *David Copperfield*'s fairy-tale quality.
      He notes a folk-story rhythm of repetition, a use of
      doubles, ambiguous father figures, and Betsey Trotwood
      as good fairy. Mulvey concludes that, like the luck-child
      threatened by destruction, David survives as a hero who
      becomes a man against all odds.

430. ⸻. "Dickens and His People: Character Organization
      in *David Copperfield*, *Bleak House*, and *Little Dorrit*."
      DA, 29 (1968), 1875A (Columbia, 1968).

      Contains lengthy examination of *Copperfield*, because
      it "allows the simplest and clearest exposition of Dickens's
      method of organizing a novel around character patterns
      made of archetypes." The prevalent pattern Mulvey finds
      is the family one of father, mother, and son, and Mulvey
      cites many variations of it.

431. Murphy, Mary J. "Dickens' 'Other Women': The Mature Women
      in His Novels." *DAI*, 36 (1976), 6709A-6710A (Louisville,
      1975).

      Studies a number of characters from ten novels to "demon-
      strate that ... the distorted spinsters, the frustrated
      and masculinized 'dames', the malignant mothers, and the
      guilt-ridden wives" reflect the "maturing of the novelist's
      moral and artistic vision." Murphy cites Rosa Dartle as
      an instance of one of the women "victimized in love by

men, who revenge themselves on other women." She also
mentions Mrs. Markleham as a mother who competes with
and exploits her daughter.

432. Nash, Leslie L. "David Hero: Dickens' Portrait of the
      Artist." *DAI*, 39 (1979), 5529A-5530A (Ohio Univ., 1978).

      An epistemological reading opposing Maurice Beebe
      (223) by arguing that "the essentially imaginative charac-
      ter of the artistic act is ... common to the epistemo-
      logical processes of all men." Nash says that the artist
      is thus the model human and not the bohemian. His separate
      chapters detail how "David views and presents his life
      through the imaginative construct of the circuitous quest
      prevalent in Romantic literature." Nash also finds that
      other characters function as "reinforcing symbols of the
      artist, examples of the universality of artful processes."

433. Needham, Gwendolyn B. "The Undisciplined Heart of David
      Copperfield." *NCF*, 9 (1954), 81-107.

      Major thematic study frequently drawn upon by later
      critics; for a pointed rebuttal, see the various writings
      of James Kincaid (372-376). Needham studies the theme of
      the undisciplined heart to illuminate David's character,
      to discuss the retrospective frame structures, and to
      recognize a total effect and pervading tone. She sees
      Fielding as a probable influence because Dickens, like
      the earlier writer, presents a hero who must learn pru-
      dence; once disciplined, David gains objectivity in
      analyzing his past and present emotions. Needham thinks
      that because Dickens deals with "simple fundamentals," he
      does not present a profound character study but portrays
      a very human hero who struggles with wasted opportunities.
      She shows other characters reflecting aspects of the
      central theme, and she thinks the book concludes with an
      affirmation not to be dismissed as shallow optimism.

434. Neill, Diana. *A Short History of the English Novel*. New
      York: Collier, 1964, pp. 165, 169.

      Sees Dickens's adolescent sufferings turned to good
      account in *Copperfield*, a book which brings to literature
      a new imaginative understanding of the child's point of
      view. Even for a survey of Dickens and English fiction,
      Neill's work is too brief to be as useful as Allen's
      (208).

435. Nelson, Carolyn C. "Patterns in the *Bildungsroman* as
      Illustrated by Six English Novels from 1814 to 1860."
      DAI, 33 (1973), 3597A-3598A (Wisconsin, 1972).

      Argues that with *Jane Eyre*, *David Copperfield* portrays
      "the inadequacy of the social institutions in the life
      of the individual" and demonstrates that "he must with-
      draw into a much smaller group, the family, to achieve
      happiness and fulfillment."

436. Nevins, Allan. "Introduction." In 1928 Macmillan Edition,
      pp. v-xii (56).

      Claims that despite the broad assumption that the novel
      is autobiographical, three fourths of the characters are
      wholly fictitious. Nevins traces the life of young Dickens
      as portrayed in the novel and believes the parallels
      end in the marriage of David to Dora. Of all its qualities,
      the novel's "reality" most impresses Nevins, for he finds
      the novel intensely describing the emotions of a pre-
      cocious childhood. Many of the fine characterizations
      contribute to the "reality" which Nevins finds, and he
      mentions Betsey as "a figure as only the tradition of
      Sterne and Dickens would be likely to give us." Micawber,
      he thinks, is the greatest triumph and Nevins agrees with
      Gissing (321) that Dickens's idealized portraitures often
      convey essential truths.

437. Noonan, William F. "The Comic Artist in the Novels of
      Charles Dickens." *DAI*, 35 (1975), 7263A (Ohio State,
      1974).

      Includes Mr. Micawber among artists from various other
      Dickens novels who "invent an imaginary ideality of youth,
      freedom, and individuality that replaces conventional
      reality."

438. Norris, E. Ashby. "The Domestic Atmosphere in Dickens's
      Books." *Dickensian*, 4 (1908), 288-290.

      Brief, appreciative mention of a "pervading atmosphere
      of domesticity" in *David Copperfield*.

439. Nunn, Robert C. "Remembering, Forgetting, and Uncanny
      Repetition in *Dombey and Son*, *David Copperfield*, *Great
      Expectations*, and *Our Mutual Friend*." *DAI*, 37 (1977),
      6506A (Toronto, 1974).

      Discusses "forgetting as a mechanism of repression,
      involuntary and incompletely-recognized reanimations of
      the buried past." Nunn's Freudian reading shows "in

David Copperfield the restoration of the past in memory ...
identified not only with the achievement of psychic
wholeness but also with the creative process."

440.   Oddie, William. "Mr. Micawber and the Redefinition of
       Experience." *Dickensian*, 63 (1967), 100-110.

Suggests three related problems posed by Micawber--the
extent to which he represents Dickens's "working out to
himself of his father," the source of Micawber's humor,
and how we are to relate his comedy to his capacity for
redefining painful experience. Oddie concludes that although the character may represent the evasion of a moral
problem for Dickens, Micawber makes us "for the moment
accept his substitution of accidentals for substance as
a real way of meeting" life's challenge. For a contrasting view of the effectiveness of comic redefinition see
Kincaid's study of the novel's subversive humor (374).

441.   [Oliphant, Margaret]. "Charles Dickens." *Blackwood's
       Magazine*, 109 (1871), 673-695.

General essay notable for its recognition of the Micawbers as great but "not pathetic: there is not in them
that deeper touch which dignifies the laughter." Oliphant
gives four pages to this point and notes that *David
Copperfield* has many of Dickens's best characters, and
"even the hero himself is capable of attracting us."
She finds Betsey Trotwood the best of Dickens's women but
thinks the presence of Steerforth, Rosa, and Little Em'ly
regrettable, for the strength of Dickens was not in these
characterizations. Oliphant, like many early readers who
preferred the more comic novels, believes Dickens's genius
culminated in *Copperfield*, for in later works "the impulse
and spontaneity are gone." Oliphant's article apparently
was written soon after Dickens's death but was held back
from publication for nearly a year. K.J. Fielding, writing
in the *Dickensian*, 66 (1970), 87, calls Oliphant's work
"an extraordinary exercise in damning criticism and grudg-
ing praise."

442.   O'Mealy, Joseph H. "Charles Dickens' Sense of His Past."
       DAI, 36 (1976), 6118A (Stanford, 1975).

Traces the progress of Dickens's "thoughts about the
influence of the past, for good or for ill, on a person's
development." O'Mealy shows that after his trip to America
Dickens "shifts from reminiscence and memory to self-examination, from outward reconstruction of the past to in-

ward exploration of its properties." O'Mealy thinks *Copper-field* advances a step beyond earlier Dickens fiction by its investigations into the author's personal history.

443. Orwell, George. "Charles Dickens." In *Inside the Whale*. London: Victor Gollancz, 1940, pp. 9-85. Reprinted in *Dickens, Dali and Others*. New York: Reynal and Hitch-cock, 1946, pp. 1-75.

Important essay because with Edmund Wilson's "Dickens: The Two Scrooges" (536) it has initiated modern study of Dickens as a serious writer. Orwell praises the excellence of Dickens's portrayal of childhood. Alert, as is Wilson, to many of the paradoxes of Dickens's artistry, Orwell notes that Dickens seems hampered at times by the very fertility of his invention, because it leads to over-writing. Orwell grants Dickens's stature as a humorist but insists that he is also a moralist. In his remarks on *David Copperfield* Orwell anticipates Kincaid's dis-cussion of the book's subversive humor (374) because, like Kincaid, Orwell refuses to read Dickens as merely a comic writer. According to Orwell, Dickens lacks con-structive suggestions for social improvement and has only an emotional perception that something is wrong. Here Orwell differs from such critics as T.A. Jackson (353) who argue that Dickens was a more deliberate revolutionary; Orwell comments that the vagueness of Dickens's discon-tent is the mark of its permanence. Orwell notes that in the ending of *David Copperfield* Dickens's intuitive sym-pathy for the underdog becomes confused once the down-trodden receive their rewards. Although Orwell does not discuss *David Copperfield* separately, his entire essay is a useful study for readers interested in Dickens's social consciousness.

444. Patten, Robert L. "Autobiography Into Autobiography: The Evolution of *David Copperfield*." In *Approaches to Vic-torian Autobiography*. Ed. George P. Landow. Athens: Ohio Univ. Press, 1979, pp. 269-291.

One of the most thorough discussions of the relation-ship of *David Copperfield*, the autobiographical fragment, and *Dombey and Son*. Patten shows that throughout the 1840's Dickens was attempting "to come to terms with the past--with revolution, romanticism, pre-industrialism, his own life." Patten says that in *Dombey* Dickens had opted for a past and dying world and had left his auto-biography incomplete with "no connection to the future life of the child or the present life of the adult."

Copperfield, Patten points out, was Dickens's "third version of the abandoned child, another try at connecting
past to present and writing oneself into adequacy." Patten
briefly discusses "a therapeutic model in the moral of
The Haunted Man," and he argues that the fictional character in *Copperfield* permitted Dickens to establish "a
cordon sanitaire between the 'I' of David and the 'I' of
Dickens." Patten is one of few commentators to consider
the difficulty Dickens had selecting a title, and he
recognizes how the many versions of the title and of the
main character's name signal changes in Dickens's concep-
tions of the novel's form. The final part of Patten's
essay argues that David not only becomes "an adequate
writer, but also he becomes a hero, if at all, through
the writing of his life," because he "creates the world
of his desire and discovers for himself and us its design
and meaning."

445. Pattison, Robert. *The Child Figure in English Literature*.
      Athens: Univ. of Georgia Press, 1978, pp. 122-127.

      Brief consideration of *David Copperfield*, arguing that
      the novel "looks at adult life through the eyes of child-
      hood and rejects it," viewing the world more sorrowfully
      than angrily. Pattison thinks Steerforth's story shows
      the problem of becoming an adult, and Dora "illustrates
      the impossibility of remaining one type of eternal juve-
      nile." Pattison says that despite David's attraction to
      both Steerforth and Dora, David steers clear of both ex-
      tremes, growing up yet still remaining open to his child-
      hood.

446. Pavese, Cesare. "Preface to Dickens: *David Copperfield*."
      In *Cesare Pavese: American Literature: Essays and
      Opinions*. Trans. Edwin Fussell. Berkeley: Univ. of
      California Press, 1970, pp. 206-210.

      English translation of Pavese's 1939 preface to an edi-
      tion of *David Copperfield* in Italian. He notes that the
      twentieth century lacks the necessary naiveté to write
      "human comedies," and finds *Copperfield* the Dickens novel
      "in which the characterization is most capricious and the
      futility of plot most enjoyable." Pavese thinks *Copper-
      field* too moralistic and founded on fairy tale, a "novel
      of delayed development and of the hero's good intentions
      of making a man of himself."

447. Pearlman, E. "David Copperfield Dreams of Drowning." *AI*,
      28 (1971), 391-403.

Valuable psychoanalytic study because it recognizes
subtle interrelationships between David, Heep, and Steerforth. Pearlman suggests that David's dream of drowning
may be "a path into the central structural pattern of the
novel, which is the rich and complex relationship" between
him and these complementary characters. Pearlman finds
Dickens's psychological vision "dense with the involuted
analysis of personality and motive." For a less psychologically centered discussion of Steerforth's importance
to the book's structure see Marshall (413) and for a
more general psychoanalytic reading that finds less
subtlety in the characterization of David see Manheim
(406).

448. ————. "Inversion in *Great Expectations*." *DSA*, 7 (1978),
190-202.

One of the most detailed considerations of the similarities and differences between *David Copperfield* and
Great Expectations. Pearlman says that although Dickens
repeats himself in a number of ways in all his books, in
producing *Great Expectations* he stands "the structure of
David Copperfield on its head." Pearlman considers three
sorts of structural inversion: the transformation of Clara
Copperfield and Mr. Murdstone into Joe and Mrs. Joe; the
transformation of Betsey Trotwood into Miss Havisham; the
more complex presentation of Dora and Agnes, Biddy and
Estella as "equivalent and opposed versions of a single
psychological pattern." Although not altogether convincing in suggesting that Estella combines the two women
David desires (Dora and Em'ly), Pearlman does show that
however Dickens inverted the *Copperfield* relationships
in *Great Expectations* he did avoid the conventional
moralizing that ended the earlier novel.

449. ————. "Two Notes on Religion in *David Copperfield*."
VN, 41 (Spring, 1972), 18-20.

Shows the novel infused with religious material and
having a morality play structure in which Agnes is the
moral guide. The second note acknowledges that Dickens's
religion stresses bounteousness and is theologically
simple. According to Pearlman, Mr. Peggotty develops into
a mystic and prophet, evincing "a humanity that grows
and deepens with suffering."

450. Pearson, Hesketh. "'Most Popular Masterpiece of Fiction.'"
Listener, 41 (1949), 1030-1031.

Describes principal autobiographical elements and discusses the conditions under which Dickens worked while
writing the novel. Pearson concludes that as "autonovel"
David Copperfield is more true to life than most autobiog-
raphies.

451. Perry, Donna M. "From Innocence Through Experience: A Study
      of the Romantic Child in Five Nineteenth Century Novels."
      DAI, 37 (1976), 3599A (Marquette, 1976).

      Studies *David Copperfield* with *Jane Eyre*, *The Mill on
      the Floss*, *Great Expectations*, and *What Maisie Knew* to
      trace "the way ... innocence of vision ... accommodates
      experience with the world." Perry claims that like the
      narrator of *Jane Eyre*, David is a "wish-fulfillment
      figure" retaining innocence despite overwhelming odds.
      All five books suggest to Perry "ambiguities of inno-
      cence--to some extent David's marriage to Agnes is a
      retreat from adulthood and into false security."

452. Peyrouton, Noel C., moderator. *Dickens Criticism: Past,
      Present, and Future Directions. A Symposium with George
      H. Ford, Edgar Johnson, J. Hillis Miller, and Sylvère
      Monod*. Boston: Charles Dickens Research Center, 1962,
      pp. 37-38.

      Edgar Johnson divides *David Copperfield* "into three
      symphonic movements, of which the first comes to an end
      when David rebels against his incarceration in the bottling
      factory and flees to appeal to his aunt, Miss Betsey
      Trotwood, of which the second comes to an end with the
      climactic stroke of Steerforth's seduction of Little Emily
      and their flight, and of which the third movement occupies
      all the remaining half of the book."

453. Pope, Norris. *Dickens and Charity*. New York: Columbia
      Univ. Press, 1978, pp. 122-126.

      Notes that the description of the model prison in
      Copperfield's final number is consistent with Dickens's
      other comments on prison reform. See also Collins (264)
      and Oddie (684).

454. Pratt, Branwen B. "Dickens and Love: The Other as the
      Self in the Works of Charles Dickens." *DAI*, 33 (1973),
      4430A (Stanford, 1972).

      Of obvious importance to *David Copperfield* because of
      its general psychological examination of Dickens's works
      "to understand his 'fiction of concord'--the imaginative

projection through which the artist seeks to harmonize
the world's dissonances."

455. Praz, Mario. "Charles Dickens." In *The Hero in Eclipse
in Victorian Fiction*. Trans. Angus Davidson. London:
Oxford Univ. Press, 1956, pp. 127-188.

A general and influential study of Dickens that refers
frequently to *David Copperfield*. Praz believes the story
of David upholds goodness and quiet happiness as Dickensian
ideals, but the Byronic Steerforth opposes them. The
treatment of the Strongs and of Agnes epitomizes for Praz
the Victorian idealization of women, with Agnes appearing as a wax doll. Praz reiterates an observation of one
of Dickens's earliest Continental critics, Taine (199),
saying that Dickens, at his best as caricaturist, "with
a tendency to hallucination," captures his characters'
"picturesque essence." Praz cites Heep and Betsey Trotwood as the best examples of Dickens's caricature, and
he finds Mr. Pickwick and David slightly different from
Dickens's usual puppet-like heroes. Praz concludes by
pointing out a number of the novel's memorable genre
pictures; like popular genre painters Dickens exploits
"the eloquence of external things."

456. Priestley, J.B. "Mr. Micawber." In *The English Comic
Characters*. New York: Phaeton Press, 1972, pp. 211-242.

Terms Mr. Micawber the greatest of Dickens's comic
characters, droll both in nature and in speech. Priestley
ranks Micawber second only to Falstaff among English comic
characters. He thinks too much has been made of Micawber's
mere optimism; Priestley considers him to have an "elas-
tic" temperament, varying from despair to the height of
gaiety. Mrs. Micawber shares this temperament, and
Priestley goes on to say that her "logical" outlook
complements her husband's "imaginative" one so that the
two "act as both a check and a stimulus upon one another."
Priestley does not think Micawber's role in castigating
Uriah Heep is defensible, for Micawber simply is not a
credible "financial detective."

457. ————. "The Wonderful World of Dickens." In *English
Humour*. London: Longmans, Green, 1930, pp. 150-162.

Cites Mr. Micawber as an instance of the comic character existing in a self-enclosed atmosphere. Priestley
thinks it a mistake for Dickens to have sent the Micawbers to Australia. Micawber, for Priestley, is the "ro-

mantic adventurer and orator"; his wife is "the clear-
sighted practical helpmate" (surely one of the most positive tributes paid her by any commentator).

458.   Quiller-Couch, Sir Arthur. "Dickens." In *Charles Dickens
       and Other Victorians*. Cambridge: Cambridge Univ. Press,
       1925, pp. 1-100.

       Series of lectures on Dickens with a few citations from
       David Copperfield to substantiate his defense of Dickens's
       prose style. He resists the view that Dickens was a care-
       less writer, noting especially the description of young
       David's reading in the fourth chapter of *Copperfield*.
       Like Gissing (321), Quiller-Couch praises the account of
       David's journey to Dover, considering it "as good a piece
       of narrative prose as can be found in English."

459.   Quirk, Randolph. *Charles Dickens and Appropriate Language*.
       Durham: Univ. of Durham, 1959, passim.

       Suggests that *David Copperfield* was Dickens's first
       opportunity to indulge rhetorically in verbs even though
       many of the "Retrospect" chapters have verbless sentences.
       Quirk's twenty-six-page article was originally a lecture.

460.   ———. "Some Observations on the Language of Dickens."
       REL, 2 (1961), 19-28.

       Draws upon a number of the novels to show Dickens em-
       ploying "multifunctional" language to individualize charac-
       ters and to experiment. Quirk mentions the language of
       Uriah Heep and considers the book's occasional use of the
       historical present tense.

461.   Raina, Badri. "Charles Dickens: The Dialectic of Self."
       DAI, 37 (1976), 3648A (Wisconsin, 1976).

       Describes a contradictory structure of feeling in
       Dickens's "ambivalence toward bourgeois Victorian culture
       and ... toward himself." Raina gives particular attention
       to David, Steerforth, and Uriah Heep.

462.   Raleigh, John D. "Dickens and the Sense of Time." *NCF*,
       13 (1958), 127-137. Reprinted in *Time, Place, and Idea:
       Essays on the Novel*. Carbondale: Southern Illinois
       Univ. Press, 1968, pp. 126-136.

       Discusses the concrete and philosophical senses of time
       in Dickens, finding in his first-person narratives "a
       compound of memory and desire ... added on to the temporal

implications of the involved plotting." Raleigh argues
that *David Copperfield* blends its skillful evocation of
modes and habits of memory with accurate descriptions of
change, and David provides a valuable temporal perspective.
For a more far-reaching analysis that disagrees with
Raleigh's conclusions about the novel's success in coping
with the sense of time, see Lougy (391).

463. Reed, John R. "Confinement and Character in Dickens's
Novels." *DSA*, 1 (1970), 41-54.

Considers themes of imprisonment, in which dynamics of
constraint and of freedom crystalize character in Dickens.
Such themes are most evident for Reed in *David Copperfield*,
which reveals Dickens's attitudes toward writing. Reed
states that "the novel's web of incident controlling its
characters was the constraint by which he confronted himself." Like Hornback (344) Reed is interested in the relationship between David's moral and artistic self-disci-
pline.

464. ———. *Victorian Conventions*. Athens: Ohio Univ. Press,
1975, passim.

Makes frequent mention of *David Copperfield* in his
survey of conventional female character types. Agnes
combines qualities of types Reed identifies as the pur-
sued innocent (the "Susannah") and the successful domestic
saint. It is not altogether clear why Reed regards Rosa
Dartle as "potentially malign," for most readers see her
potential fulfilled at least in her self-torment. Reed
observes that with Martha, Dickens turns the conventional
bitter end for the fallen woman to a more generous conclusion. Reed notes the novel's deathbed scenes and comments also on its use of the orphan figure.

465. Rigg, Ronald E. "The Fascination of the Sea." *Dickensian*,
40 (1944), 89-96.

Of little direct critical interest but shows readers
interested in *Copperfield*'s imagery that Dickens in a
number of books regarded the sea as "sublime and wonderful."

466. Robison, Roselee. "Time, Death, and the River in Dickens'
Novels." *ES*, 53 (1972), 436-454.

Studying Dickens generally, Robison briefly mentions
Dickens's use of water imagery to sustain an elegaic tone
in *David Copperfield*.

467.   Romanofsky, Barbara R. "A Study of Child Rearing Practices
       in the Middle Novels of Charles Dickens." *DAI*, 38 (1978),
       4853A (CUNY, 1977).

       Catalogues the parents in Dickens's novels and examines
       methods by which children overcome abuse. She thinks *David
       Copperfield* "explores the positive mother figure," with
       three women forming a composite of ideal motherhood—Clara
       Copperfield, Clara Peggotty, and Betsey Trotwood.

468.   Romig, Evelyn M. "Women as Victims in the Novels of Charles
       Dickens and William Faulkner." *DAI*, 39 (1978), 1600A
       (Rice, 1978).

       States that for both novelists, "the victimized woman
       is often an unhappy wife or sweetheart, and domestic con-
       flict between male and female wills is a central theme."
       Romig notes that in *Copperfield* "structures of traditional
       romance are inverted to show that love assures no happy
       endings in real domestic life."

469.   Rooke, Eleanor. "Fathers and Sons in Dickens." *E&S*, NS 4
       (1951), 53-69.

       Observes the absence of fathers for most of Dickens's
       heroes and discusses Dickens's relationship with his
       father and with his own sons. Her essay has little directly
       concerning *David Copperfield*, but Rooke considers Micaw-
       ber a good father and a sympathetic portrait of John
       Dickens, although admittedly "it is not primarily as a
       father that we regard Mr. Micawber."

470.   Roulet, Ann E. "Dickens: The Controlling Voice of the
       Artist." *DAI*, 32 (1971), 3267A-3268A (Case Western
       Reserve, 1971).

       Traces Dickens's "evolving skill in the use of point
       of view" in the major novels from *Martin Chuzzlewit*
       through *Bleak House*. In *David Copperfield*, Roulet says,
       the first-person point of view provides "not a single
       voice but a double perspective." She argues that Dickens's
       mastery of double perspective comes later in *Bleak House*.

471.   Saha, Narayan. "Dickens's Treatment of Child-Psychology—
       and *David Copperfield*." *Bulletin of the Department of
       English* (Calcutta Univ.), 6 (1970-1971), 26-28.

       Without close study claims that Dickens put story first
       and psychology second, although they intermingle. Saha
       notes that David demonstrated the child's instintive love
       and hate.

472. Saintsbury, George. "Charles Dickens." In *Corrected
      Impressions: Essays on Victorian Writers*. London:
      Heinemann, 1895, pp. 117-137.

      Acknowledges the difficulty of writing about Dickens
      at a time when there are differing opinions about him
      but thinks his fame must rest on the novels from *Nicholas
      Nickleby* or *David Copperfield*. Saintsbury notes especially
      the divided critical opinions concerning Agnes, and he
      resists vigorously any suggestion that she is charming.
      In his article on Dickens in Vol. XIII of *The Cambridge
      History of English Literature* (1917), Saintsbury acknow-
      ledges the importance of *Copperfield* as a projection of
      "what Dickens could not be and would have liked to be."
      It is, says Saintsbury, his most varied, most serious,
      and most sustained novel.

473. Saks, Irene J. "Charles Dickens and the Self-Made Man."
      DAI, 36 (1975), 1535A (CUNY, 1975).

      Argues that characters in the novels reflect Dickens's
      ambivalence in reconciling his "self-made, aggressive
      and effective" identity with "Christian ideals which he
      saw as man's salvation." In some of the books Saks finds
      "an inversion ... employing adoption as the means of
      raising the hero's station. In these ... the villains are
      willful and aggressive men." It is not clear how much
      attention Saks gives *Copperfield* but her general subject
      has obvious bearing on the novel.

474. Schilling, Bernard N. "Mr. Micawber's Difficulties" and
      "Mr. Micawber's Abilities." In *The Comic Spirit:
      Boccaccio to Thomas Mann*. Detroit: Wayne State Univ.
      Press, 1965, pp. 98-144.

      Two essays on Micawber within *The Comic Spirit*'s more
      general examination of how humane comic experience senses
      "the richness of life." Schilling makes the moral prob-
      lem of whether Micawber is absurdly inept or cunningly
      knavish the focal point of "Mr. Micawber's Difficulties."
      He says Micawber cannot perform what he professes but
      depends upon his troubles and takes pleasure in drama-
      tizing them. The one "flaw" Schilling notes in Micawber's
      "otherwise boundless ineptitude" is his work for others,
      and he is the ideal character to denounce Uriah Heep.
      Schilling thinks that Dickens's sending of Micawber to
      Australia was a fitting termination to the comedy, but
      allowing him to succeed there was a mistake. Continuing
      this discussion in his second essay, Schilling acknow-

ledges that some readers find Micawber too sympathetically
presented but insists that "Dickens's sympathy for Micawber keeps within Micawber's world." Schilling concludes
that as a comic writer, "Dickens was too generous to do
his best work in the harshest satiric terms. He had immense
energy and a militant temper, but especially in the early
novels he could not escape his human pity, his open-
hearted sympathy with life. Of this temper, Micawber is
the highest achievement."

475.   Schmidt, Julian. "Comment on *David Copperfield*." In 1919
       Readers' Classics Edition, pp. 38-39 (55).

       In this piece, written first for a German magazine in
       1870, Schmidt does not find *David Copperfield* to be
       Dickens's masterpiece because "the fantastic nature of
       his characters can only be justified by the very extreme
       of his boldness."

476.   Secor, Marie J. "Dickens' Rhetoric: A Study of Three
       Bildungsromans." *DAI*, 31 (1971), 4732A-4733A (Brown,
       1969).

       Considers *Oliver Twist* and *Great Expectations* in addi-
       tion to *David Copperfield*. In the latter, Secor finds
       "veracity and appeal ... established by a rhetoric which
       simultaneously creates its own reality and insists on
       its objective validity."

477.   Shaw, George Bernard. "Foreword." In *Great Expectations*.
       London: Hamish Hamilton, 1947, pp. v-vi.

       Finds Dickens's tremendous growth beginning with *Hard
       Times* and *Little Dorrit* and wonders whether "in that
       immensely broadened outlook and knowledge of the world ...
       he may not have come to see that making his living by
       sticking labels on blacking bottles and rubbing shoulders
       with boys who were not gentlemen, was as little shameful
       as being Spenlow's genteel apprentice or a shorthand
       writer." Shaw contrasts Micawber with William Dorrit to
       discuss a "tragic change" in Dickens's valuations; in
       comparison Micawber becomes "a mere marionette pantaloon
       with a funny bag of tricks which he repeats until we can
       bear no more of him." Similarly, Shaw's contrast of David
       and Pip suggests that the adult David becomes what "stage
       managers call a walking gentleman." Shaw thinks the
       reappearance of Dickens in the character of a blacksmith's
       boy may be regarded as "an apology to Mealy Potatoes."
       Shaw's point is that in *Copperfield* Dickens's snobbish-

ness affected his fictional treatment of his unhappy days
in the blacking warehouse.

478. ———. "George Bernard Shaw on *David Copperfield*."
      Dickensian, 45 (1949), 118.

      Comments briefly that *Great Expectations* "wiped out"
      David Copperfield and that the adult disillusion over
      young love seen through the characterization of *Little
      Dorrit*'s Flora was more impressive than the illusions
      of David concerning Dora. Shaw hastily concludes, "There
      is more to be said about David; but I have no time to
      say it."

479. Shore, W. Teignmouth. "*David Copperfield* as an Example
      of Dickens' Genius." In *Dickens*. London: George Bell
      and Sons, 1904, pp. 69-80.

      Claims that the novel contains farce, comedy, and
      tragedy of uneven quality but that overall *David Copper-
      field* is Dickens's finest achievement. Shore notes that
      the plot does not easily connect the actions of the two
      sets of characters in the David and the Steerforth stories.
      Shore does not think Steerforth's attractiveness to David
      is credible, and he thinks Little Em'ly is a stock figure
      of melodrama. Agnes' perfection is exasperating to Shore,
      who says that "we almost believe that David must have
      repented of his bargain." Dickens's chief strength, con-
      cludes Shore, is his delicate pathos and comedy, farce
      and caricature.

480. Sitwell, Osbert. *Dickens*. London: Chatto and Windus,
      1932, pp. 22-24.

      Has high but not well-defined praise for Dickens as
      "an inventor of 'expressionism'" in fiction. Sitwell
      mentions Dickens's description of Miss Murdstone as an
      example.

481. Smith, Sheila M. "Anti-Mechanism and the Comic in the
      Writings of Charles Dickens." *Renaissance & Modern
      Studies*, 3 (1959), 131-144.

      Little directly concerning *David Copperfield*. Smith
      cites Dora and Agnes as conventional figures too sacred
      for Dickens's comic spirit to play upon. Her point is
      that although the novel has "anti-mechanist" arguments,
      Dickens presented these characters mechanically. Few
      readers would argue with Smith about Agnes, but most
      would wonder why she ignores the praise critics have long
      accorded Dickens's humorous portrayal of Dora.

482. Snow, C.P. "Dickens." In *The Realists: Portraits of Eight
      Novelists*. London: Macmillan, 1978, pp. 62-83.

      General essay with little direct mention of *Copperfield*.
      Snow observes how much more gentle Dickens was toward Mi-
      cawber than toward any of his other major comic figures.
      He notes that Dickens's glaring weakness was his inability
      to portray deep relationship between men and women.

483. Solomon, Pearl C. *Dickens and Melville in Their Time*.
      New York: Columbia Univ. Press, 1975, pp. 38-39, 103,
      134-153.

      Includes Uriah Heep in a survey of clerk characters but
      favors Bob Cratchit as more realistic. Solomon sees David
      as the only artist in Dickens's fiction who takes as much
      pleasure in his work as some businessmen take in theirs.
      She traces autobiographical elements to show Dickens
      changing his own story. Solomon generalizes David's life
      in cultural terms: David's "childhood is England's pre-
      industrial past; his youth is his initiation into the
      modern world; his maturity is his acceptance of the terms
      of the industrial world through his own effort and hard
      work." Making an intriguing case for Betsey Trotwood as a
      surrogate father, Solomon shows David's considerable con-
      fusion of father figures and concludes that Dickens does
      not face David's adult inner life clearly. Extensive com-
      parison with *Great Expectations* provides support for
      Solomon's observation that Dickens's criticism of society
      deepened in that novel. Reviews: Richard J. Dunn, *SNNTS*, 8
      (1976), 223-233; H. Bruce Franklin, *NCF*, 30 (1976), 547-
      553; Lauriat Lane, Jr., *DSN* 7 (1976), 46-48 and *Extracts*
      (Melville Soc.), no. 23 (Sept. 1975), 14; Joseph Schifman,
      AL, 47 (1975), 457-458.

484. Sowter, Eadgyth. "The Dark Lady of Dickens." *Dickensian*,
      25 (1929), 204-206.

      Primarily interested in Lady Dedlock of *Bleak House*
      but cites Rosa Dartle as an instance of a Dickens woman
      standing out because "of a strange face that she seems
      to possess."

485. Spengemann, William C. "Poetic Autobiography: *David
      Copperfield*." In *The Forms of Autobiography: Episodes
      in the History of a Literary Genre*. New Haven: Yale
      Univ. Press, 1980, pp. 119-132, 233-236.

      Concentrates on the first fourteen chapters, arguing
      that the novel "is autobiographical only to the extent

that it expresses through the deployment of conventional
narrative *personae* and through the allegorical tenor of
its language Dickens's over-riding concern with the realization of his self." Spengemann discusses in detail his
sense of Mr. Dick as a link between the young David and
the older narrator, for Mr. Dick is a "transparent
biographical allegory." Spengemann thinks that in the
novel's final domestic circle Dickens resolves his book
in entirely poetic terms, because Dickens's "several past
and present selves assume the guise of characters in a
domestic novel and commune among themselves in that in-
vented world." In a brief bibliographical essay Spengemann discusses criticism of *Copperfield*'s autobiographical
aspect, calling attention to work of Collins (263),
Manheim (406), Spilka (486), J. Hillis Miller (419), and
mentioning particularly Westburg's (527) and Tick's (509)
writing about the autobiographical importance of Mr.
Dick.

486. Spilka, Mark. "*David Copperfield* as Psychological Fiction."
      CritQ, 1 (1959), 292-301.

      Regards *Copperfield* as a "projective" novel in which
surface life reflects inner self. Spilka says that Dickens's
projected feelings make real outer scenes seem fantastic,
and he finds the effect, though not the method, similar
to Kafka's. To Spilka both novelists present a surface
"charged with baffling implications." Spilka discusses a
number of the novel's key relationships. He notes that
in David's eyes Mr. Murdstone becomes a revengeful father;
"the boy's hostility and fear suffuse the outward scene."
From Steerforth David seeks power, but Spilka observes
that for David and Steerforth "the projective paths to
mother-love are varied." Spilka thinks that even the
book's "comedy thrives upon the original psychic thrust,"
and he believes that the nostalgia also relates to Dickens's childhood anguish and his attempts to escape its
pain.

487. ———. *Dickens and Kafka: A Mutual Interpretation.*
      Bloomington: Indiana Univ. Press, 1963, passim.

      Incorporates Spilka's earlier psychological and literary
influence studies. The subtitle fitly designates this as
an interpretive work. Spilka's first section, "A Child's
View of the Universe," notices the writers' senses of
familial exclusion, "its commercial reinforcement, and
its damaging effect on their relations with women." His
second edition, "The Technique of the Grotesque," deals

less specifically with *David Copperfield*, but his third
part, "*Copperfield* and *Amerika*," makes extensive comparative analysis, reviewing and expanding E.W. Tedlock's
findings (691). Spilka observes that through an infantile
perspective, the outcast child may find a sense of "sin-
fulness without guilt." Spilka speaks of *Copperfield* as
a "progress toward maturity through identifications and
displacements." He thinks the book thus gains "unifying
power from psychological sources." Because of these views
Spilka has given significant impetus to readings of David
as a modern hero "whose dreamlike progress furthers the
development of modern forms." A final chapter summarizes
Spilka's argument that *Copperfield* "is projective fiction
of the Kafkan order," with David "a psychological center
for the life around him." Spilka's study is useful for
any readers interested in the novel's psychological intensity, although obviously he is most helpful to readers
acquainted with the work of both Dickens and Kafka. Reviews: Sheridan Baker, *MQR*, 5 (1966), 68-69; M. Ann Houk,
L&P, 14 (1964), 37-39; J. Hillis Miller, *NCF*, 18 (1965),
404-407; N.C. Peyrouton, *Dickensian*, 60 (1964), 115-116.

488.   Stedman, Jane W. "Child-Wives of Dickens." *Dickensian*,
        59 (1963), 113-118.

        Considers Dora and child-wives from other novels as
characters toward whom Dickens sooner or later establishes
a sympathetic attitude by equating "innocence with im-
practicability, intellectual or emotional immaturity,
and sexlessness." Stedman thinks that Clara Copperfield
and Annie Strong, with Dora, form a triad of child-wives,
but only Annie grows up. Stedman finds Dickens giving
new dimensions to the fictional convention of the child-
wife.

489.   Steig, Michael. "*David Copperfield*: Progress of a Con-
        fused Soul." In *Dickens and Phiz*. Bloomington: Indiana
        Univ. Press, 1978, pp. 113-130.

        This chapter incorporates and expands material from
Steig's earlier essays to give the most detailed critical
reading of *David Copperfield*'s illustrations as integral
to the novel's structure and meaning. Steig shows the
illustrations providing details of their own for serious
or comic comment upon characters and events. Themselves
rich with allusions, the illustrations, as Steig so well
shows, anticipate plot developments and form "part of the
evidence of what the novel *is*." One of Steig's most original observations is that the illustrations play down

the role of Agnes as dominant female by giving prominence
to Dora and Little Em'ly. He thinks the depiction of the
women in David's life was "Browne's major contribution
to the visual progress of David Copperfield." Steig reproduces a number of plates and includes several of the
sketches for the plates. Reviews: Anthony Burton, *VS*, 23
(1980), 280-283; John Dixon Hunt, *Dickensian*, 76 (1980),
51-52; Robert L. Patten, *NCF*, 34 (1979), 224-228.

490.   ————. "Dickens' Characters and Psychoanalytic Criticism."
       HSL, 8 (1976), 38-45.

       Discusses much else in Dickens but is applicable to
       David Copperfield because Steig warns critics and readers
       to consider Dickens's own awareness "of some of the com-
       plex psychological insights his characters provide."

491.   ————. "The Iconography of *David Copperfield*." *HSL*, 2
       (1970), 1-18.

       Considers critically the allegorical details of illustra-
       tions to show how they clarify David's early relationship
       to his mother and the Murdstones, his later attempts to
       discover a mature identity, and his relationships with
       Em'ly and Dora and Agnes. See Steig's later note on Plate
       1 (30) for a supplemental point to this article.

492.   ————. "The Whitewashing of Inspector Bucket: Origins
       and Parallels." *Papers of the Michigan Academy of
       Science, Arts, and Letters*, 50 (1965), 575-584.

       Includes Steerforth among the characters Dickens changes
       from monsters to heroes. According to Steig, Steerforth
       is the first upper-class character in Dickens to have
       qualities of social adaptability and general competence.
       Steig thinks Dickens deliberately undercut David's adula-
       tion of Steerforth, partly because "while he has plenty
       of upper-class snobbishness, and brutality, he has none
       of the revolutionary spirit that characterizes the true
       Byronic type."

493.   Stevenson, Lionel. *The English Novel: A Panorama*. Boston:
       Houghton Mifflin, 1960, pp. 285-287.

       Thinks there is less specific social crusading in *David
       Copperfield* than in Dickens's other novels, "but his
       preoccupation with the problems of opportunity and social
       prejudice was under the surface throughout." Stevenson
       says that Dickens's "technique of characterization by
       humours" reached its peak of creativeness with Uriah Heep

and Mr. Micawber. Stevenson concludes with some general
comparisons of *Copperfield* and *Pendennis*.

494. Stevenson, Robert L. "Some Gentlemen in Fiction." *Scribner's Magazine*, 3 (1888), 766-767.

Admits Dickens's long inability to portray a gentleman,
although finally "David Copperfield scrambled through on
hands and knees; it was at least a negative success."
Stevenson states that conventionally the gentleman is
inconspicuous and hardly worth drawing by any artist who
individualizes characters to the extent Dickens does, and
he hypothesizes that Dickens's difficulty may have been
that of refusing to be "content to draw a hero and a
gentleman plainly and quietly." Curiously, Stevenson does
not discuss Dickens's portrayal of Steerforth, a matter
of some concern for later readers interested in Dickens's
gentlemen—see Moers (424).

495. Stewart, Garrett. *Dickens and the Trials of the Imagination.* Cambridge, Mass.: Harvard Univ. Press, 1974,
pp. 136-143, 164-166, 180-182, 237-240.

Stewart's work centers on Dickens's earlier novels to
argue that Dickens's creative energies wane after *Pickwick.* Without giving a separate discussion of *Copperfield*,
Stewart in passing mentions it as a search for stylistic
authenticity as David feels "his way toward expressive
self-reliance." Stewart cites Mr. Micawber as an example
of "indulgent, sometimes dangerously negligent loquacity."
He regards Micawber as "a commanding stylist against whose
prose David must define his own expressive tendencies."
Stewart thinks that David is "a transitional figure in
that reluctant devaluation of verbal fancy which under-
mines the life of words in Dickens's later novels." In
an appendix Stewart discusses the novel's "secret prose,"
its "lyric inwardness of style" that makes possible some
brief moments of self-recognition. Stewart's reading of
Dickens received mixed reviews: Philip Collins, *TLS*, 19
Sept. 1975, p. 1066; Richard J. Dunn, *SNNTS*, 8 (1976),
223-233; Robin Gilmour, *Dickensian*, 72 (1976), 39-40;
Bert G. Hornback, *DSN*, 7 (1976), 81-83; James R. Kincaid,
NCF, 30 (1976), 535-538.

496. Stone, Harry. "*David Copperfield*: The Fairy-Tale Method
Perfected." In *Dickens and the Invisible World: Fairy
Tales, Fantasy, and Novel-Making.* Bloomington: Indiana
Univ. Press, 1979, pp. 193-278.

In the most complete study of Dickens and the fairy
tale, Stone uses *Copperfield* as the primary example of
Dickens's fairy-tale art. Incorporating and expanding
his earlier articles on the novel, Stone discusses many
details of character, scene, and technique. He calls it
a novel of "myriad confluences and portents of the puissant
invisible world." He is especially concerned with the
nightmare of David's childhood, which Stone finds changing to the "dream of David's youth." He discusses the
fairy-tale aura surrounding Steerforth and Rosa Dartle
and finds fairy-tale details heightening Dickens's
psychological realism in these characterizations. Stone
mentions many other characters that seem in part con-
ceived by Dickens as fairy-tale figures and finds it
particularly useful to recognize the Murdstones and Uriah
Heep in this way. The fairy tale in Dickens, as Stone
shows, is not simply present in the characterization of
story-book characters but is also evident in Dickens's
attention to setting. Stone thus speaks of the "Tempest"
chapter as one "densely fraught with witching energies
and with reverberations of the irrational." He acknowledges this as a chapter of formal climax to many of the
book's themes and argues that as the book's great organizing principle the fairy-tale structure carries through
the chapters after the tempest. In discussing the ending
Stone calls Agnes "a fantasy substitute," but he thinks
that symbolically Dora and Agnes "express two aspects of
a single experience of womanhood for David." Stone grants
that however magnificently the "Tempest" chapter incorporates the "deeply symbolic and profoundly psychological"
dimensions of David's experience, the remainder of the
novel seems more superficial because it rewards David
"with the same promise of romantic fulfillment that has
elsewhere been his nemesis." Reviews: Charles Bishop,
Library Journal, 104 (1 Sept. 1979), 1700; Peter Keating,
TLS, 18 Apr. 1980, p. 444.

497.   ———. "Dickens and Fantasy: The Case of Uriah Heep."
        Dickensian, 75 (1979), 95-103.

Shows fantasy playing a deceptive role in the process
of Dickens's probing and conveying of Heep's character.
Stone shows how physically Uriah seems more than an ordinary mortal; Dickens employs a number of supernatural
devices for this effect. Part of what Stone calls Heep's
"menacing reality" is his resemblance to the devil. Stone
claims that Heep's unmasking occurs in a scene filled
with the novel's seemingly warring modes of realism, bur-

lesque, and diablerie. Stone outlines a fairy-tale pattern
of doubling of David and Uriah which adds further complexity to him as David's rival. As have a number of
readers, Stone mentions Heep in connection with Steerforth,
for both personify evil. In Stone's view fantasy enlarges
this evil and the threat it poses to society; "by distort-
ing reality, Dickens helps us grasp reality."

498.   ———. "Fairy Tales and Ogres: Dickens' Imagination
       and *David Copperfield*." *Criticism*, 6 (1964), 324–330.

Identifies a range of fairy-tale elements in the novel
and shows the impact of fairy tale on Dickens's imagination. In *David Copperfield* Stone thinks Dickens's "own
life becomes a fairy tale in ways that intensify reality."
Stone speaks of the episode in which David encounters the
clothing dealer as an instance of Dickens's "expression-
istic objectification" of a nightmare fairy-tale world.

499.   Strong, L.A.G. "*David Copperfield*." *Dickensian*, 46 (1950),
       65–75.

Reproduces lecture presented to Dickens Fellowship.
Strong sees much unconscious venom in the portrait of
Dora and does not think the novel has anything to say
about marriage or the relationship of woman to man. But
he praises an "irrepressible munificence" in Dickens's
handling of minor characters.

500.   Sucksmith, Harvey P. *The Narrative Art of Charles Dickens:
       The Rhetoric of Sympathy and Irony in His Novels*. Ox-
       ford: The Clarendon Press, 1970, passim.

A major study of Dickens's artistry with attention to
many characters and incidents in *David Copperfield*. Although the *Copperfield* material is easy to locate in
Sucksmith's fine index, readers would do well to read
the entire study, as the *Copperfield* material is best
understood in the context of the larger argument. Sucksmith concludes that Dickens's rhetoric of sympathy and
irony presents an "extroverted vision of a spiritual
universe pervading the material world." He compares manuscripts and proof revisions with text to show Dickens
communicating "a vision of life" even as he argues
specifically for such concerns as humane treatment of
the insane (Mr. Dick). Sucksmith thinks that because he
was dealing with his own life Dickens added the character of Mr. Micawber to make his narrator's self-pity
more bearable; from the first Micawber functions as a

parody of David's genteel pretensions. Revisions which
Sucksmith examines show Dickens employing complex rhetoric
to maintain ironic distance in characterizing Dora and
to suggest the attraction-repulsion of David to Uriah.
Noticing many of the characters and places and attending
to such qualities as the author's self-pity, wounded
pride and snobbishness, Sucksmith effectively combines
textual and critical study and offers substantially fresh
insights about the novel's imaginative sources, composition history, and rhetorical tensions. Reviews: Duane
DeVries, *JEGP*, 71 (1972), 152; Lauriat Lane, Jr., *SNNTS*,
5 (1973), 125-138; Robert B. Partlow, Jr., *NCF*, 26 (1972),
494-497; Grahame Smith, *Dickensian*, 67 (1971), 49-51;
Richard Stange, *DSN*, 1 (1970), 5-7.

501. Swinburne, Algernon C. *Charles Dickens*. London: Chatto
and Windus, 1913, pp. 25, 33-35.

Thinks Dickens was probably right in preferring *David
Copperfield* to all his other books. In Swinburne's opinion,
"the narrative is as coherent and harmonious as that of
Tom Jones," and Micawber and Miss Trotwood surpass any
of Fielding's comic figures.

502. Symons, Julian. *Charles Dickens*. London: Arthur Baker,
1951, pp. 42-43, 63-66.

Claims Dickens's interest was truly engaged by David's
emotional relationship with Dora and Steerforth. Symons
notes varieties of sadism in Mr. Murdstone, Creakle, and
Rosa Dartle and views the latter as the most notable
portrait.

503. Talbot, Norman. "The Naming and the Namers of the Hero:
A Study in *David Copperfield*." *SoR*, 11 (1978), 267-
282.

Argues that in each of the interlocked plot structures
David has one crucial good name and one ill name and
there are "three periods in which ... inaccurate names,
confusions of identity and threats of absolute anonymity
afflict the hero." Talbot provides especially useful
discussion of the Biblical associations for David, Uriah,
and Agnes, and he avoids the dangers of reductive allegorical criticism—contrast Vogel (517). Talbot thinks
Dickens took great care to provide suitable names for
his characters and concludes that none of his other books
has "such powerful interchanging and contrasting names";
the "arcane implications of mythic naming" are important
throughout *David Copperfield*.

504.   Tewari, R.P. "The Treatment of Fallen Women in the Novels
        of Dickens and Mrs. Gaskell." *Agra Univ. Journal of Re-
        search (Letters)*, 19 (Jan. 1971), 43-51.

        Thinks *David Copperfield* marks a departure in Dickens's
        treatment of the fallen woman, for in portraying Martha
        and Little Em'ly he avoids the inevitability of death
        as the fate of such characters. Tewari notes that although
        social norms and literary clichés of his age prevented
        Dickens from revealing the whole truth about the plight
        of fallen women, the novel shows him moving "in the direc-
        tion of the rescue and rehabilitation" of them.

505.   Thirkell, Angela. "*David Copperfield* Reconsidered."
        Dickensian, 45 (1949), 119-122.

        Rather than reconsider the book in detail, Thirkell
        simply mentions that the novel's sensitive picture of
        childhood suffering appeals to adult as well as to younger
        readers.

506.   Thomson, Patricia. *The Victorian Heroine. A Changing
        Ideal 1837-1873*. London: Oxford Univ. Press, 1956, pp.
        93, 123-124.

        No extended discussion of Dickens but mentions *David
        Copperfield* characters in classifying Dickens's heroines
        as either "tall, composed, steadfast and sensible" or
        "small, fluttering, playful and dependent." Thomson notes
        that Martha's character "is obscured by conventional
        darkness and gloom," and she mentions similar portrayals
        of prostitutes by several minor poets. See also Basch
        (220).

507.   Threapleton, Mary E. "Introduction." In 1965 Airmont
        Edition, pp. 1-5 (68).

        Gives nearly half of its attention to a biographical
        sketch of Dickens. Threapleton regards David as "perhaps
        the least interesting character" and suggests that Dickens's
        hesitancy over Dora's death may have indicated his in-
        decision about permitting her to live on with Agnes as
        her adviser. Threapleton does not support this contention
        by any mention of the number plans. For a closer study
        of Dickens's hesitation concerning Dora see Vann (514).

508.   Thurley, Geoffrey. "*David Copperfield*." In *The Dickens
        Myth: Its Genesis and Structure*. New York: St. Martin's
        Press, 1976, pp. 132-172.

Finds *David Copperfield* is absolutely central to an understanding of Dickens's development and thinks it a mistake to regard the novel "as falling away from the childhood experiences into something less worthy of our attention." Thurley makes an extensive and original comparison of Dickens's and Joyce's treatment of childhood recollections and identifies a "polyphonic strategy" in the structuring of *Copperfield*'s story strands. Thurley finds the book's real quality in its "strange marriage of contraries." He shows Mr. Micawber poised upon the class-divide and David and Traddles insecure members of the middle class. The characterizations of Heep and Mr. Spenlow to Thurley indicate Dickens's interest in hollowness, and he feels that "Dickens did nothing better than the domestic anarchy of David and Dora's so-called marriage." Thurley opposes readings that stress the "disciplined heart" theme—see Needham (433)—because "the *disciplined* heart in the Dickens world is simply a contradiction in terms." There is, he thinks, a unity of character and morality in the person and career of David. Thurley says, "There is no other work in the language ... in which this profound commonplace—that life is the sum of what happens to us, and should be lived to the fullest, without evasion or question—is so irresistibly urged." Reviews: Peter Christmas, *DSN*, 9 (1978), 50-52; Richard J. Dunn, *Review*, 1 (1979), 91-104; Robin Gilmour, *Dickensian*, 73 (1977), 116-117; Robert L. Patten, *Novel*, 12 (1979), 254-259.

509. Tick, Stanley. "The Memorializing of Mr. Dick." *NCF*, 24 (1969), 142-153.

Finds Mr. Dick a critically neglected figure who merits attention as a would-be autobiographer, an authorial self-portrait, and as an instance of the function of metaphor. Tick thinks that Mr. Dick is possibly a parodic figure because he "defines in part the abstraction Charles Dickens." In particular, Tick argues that like Dickens Mr. Dick cannot present the truth of his past directly, and he fits well into a novel "preoccupied with the role and power of memory."

510. ———. "On Not Being Charles Dickens." *Bucknell Review*, 16 (1968), 85-95.

Suggests that the creative experience of *David Copperfield* made possible in large part Dickens's more equivocal conclusion in *Bleak House*. Tick's principal argument is that the narrator, closer to other characters than to the

novelist himself, commands only limited authority for
observation and explanation. He agrees with Garis (319)
and Lubbock (392) that David is remote from Dickens. Tick
says David does not acknowledge the force of history or
impress readers with any sense of his history as ongoing
experience. Thus, for Tick this is not a psychologically
realized novel but is the last for Dickens "in which the
past is at all points successfully overcome." Other
critics of the first-person narration, the function of
memory, and the complexity of David continue to debate
the extent to which *Copperfield* is a psychological novel
bound by its narrator's sense of his escapable or in-
escapable past.

511.   ————. "Toward Jaggers." *DSA*, 5 (1976), 133–149.

Traces Dickens's handling of guilt and secrecy from
David Copperfield through *Great Expectations*. Tick argues
that it was not the blacking factory experience but the
suppression of it that elicited Dickens's guilty feelings.
He discusses the fragmentary autobiography and *Copperfield*
as Dickens's first attempts to come to terms with his
troubled conscience. Tick finds David becoming less honest
with himself and his readers as he grows older, and "a
fantasy of wish fulfillment directs" the book's ending.
He also observes that unlike later novels *Copperfield*
lacks a consistent metaphor for secrecy.

512.   Tillotson, Kathleen. "The Middle Years from the *Carol* to
Copperfield." *Dickens Memorial Lectures 1970*. *Dickensian*,
65, supplement (September 1970), 7–19.

Brief but incisive recognition of *Dombey and Son* and
A Christmas Carol as providing implicit impetus for *Copperfield*. Tillotson shows that with memory providing "the
very form of the novel," Dickens balanced the reader's
consciousness between David remembering and David remembered. She asserts that unlike the novel and story pre-
ceding it, *David Copperfield* supplies often "the sense of
alternative futures within this life." She says it is
"resonant memory" that makes this Dickens's most poetic
novel--see Easson (291) and Gilmour (320) on memory.

513.   Tomlin, E.W.F. "The Englishness of Dickens." *EA*, 23 (1970),
113–124.

Shows Dickens as "a complete Londoner," distinguished
by his capacity for concrete observation. Tomlin regards
Dickens's humor as one of his most English qualities and

says that for the most part this humor comes through
Dickens's characterization, with Mr. Micawber as one of
his greatest creations. Tomlin considers Micawber as a
man of his time and says "it would have been difficult
to invent Mr. Micawber in a society less hierarchical
than that of England in the mid-nineteenth century."
Tomlin probably is alone in his opinion that Uriah Heep,
portrayed without humor, is a failure because he does
not seem human, but Tomlin may be speaking of the failure
of Heep's schemes and not the failure of Dickens to make
him believable. Tomlin also notes that Dickens's childhood employment in the blacking factory "was not so much
his undoing--a lapse into ignominy and horror which should
never have been allowed to occur--as the making of him."
For further discussion of this final point see Hutter
(737).

514. Vann, J. Don. "The Death of Dora Spenlow in *David Copperfield*." *VN*, 22 (Fall 1972), 19-20.

Thinks the haphazard structure of Part XIV and the external evidence that Dickens was having difficulty with
his novel indicate that both the marriage and the death
of Dora were contrived because Dickens had no fresh
material at hand.

515. Vašata, Rudolf, pseud. [Rudolf Popper]. "*Amerika* and
Charles Dickens." In *The Kafka Problem*. Ed. Angel Flores.
New York: New Directions, 1946, pp. 134-139.

Brief essay which is less substantial than Spilka's
later discussions of the *Copperfield-Amerika* parallel
(487). Vašata quotes Kafka's diary entry indicating that
"The Stoker," which became the first chapter of *Amerika*,
was an imitation of *David Copperfield*. Vasata finds a
much broader optimistic outlook in Kafka's book than in
Dickens's, even though Dickens's hero escapes the contra-
dictions and shortcomings of his world. He thinks the
writers differ most in their handling of symbolism;
Dickens's hidden meanings lie beneath a generally realistic
surface, but Kafka's surface is one of strange and unreal
events.

516. Vega-Ritter, Max. "Etude Psychocritique de *David Copper-
field*" [with English abstract]. In *Studies in the Later
Dickens*. Ed. Jean-Claude Amalric. Centre d'Etudes et
Recherches Victoriennes et Edouardiennes. Université
Paul Valéry: Montpellier, [1973], pp. 11-70.

Applies the "psychocriticism" of Mauron and also Freud's
general view of fiction to a discussion of *David Copperfield*. Vega-Ritter sees David beginning in a sort of
secluded Eden and lacking a father model; Murdstone appears
as the intruder persecuting the helpless child; and Dr.
Strong ultimately becomes a friendly father figure of
the type Dickens would have earlier totally endorsed. At
this point Vega-Ritter sees a division in David's personality caused by repression of his past self. Yet he
finds hidden connections remaining in the similarities of
David's desires with Jack Maldon's, Uriah Heep's, and
Steerforth's. With his fellow Continental readers Taine
(199) and Praz (455), Vega-Ritter is interested in David
as a hero and says that like other Dickens heroes, David
seems poised between submission and rebellion. As Vega-
Ritter observes, David chooses the shelter of law, bury-
ing his past in conformity and sentimentality until the
world of his refuge collapses and the difficulty with
Dora reveals his psychic conflict "between the immature
and the more mature self." Her death, argues Vega-Ritter,
is not only convenient for the plot but also reveals an
underlying urge of David "to destroy what is most cherished." Vega-Ritter thinks the novel ends ambiguously,
but he feels that at the end Dickens shows a more emanci-
pated hero than in earlier novels; "having deposed of the
father figure he sets out to probe the crises of a young
adult."

517. Vogel, Jane. *Allegory in Dickens*. University: Univ. of
      Alabama Press, 1977. 347 pp.

      First advertised as *Allegory in David Copperfield*, the
      book centers on that novel in an elaborate effort to
      understand Dickens as a "devout Christian novelist and
      moralist." Vogel contends that "while David Copperfield
      is a living, breathing child of his time, ... he is also
      magically endowed with a pilgrim *David* life that takes
      the long way the spiritual consciousness of Western man
      itself took." With apparently unintended irony, Vogel's
      prefatory statement gives fair warning to readers of her
      single-minded study: "Whether the following work can
      prove its thesis; whether it can explain the knotty
      matter of why Dickens kept the secret of his allegory,
      while asserting it was, first and last, his chief and
      abiding love, interest, and aim, these pages must show."
      Bert G. Hornback, reviewing Vogel, describes this book
      as "almost an affront to serious scholarly endeavor," in
      DSN, 2 (1978), 53-54. Reviews: Richard J. Dunn, *Review*,

1 (1979), 91-104; D.A. Miller, *VS*, 22, (1979), 473-474;
Allen Samuels, *Dickensian*, 74, (1978), 111-113.

518. Wagenknecht, Edward. "Life and Works of Charles Dickens."
      In *Cavalcade of the English Novel*. New York: Henry
      Holt, 1954, pp. 213-233.

      First published in 1943; revised in 1954. Wagenknecht
      declares *David Copperfield* to be "the most beloved piece
      of fiction in the English language" because of its many
      memorable characters. He echoes Ernest Baker's praise
      for the "enchanting idyll" of David and Dora (214).
      Wagenknecht thinks Dickens's error in making Micawber
      end so prosperously may have been the result of Dickens's
      hurried acceptance of the conventional happy ending.

519. Walker, Susan. "The Artistry of Dickens as an English
      Novelist." *Dickensian*, 51 (1955), 102-108.

      Cites the latter part of the thirty-third chapter as
      an illustration of Dickens's minute analysis and economy
      of words. Walker shows Dickens intensifying the emotions
      of Mr. Peggotty and David when they learn of Em'ly's
      flight and producing an effective composite vision of
      them.

520. Wall, Stephen, ed. *Charles Dickens: A Critical Anthology*.
      Harmondsworth: Penguin, 1970, passim.

      Selections from Dickens's letters speeches, and other
      writings as well as selections from major Dickens critics.
      Wall's anthology is well indexed. There is no separate
      division for *David Copperfield* and there is less direct
      focus on *Copperfield* than in Collins's *Dickens: The Cri-
      tical Heritage* (189). An appendix lists the number divi-
      sions for all of Dickens's novels.

521. Walther, Luann. "The Invention of Childhood in Victorian
      Autobiography." In *Approaches to Victorian Autobiography*.
      Ed. George P. Landow. Athens: Ohio Univ. Press, 1979,
      pp. 64-83.

      Discusses the imaginative pleasures of memory and says
      that narrative memorialization of the past "creates not
      only a pleasant sense of nostalgia, but can also confer
      the energy and the purity of the former time to the
      present." Walther notes in passing that social historians
      relying on such factual works as Augustus Hare's *The
      Story of My Life* may misunderstand the nature of a liter-
      ary imagination unless they realize that the young Hare
      "often bears an uncanny resemblance to David Copperfield."

522. Ward, Adolphus W. "*David Copperfield.*" In *Dickens.* London:
      Macmillan, 1882, pp. 85-107.

      Supplies biographical information about Dickens's many
      activities in the late 1840's and early 1850's and a few
      brief critical comments about the novel. Ward is one of
      the first commentators to argue for the separability of
      actual and fictional autobiography. He considers the
      Peggotty-Little Em'ly story the best-constructed part
      and the Rosa Dartle story the most extraneous. The novel's
      "reality" is for him its most striking quality, and
      closer acquaintance shows him its "wonderful *art.*"

523. Waugh, Arthur. "Dickens's Lovers." *Dickensian*, 15 (1919),
      8-18.

      Finds Dickens expressing typically theatrical early
      Victorian attitudes toward love and thinks that although
      he presents a number of comic lovers, Dickens usually sees
      love leading to respectable citizenship. *David Copperfield*
      contains what Waugh calls "an odyssey of youthful suscep-
      tibilities."

524. Welsh, Alexander. *The City of Dickens.* Oxford: The Claren-
      don Press, 1971, pp. 105, 155-158, 180-183.

      Without devoting a separate section to *David Copperfield*,
      Welsh's critically incisive study is useful for under-
      standing the novel's hero and heroine. He notes a pattern
      of wronged heroes in Dickens; the trail of wrongs in
      David Copperfield extends beyond David's childhood suffer-
      ings to later times when "each death in the novel answers
      in some respect to an injury to the hero." Welsh discusses
      Dickens's need of transmuting "sweethearts and wives into
      sisters and daughters, or of living snugly with sisters
      ans daughters as well as wives, ... not necessarily to
      substitute one for the other female relation, but ideally
      to enjoy both, or all three relations in the enclosure
      of the hearth." One of few commentators to consider
      closely the book's final lines, Welsh suggests that Agnes's
      apparent relation to the Divine bears on the problem of
      the hero's death, because "the power of an angel to save
      implies, even as it denies, the eventuality of death."
      Reviews: James R. Kincaid, *DSN*, 3 (1972), 81-84; Lauriat
      Lane, Jr., *SNNTS*, 5 (1973), 125-138; Michael Slater, *NCF*,
      26 (1972), 492-494; Raymond Williams, *Dickensian*, 68
      (1972), 53-54.

525. Wenger, Jared. "Character-Types of Scott, Balzac, Dickens, Zola." *PMLA*, 62 (1947), 213-232.

Mentions Mr. Micawber as the apotheosis of the Dickensian monomaniac and notes that he has his counterpart in a peasant in Zola's *La Terre*. Wenger says that both characters form a large part of the authors' playworlds. He notices the masochistic tendencies of Mrs. Micawber and Mrs. Gummidge and the sadism of Rosa Dartle. Wenger thinks that despite his "Puritan caution, Dickens succeeded in creating a female who was anything but flaccid."

526. West, Rebecca. Quoted in "The Gossip Shop." *Bookman*, 52 (September 1920), 94-95.

In a lecture to the Women's Freedom League, West remarked that "it was a real terror of women that led Dickens into enthusiasm over semi-idiots like Dora." William Archer replied in the *Dickensian*, 16 (1920), 117, that West must not have read *Copperfield* since her childhood, for "Dora is satirically drawn from first to last."

527. Westburg, Barry. "David Copperfield: 'The Prismatic Hues of Memory'" and "*David Copperfield* and the Aesthetics of Education." In *The Confessional Fictions of Charles Dickens*. DeKalb: Northern Illinois Univ. Press, 1977, pp. 33-114.

A major study of *Copperfield*, *Oliver Twist*, and *Great Expectations* as Dickens's confessional trilogy. Westburg argues that Dickens developed most as a writer "each time he posed development itself as his theme." Noting the repetitive objects of David's memory, Westburg points out an opposition between memory and the current that pulls David into the future. He disputes Garis's (317) discrediting of Dickens as a psychological novelist, for without providing direct insights into psychology Dickens's novels do reveal "a subtle imaginary psychology, which offers an interesting repertory of behavior for a consciousness threatened by change and time." Westburg contends that Dickens distinguishes between the narrator's and the hero's memories, with the former's as the more complete attempt at self-knowledge. Westburg demonstrates that the novel's educative experience involves the connected growth of imagination and memory. He discusses a number of revelatory mirror-images in *Copperfield*, because he believes it important to recognize "the narcissism of symbol-using ... as an alternative to intimate human interrelationships." Also Westburg considers the self-con-

sciousness of David's language; David "grows by means
of difficult encounters with words." His total experience
is circular but his verbal self-recreation succeeds only
partially, because the hold of his past is persistent.
As reviews show, readers take issue with some of Westburg's
argument, but his approach makes fresh use of biographical
and psychological materials in studying fictional structure. See also Westburg's "Studies in Personal History:
Oliver Twist, David Copperfield, Great Expectations,"
DA, 28 (1967), 2269A-2270A (Cornell, 1967). Reviews:
Richard J. Dunn, *Review*, 1 (1979), 91-104; Jerome H.
Buckley, *NCF*, 33 (1979), 508-512; David Parker, *MLQ*, 39
(1978), 79-82; Robert L. Patten, *Novel*, 12 (1979), 254-
259; Paul Schlicke, *Dickensian*, 74 (1978), 113-115.

528.   Weygandt, Cornelius. "Dickens and the Folk-Imagination."
       In *A Century of the English Novel*. New York: The Century
       Company, 1925, pp. 63-82.

       Makes only passing mention of *David Copperfield*, de-
       scribing it as the work of a realistic novelist and claim-
       ing that Dickens told "his own story in the scenes of
       David's maturity as well as in the scenes of David's
       childhood."

529.   Whipple, Edwin P. "Preface." In 1877 New Illustrated
       Library Edition, pp. xiii-xxxvi (43).

       Perceptive early recognition of the novel's blend of
       fact and fiction, seeing Dickens combining what he
       "achieved in practical life ... with what he wished to
       achieve in the sphere of the affections." Whipple finds
       Traddles lacking the fine mind of Dickens's friend Tal-
       fourd--see Clark (605). He notes that the Micawbers live
       on "nothing a year," in Thackeray's phrase, and suffer
       rapid alternations of delight and despair. For Whipple,
       Heep is one of the most elaborately developed of Dickens's
       villains and the most intensely realised character in
       the novel. Like G.H. Lewes (389), Whipple praises the
       hallucinatory quality of Dickens's imagination, especially
       in the "Tempest" chapter. In what must be one of the
       safest predictions ever ventured, Whipple states his cer-
       tainty that Dickens's works will outlive those of such
       other popular writers as G.P.R. James.

530.   Widdemer, Margaret. "Dickens's Dolls." *Literary Review*
       [of the New York *Evening Post*], 1 (18 June 1921), 1-2.

       Defends Dickens's women against notions that he did not
       "draw a live woman outside of his grotesques." Widdemer

observes that Dora, like characters of Scott Fitzgerald
and Booth Tarkington, proves writers may take seriously
love experienced by characters younger than twenty-five.

531. Williams, Ioan. *The Realist Novel in England*. London:
Macmillan, 1974, pp. 124, 153-155.

Considers it ironic that at the point Dickens achieved
control over his art he came under serious attack. Williams
thinks *David Copperfield* stands out as Dickens's most optimistic novel, the one in which his idiosyncrasies are
least evident. Williams discusses its optimism as a
convention of Victorian realism. With this realism such
evils as the Strongs' domestic problems can be met directly,
and it seems to Williams that Dickens worked out "his
deepest fears on the basis of a firm confidence in the
nature of social life." He discusses Dickens generally
and is not of great help in the question of the mixture
of realism and fantasy in *Copperfield*.

532. Wilson, Angus. "Charles Dickens: A Haunting." *CritQ*, 2
(1960), 101-108.

The discussion of individual novels is brief in this
survey of Dickens's imaginative pull on Wilson's imagination. Wilson grants *Copperfield* to be Dickens's best work
of art in many respects, yet he feels the novel has a
complacency that keeps it from being "great in the sense
of *Anna Karenina*." Wilson acknowledges an exception to
this complacency in Steerforth and all the scenes that
concern him.

533. ————. "*David Copperfield*." In *The World of Charles
Dickens*. New York: Viking, 1970, pp. 211-216.

Reprinted as the introduction to the 1971 Watts Ultratype Edition, pp. vii-xvii (71). Wilson's is one of the
better condensed critical discussions of *Copperfield*.
Wilson notes that the first fictional characters which
derived directly from Dickens's childhood appear in
Dombey and Son and that *The Haunted Man* reflects his bitterness about his childhood. He shows that these works and
the autobiographical fragment led Dickens to *David Copperfield*. Wilson discusses the difference between Dickens's
writing about and actual conduct toward fallen women,
observing that his nonfictional rhetoric in an "Appeal
to Fallen Women" (34) seems to contradict the good sense
with which he administered a home for them, but the
extravagant rhetoric of the "Appeal" may help explain his

disappointingly conventional treatment of Martha and
Em'ly. The subject of fallen women, as well as the topics
of Australian emigration and model prisons, seem intrusions
to Wilson, for he thinks *Copperfield* a more metaphysical
than social novel. Wilson calls the book "Dickens's great
internal--what used to be called 'psychological'--novel,
a Proustian novel of the shaping of life through the echoes
and prophesies of memory." Wilson admits that the adult
David remains too complacent; as a novelist he "is too
much like Trollope as he tells us he was in his autobiography." Wilson includes an excellent discussion of the
ending, "the epitome of Victorian bourgeois morality,"
and finds in Steerforth "one of the finest portrayals in
fiction of that secular semblance of grace, called charm."
Himself a novelist, Wilson says he is tempted to make
separate novels of David's childhood and Steerforth's
story.

534. ————. "Dickens on Children and Childhood." In *Dickens
  1970*. Ed. Michael Slater. London: Chapman and Hall,
  1970, pp. 195-227.

Shows that the novel's portrayal of childhood draws
both on Dickens's obsession with the incidents of his
own childhood and on a more general contemporary effort
to determine the meaning and value of childhood as an
ideal in opposition to the industrial exploitation of
children. Wilson discusses the threat Murdstone's Calvinism
poses to the nineteenth-century ideal of childhood. In
considering the power of autobiographical obsession in
Dickens's characterization of David, Wilson finds David
less morbid than a number of other Dickens child-heroes.
Wilson mentions David's connection with the Micawbers
as Dickens's "most autobiographical sketch of a parent-
child relationship," and Wilson thinks that Wilkins
Micawber, Junior, may represent a comic version of Dickens's
own boyhood self. But, as Wilson adds, the novel, while
idealizing Micawber as David's surrogate father, does
not consider the effect of Micawber on his own children.

535. Wilson, Arthur H. "The Great Theme in Charles Dickens."
  Susquehanna Univ. Studies, 6 (1959), 422-457.

Bringing to more recent criticism the kind of generalized sociological reading more common in the 1930's and
earlier, Wilson acknowledges *Copperfield* to be a departure
from Dickens's great social novels. He follows but does
not match in critical insight Edgar Johnson's (357) and
Edmund Wilson's (536) readings of *Copperfield*.

536. Wilson, Edmund. "Dickens: The Two Scrooges." In *The Wound and the Bow*. Cambridge, Mass.: Houghton Mifflin, 1941, pp. 1-104.

A psychological study of Dickens especially important to *David Copperfield* readers because of the attention Wilson gives to Dickens's divided nature throughout his career. He describes the complexity of the novelist's life and work, finding his books a continuing "attempt to digest those early shocks and hardships, to explain them to himself, to justify himself in relation to them, to give an intelligible and tolerable picture of a world in which such things could occur." Although he grants that *David Copperfield* idealizes the fears and wonders of childhood, Wilson does not consider it the deepest of Dickens's books. He devotes only a paragraph to it specifically, but his entire essay remains essential for anyone considering the relation of fiction and autobiography in *Copperfield*.

537. Wing, George. *Dickens*. Edinburgh: Oliver and Boyd, 1969, pp. 49-52.

Follows John Jones's division of the novel into the trials of David and the portrait of the artist (361). Wing treats the book as a memoir of younger experiences and also as a reflection of the uncertainties in Dickens's married life. Wing's discussion of *Copperfield* is very brief.

538. Woolf, Virginia. "*David Copperfield*." *Nation and Athenaeum*, 37 (1925), 620-621, 699. Reprinted in *The Moment and Other Essays*. London: Hogarth Press, 1947. Also in *Collected Essays*, London: Hogarth Press, Vol. I., 1966.

Asks what impression *David Copperfield* makes upon adult readers when raised from the "hazy atmosphere" of childhood reading--cf. Mansfield (568). Woolf thinks Dickens lacks charm and idiosyncrasy. In one of the most curious comments ever made about Dickens's most autobiographical novel, she claims that Dickens is not as personally present in his books as other great writers are in theirs. Rather than probe the nature of Dickens's self-distancing or self-disguising, Woolf notes that the combination of Dickens's literary fecundity and apparent lack of reflection have the strange effect of making creators of his readers. She notes also that Dickens avoids fragmentation of his work by enveloping the tumult with "some common feeling--youth, gaiety, hope." Her letter, page 699,

clarifies her preference for Dickens's novels but puts
him "nowhere at all" when ranking Shakespeare, Scott,
and Dickens as men.

539.   Woollen, C.J. "Some Thoughts on Dickens's Women."
       Dickensian, 36 (1940), 178-180.

       All too brief mention of Betsey Trotwood as the strongest
       of Dickens's women characters. Woollen says that because
       he was generally limited by convention, Dickens did not
       purport "to paint real women." She has some praise for
       Clara Peggotty, Clara Copperfield, and Dora as believable
       portraits of weakness.

540.   Worth, George. "The Control of Emotional Response in
       David Copperfield." In *The English Novel in the Nine-
       teenth Century: Essays on the Literary Mediation of
       Human Values*. Ed. George Goodin. Urbana: Univ. of
       Illinois Press, 1972, pp. 97-108. Revised for "*David
       Copperfield*" chapter of Worth's *Dickensian Melodrama:
       A Reading of the Novels*. Lawrence: Univ. of Kansas,
       1978, pp. 97-110.

       Argues that although novels are designed to arouse
       audience emotion, Dickens employed various strategies to
       control sentiment and melodrama. In *Copperfield* Worth
       thinks first-person narration checks emotion by convert-
       ing pathos into comedy. He argues that the novel marks
       a stage in Dickens's movement away from elemental melo-
       dramatic situations, and it mutes both heroism and villainy.
       Worth notes how such mock melodrama as Micawber's denun-
       ciation of Heep adds to the comic flavor, and he insists
       that "purely melodramatic devices are used sparingly."
       Worth's study is a good counterargument to many earlier
       readers and reviewers who were bothered by what they
       regarded as the staginess of the Peggotty-Steerforth-
       Em'ly story.

541.   Yowell, Phyllis K. "The Techniques of Characterization
       in the Novels of Charles Dickens." Dissertation. Univ.
       of Washington, 1946. 385 pp.

       Examines a number of modes of characterization, giving
       particular attention to the female characters. She argues
       that Mrs. Micawber, Dora, Agnes, and Betsey Trotwood are
       skillfully drawn characters and that "critics who dismiss
       Dora as another unbelievable heroine miss her artistic
       value entirely. She serves ... as a phase of David's
       character." David himself is, for Yowell, Dickens's first

successful hero, for his emotions and attitudes are clearly
described throughout the novel.

542. Zweig, Stefan. "Charles Dickens." Trans. Kenneth Burke.
     Dial, 74 (1923), 1-24.

     General essay observing that the episodes in *Copper-
     field* might "supply another poet with material for a life-
     time." Zweig recognizes Dickens as a visual genius, espe-
     cially in the tenacity of childhood memory standing out
     against the background of the unconscious--see Easson
     (291), Gilmour (320), and Tillotson (512). Zweig notes
     that Dickens's psychology begins with the visual and
     often (as with Uriah Heep) gives us "an embodied whim,
     a whim inside a man, moving him like a mechanic doll."
     Zweig thinks Dickens incapable of real tragedy; the gently
     touching effect of Dora's death "is the farthest reach of
     serious feeling he is capable of."

APPRECIATIONS

543. Acorn, George. "*David Copperfield*." In *One of the Multi-
     tude*. London: William Heinemann, 1911, pp. 28-39.

     Acorn recalls having spent three-pence halfpenny as a
     poor boy for a copy of *Copperfield*, having lied to his
     family about the purchase, and having been obviously moved
     by David's childhood suffering: "Dickens was a fairy
     musician to us, filling our minds with a sweeter strain
     than the constant cry of hunger, or the howling wind
     which often, taking advantage of the empty grate, pene-
     trated into the room."

544. Andelin, Helen B. "*David Copperfield*" and "Dora's Anger."
     In *The Fascinating Girl*. Santa Barbara: Pacific Press,
     1969, pp. 26-33, 186-187.

     Cites Agnes and Dora as "perfect illustration of the
     Angelic and Human woman," with Agnes as an ideal for men
     to worship. Dora fascinates and captivates, says Andelin,
     who mildly complains of Agnes's independence and lack of
     gentle "little ways that stir a man's heart." This book
     uses the Dickens characters as examples of the "ideal
     woman from a man's point of view," and Andelin insists
     that both Agnes and Dora remain valid examples for the
     twentieth century. Andelin's least controversial point is

probably her passing notice of Dora's reliance on pet
adjectives.

545. Armitage, Harold. "Micawber Mansions." *Dickensian*, 42
      (1946), 154-156.

      Describes Micawber as an untiring worker for other
      people and proposes a memorial square dedicated to him
      in a rebuilt City Road housing project. This proposal
      was not acted upon.

546. Ashby-Norris, E.E. "The Domestic Atmosphere in Dickens's
      Books." *Dickensian*, 4 (1908), 288-290.

      Dickensian prize essay celebrating Ashby-Norris's
      feeling that both the childhood scenes and the final
      chapters of *Copperfield* sanctify home life.

547. Bacon, Jane E.L. "A Plea for Dora." *Dickensian*, 27 (1931),
      314-316.

      Admits Dora is open to criticism but thinks her no
      fool, "for she understood and acknowledged her limita-
      tions."

548. Becker, May L. "Foreword." In 1943 Dodd, Mead Edition
      (58).

      Two unnumbered pages mentioning the novel's interweav-
      ing of truth and fiction and noting that the Dickens
      Fellowship dedicated its forty-first year to *David Copper-
      field*.

549. Bennett, James O. "Dickens' *David Copperfield*." In *Much
      Loved Books*. New York: Liveright, 1927, pp. 135-140.

      Begins with a list of memorable quotations and stresses
      the durability of the novel's world through many reread-
      ings.

550. Birch, Dennis. "Prologue." *Dickensian*, 46 (1950), 63-64.

      Verses spoken at Richard Shuckburgh's centenary recital
      of *David Copperfield*: "To celebrate the hundredth glorious
      year / Of this great story, that from the very start /
      Has found a place in every reader's heart."

551. Callaway, W.A. "Micawber as a Spiritual Force." *Dickensian*,
      20 (1924), 182-187.

Compares Micawber with Don Quixote and Falstaff to praise his unselfishness. In an aside, Callaway remarks that the phrase-making Woodrow Wilson might have taken warning from Micawber, as apparently did the more taciturn Coolidge. This discursive essay has no critical value and stands as an instance of how the character's imaginative life is sometimes projected beyond the novel. Callaway's Micawberesque conclusion speaks for itself: "To be healthy and happy it is necessary merely to wait for something to turn up, to look confidently for aid from the unseen forces that surround us."

552. Corthell, Roland. "I Meet Mr. Micawber." *Dickensian*, 17 (1921), 177.

Claims lately to have twice seen "Dear Old Micawber" in walks across London.

553. Crothers, Samuel M. *The Children of Dickens*. New York: Charles Scribner's Sons, 1925, passim.

In presenting brief character sketches of child characters in Dickens, Crothers includes David's encounter with the hungry waiter, David on the road to Dover, and Wilkins Micawber, Junior, and his parents.

554. Dickens, Sir Henry. *The Recollections of Sir Henry Dickens, K.C.* London: William Heinemann, 1934, pp. 16, 133, 302.

Resists the notion that Dickens's later novels show imaginative weakening and claims that *Pickwick* aside, Dickens said he "would place *David Copperfield* first and *Great Expectations* next to it" among his works.

555. Doran, W.J. "*David Copperfield* and Marriage." *Dickensian*, 17 (1921), 122-125.

Believing that the topic of marriage was foremost in Dickens's mind when he wrote the novel, Doran uses the moral of the David-Agnes marriage as an early warning against the increasing twentieth-century divorce rate.

556. Du Soir, A.P. "The Elfin Quality in Dickens." *Dickensian*, 23 (1926), 47-51.

Recognizes Betsey Trotwood and Dora Spenlow as "natives of fairyland."

557. Efford, Douglas. "Dickens Essays by School Children. The Book I Like Best." *Dickensian*, 9 (1913), 213-214.

A nine-year-old's admiration for a number of characters as faithful pictures of human nature.

558. Fraser, E.A. "The Psychology of Betsey Trotwood." *Dickensian*, 16 (1920), 127-129.

More appreciatively than critically, Fraser commends Dickens's delineation of both the humorous and pathetic sides of Betsey Trotwood.

559. Gerkins, J.D. d'Arnaud. "Characters from *David Copperfield*." *Dickensian*, 4 (1908), 114, 129.

Publishes a sketch of characters sent by this Dutch artist to Dickens in 1852.

560. Glaser, Robert S., and Stephen H. Roth. "In the Matter of Heep, Jaggers, Tulkinghorn & Fogg: An Unjarndyced View of the Dickensian Bar." *Rutgers Law Review*, 29 (1976), 278-297.

Includes four brief paragraphs about *David Copperfield*, noting that in it Dickens is more introspective than in any previous work. "His identification with the book hints at the emotional catharsis it generated in him ... as though this favorite child was father to Dickens' maturity as an author." There is no further discussion of this point, nor of the lawyers, nor of the legal profession in the novel.

561. Grey, Rowland. "The Boys of Dickens." *Fortnightly Review*, August 1913, pp. 254-270.

Briefly considers David as one of English literature's most memorable boys. Grey thinks Steerforth "approaches complete failure" and should have been a Thackeray character.

562. Jerome, Jerome K. "My Favorite Novelist and His Best Book." *Munsey's Magazine*, 19 (1898), 28-32.

Cites a number of books and authors he admires and says that *Copperfield* is his most worn book. Like much of the earlier appreciative commentary, Jerome's article celebrates Dickens's success with many of the characters, noting the joy and sadness of this "plain tale, simply told." He does remark that Dickens's good women are "too good for human nature's daily food."

563. Kirkus, William. "On Some of the Later Works of Mr. Charles Dickens." In *Miscellaneous Essays, Critical and Theo-*

logical. London: Longman, Green, Longman, Roberts, and Green, 1863, pp. 65-76.

Resounds with praise for *David Copperfield* as Dickens's "most beautiful story" and concludes with Kirkus's expectation that "Agnes will live long in our memories, a good angel to us also."

564. Lambert, Grace. *"David Copperfield."* In *Bookland and Some People We Meet There.* London: Elliot Stock, 1912, pp. 129-140.

Approaches the novel with a reverence that inhibits any full evaluation. Lambert's discussion centers on the "loving, pitiful spirit" emanating "from every line." She is mistaken in claiming that Dickens stayed in the Blundeston rectory while writing the novel, because if he visited Blundeston at all it was well before he began writing his book.

565. Langstaff, John B. *David Copperfield's Library.* London: George Allen and Unwin, 1924. 157 pp.

Lengthy account of a charitable effort to establish a children's library in Johnson Street, where as a child Dickens had so cherished his small stock of books.

566. Mabie, Hamilton W. "The Most Popular Novels in America." *Forum,* 16 (1893), 512.

Cites *Copperfield* as the fictional work most frequently checked out from main libraries.

567. MacDuffie, Marbury. "Why I Liked *David Copperfield.*" *Dickensian,* 11 (1915), 220-221.

Prize winning essay from a White Plains, New York, high school Dickens competition. MacDuffie notes that the book provides more lasting effects than popular cheap fiction designed for a few hours of amusement.

568. Mansfield, Katherine. *The Letters of Katherine Mansfield.* Ed. J. Middleton Murry. New York: Howard Fertig, 1974, p. 188.

Although Dickens was generally out of fashion at the time, Mansfield in a 22 August 1918 letter remarks, "*Isn't* David Copperfield adorable? I like even the Dora part, and that friend of Dora's--Julia--somebody, who was 'blighted'. She is such a joy to me. Yes--doesn't Charley D. make our little men smaller than ever--and such *pencil sharpeners--.*"

569. Marshall, Archibald. "Last Century's Literary Favorites:
      III *David Copperfield*." *Literary Digest International
      Book Review*, 2 (1924), 288-289.

      Presents unqualified praise for the characters and
      scenes, finding the book "as fresh and alive as any novel
      ever written."

570. Moses, Belle. *Charles Dickens and His Girl Heroines*.
      London: D. Appleton, 1911, passim.

      Historically interesting because of the subsequent
      critical interest in this subject. Moses finds Dickens's
      art never more beautiful and true "than in the creation
      of his girl heroines." Her second chapter, "The Real
      David Copperfield," does not discriminate between fiction
      and biography, and her eleventh chapter, "The Girls of
      Dickens's Day," expresses unqualified admiration for
      Em'ly, Dora, and Agnes. Her twelfth chapter, "Little
      Housekeepers in Dickens-Land," adds Mrs. Gummidge to these
      angels of the hearth.

571. Murdoch, Walter. "Laughter" and "The Book and the Island."
      In *Collected Essays of Walter Murdoch*. Sydney: Angus
      & Robertson, 1939, pp. 88-91, 311-315.

      In "Laughter" Murdoch recalls how a convalescent friend
      was pained physically by laughing at the account of Miss
      Trotwood's behavior to the doctor, but the point of the
      essay is that laughter is spontaneous and the genuine
      humorist cannot be resisted. In "The Book and the Island"
      Murdoch reports finding an imaginary island culture founded
      on *Copperfield* as "the Book of Books." From Murdoch's
      fictional islanders' point of view "all the guidance we
      require is in the Book."

572. Norris, E. Ashby. "Dickens and Children II." *Dickensian*,
      7 (1911), 190-193.

      Claims that young David, like children in other Dickens
      novels, moves readers to value the simple joys and plea-
      sures of childhood.

573. ————. "Mr. Peggotty, Gentleman." *Dickensian*, 5 (1909),
      241-244.

      Insists, as part of an appreciative statement, that in
      the truest sense of the word Mr. Peggotty is a gentleman.
      Much later biographers have been interested in Dickens's
      concept of a gentleman, a subject most often considered
      by readers of *Great Expectations*.

574. Obermeir, Thomas F. "Mr. Micawber." In *Characters of Charles Dickens*. Deerfield, Illinois: Privately Printed, 1970, pp. 104-120.

Intends to provide readers with "the flavor" of Dickens by selecting characters and presenting them in Dickens's words. This chapter retells the Micawber story through extracts and brief connecting narrative.

575. Rideal, Charles F. *Charles Dickens' Heroines and Women-folk: Some Thoughts Concerning Them. A Lecture*. London: The Roxburghe Press, n.d. 63 pp.

Disappointingly sparse in critical observation. Rideal cites the familiar prototypes for Dora, Miss Mowcher, and Rosa Dartle, evidently drawing mainly on Forster (730).

576. Romayne, Leicester. "The Survival of Mrs. Crupp." *Dickensian*, 1 (1905), 174-176.

Ruminates about whether many Copperfields have lodged with such landladies as David's and admonishes his readers that "Mrs. Crupp must be taken ... as a bit of London, a little dingy ... but of an interesting rustiness."

577. Rust, S.J. "David Copperfield and His Friends: What They Did in the Great War." *Dickensian*, 16 (1920), 135-138.

Fanciful projection of *David Copperfield* characters into World War I setting.

578. ――――. "The Education of David Copperfield." *Dickensian*, 31 (1934), 46-50.

Finds the whole education of David--at home, Salem House, Murdstone and Grinby's, Dr. Strong's--interesting because "the nature of teaching is changing rapidly now." Rust believes that under Dr. Strong David learned "to become a great thinker and a great author."

579. Sanders, Henry S. "The Delightful Scamp." *Dickensian*, 28 (1931), 27-31.

Places Mr. Micawber with Don Quixote and Falstaff as a foremost humorous creation but thinks Dickens mistaken in allowing Micawber success in Australia.

580. Schofield, Guy. "A Hundred Years of--*David Copperfield*." *Evening News* [London], 26 April 1949, p. 2.

Regrets the absence of any national centenary celebration of the novel's publication. Had Dickens been a Russian,
Schofield thinks the state surely would have commemorated
his greatest work. Although he finds it deficient in form,
Schofield states that *Copperfield* "confers, in imagination, *a second life*" in its intense portrayal of life.

581. Sen, S.C. "Dickens the Conjurer." *Bulletin of the Depart-
      ment of English* (Calcutta Univ.), 6 (1970-1971), 1-13.

      Appreciative essay stating that "flat" is a fit label
      for such marvellous characters as the Micawbers, Mrs.
      Gummidge, and Uriah Heep, because lack of character devel-
      opment does not detract from the comic effects Dickens
      achieves with these characters.

582. Shuckburgh, Sir John. "Wilkins Micawber." *Dickensian*, 45
      (1949), 125-128.

      Speculates about Micawber's success in Australia, "a
      sort of antipodean utopia such as never existed." Shuck-
      burgh compares Micawber's irrepressible bouyancy, shrewd-
      ness, inner sense of propriety, sardonic humor, and
      grandiloquence with Falstaff's.

583. Simpson, Rev. T.C. "Misplaced Admiration." *Dickensian*,
      29 (1933), 147-151.

      Believes readers are too carried away by the fascina-
      tion Dickens throws over such unscrupulous characters as
      Mr. Micawber. But in spite of this complaint, Simpson
      declares he would not have the characters "in any way
      different."

584. Smithers, David W. "*David Copperfield*." In *Dickens's
      Doctors*. Oxford: Pergamon Press, 1979, pp. 52-58.

      Collects Dickens's writings about medical men and in-
      cludes Mr. Chillip's appearances in *David Copperfield*.
      Smithers remarks that cauls were advertised for sale in
      The Times while Dickens was writing this novel, and some
      were sold for as much as £39 in the middle of the nine-
      teenth century.

585. Soray, Woodford. "Dickensian Humbugs III. Uriah and Some
      Others." *Dickensian*, 2 (1906), 209-213.

      Argues that because Dickens so successfully presents
      Uriah as a moral humbug it seems unlikely that any parent
      who ever hears of the character will name a child Uriah.

Soray offers no follow-up to his prediction, and did not
live to learn that a 1970's band called itself "Uriah
Heep."

586.   S[taples], L[eslie]. *"David Copperfield* with the Scott
       Antarctic Expedition." *Dickensian*, 51 (1955), 100-101.

       Reports the presentation to the Dickens House, London,
       of the edition which had cheered the isolated explorers
       during the long Antarctic winter. See *Dickensian*, 9 (1913),
       59 and 143, and 10 (1914), 59, for accounts of the owner-
       ship of this book.

587.   Vachell, Horace A. "Dickens as a Forty-Niner." *Dickensian*,
       45 (1949), 123-124.

       For a number of fanciful reasons and because Dickens's
       works were popular in the gold camps, Vachell links the
       publication of *David Copperfield* with the discovery of
       gold in California.

588.   Van Dyke, Henry. "The Good Enchantment of Charles Dickens."
       In *Companionable Books*. London: Hodder and Stoughton,
       1922, pp. 65-102.

       Essay by an American poet and minister, who finds the
       novel's fairy-tale quality a principal element in Dickens's
       moral design. Good enchantment, for Van Dyke, is "the
       spirit of revelation, the spirit of divine sympathy and
       laughter." This essay treats Dickens as the purveyor of
       "true religion" as well as of "real democracy." Van Dyke's
       most accurate statement may be his recognition that the
       self-portrait in *David Copperfield* "is too smooth, like
       a retouched photograph," because Dickens was unable to
       admit his own humorous aspects.

589.   Watson, Gertrude. "Wilkins Micawber: A Sketch." *Dickensian*,
       14 (1918), 218.

       Wonders if all people are more or less Micawbers; Watson
       does not think him an "impossible" character.

590.   Watson, William H. "David Copperfield's Solace." *Dickens-
       ian*, 24 (1928), 192-193.

       Discusses the importance of nurses to English children
       and criticizes the role of the nurse in a recent film
       version of *Copperfield*, because it did not convey the point
       that Clara Peggotty is David's "immovable lodestone."

591.   Williams, Philip C. "Dickens's Literary Caricatures."
       Dickensian, 36 (1939), 9-11.

       Includes Mr. Micawber in a gallery of literary carica-
       tures.

592.   Wulcko, C. Tyndall. "Life's Greatest Problem: Discussed
       by Dickens in *David Copperfield*." *Dickensian*, 27 (1931),
       189-190.

       Asserts that *Copperfield* deliberately teaches the
       lesson that love can solve the problem of "what consti-
       tutes a happy marriage."

                    TOPOGRAPHY,
         CHARACTER PROTOTYPES, DIALECT

593.   Addison, William. *In the Steps of Charles Dickens*. London:
       Rich and Cowan, 1955, passim.

       Notes that like David's, Dickens's birth occurred a few
       minutes before midnight. Addison discusses William Giles's
       school as the model for the sound schooling endorsed by
       the novel, and he mentions Mrs. Dickens's unsuccessful
       efforts as the germ for Mrs. Micawber's plan for a board-
       ing school. Addison describes the book's Canterbury lo-
       cales and also some of the East Anglian settings. His work
       on East Anglia is superseded by Philip Collins's study
       (607).

594.   Allen, Edward H. "Phrase: 'To be Jorkins'd': *David Copper-
       field*." *N&Q*, 175 (1938), 350.

       Query as to whether there are any other instances of
       this phrase in literature.

595.   Ansted, Alexander. "Reminiscences of David Copperfield's
       Childhood." *Good Words*, April 1894, pp. 255-260; May
       1894, pp. 333-337.

       Describes the village of Blundeston and assumes that
       Dickens very literally describes it in his novel. Ansted's
       brief mention of Lowestoft acknowledges it as a port where
       smuggling was common. He claims that the Yarmouth of the
       1890's yet has people much like Barkis and the Peggottys.
       Ansted believes Dover was the actual site of Betsey's
       cottage, but he is unable to locate a specific house.

596. Ashbey-Sterry, J. "Miss Betsey Trotwood's." In *Cucumber Chronicles: A Book to be Taken in Slices.* London: Sampson Low, Marston, Searle and Revington, 1887, pp. 156-166.

Fanciful stroll near Dover in search of Betsey's cottage. One cottage Ashbey-Sterry mentions "is not so pleasant as it must have been formerly."

597. Bately, John. "From Blundestone to Yarmouth." *Dickensian*, 5 (1909), 232-239.

Consists of notes Bately used in guiding Dickens Fellowship members on a visit to the area. Bately reports that Dickens was once seen "perched on the end of a barrel in Marsh and Baines' bar, taking note of the words and phrases which fell from the men assembled there." He proposes a local model as his candidate for the prototype for the Peggotty house.

598. Bromhill, Kentley, pseud. [T.W. Hill]. "The 'Originals.'" *Dickensian*, 45, (1949), 161-162.

Lists numerous probable prototypes for *David Copperfield* characters (including one dog) and points out that searches for originals may have been carried too far. Bromhill admits that Dickens's characters have qualities observable in real people but argues that these qualities are "grafted on to figments of the imagination that are mostly quite unlike the persons observed."

599. Brooks, Edward D. "Charles Dickens and Blundeston." In *Blundeston and District Local Historical Information Sheet.* No. 18, January 1979, pp. 4-19.

Pamphlet at the Dickens House, London, summarizing information about the novelist's acquaintance with the village of Blundeston. Brooks thinks it likely that Dickens visited the area on several occasions. He notes that Mr. Blake, a carrier between the Plough and Yarmouth, is considered locally to be the prototype for Barkis but admits there is no Mr. Blake listed in the directory of the time. Brooks disputes the idea that Dickens drew only on a book for East Anglia dialect—see Collins (607) and Fielding (616)—because terms not in Dickens's likely source appear in the novel. Brooks includes house plans and drawings of the village in considering the accuracy of such details as Dickens's mention of the setting sun reflected on Betsey's face as she came around the south side of Blunderstone Rookery.

600.   Cardwell, Margaret. "Rosa Dartle and Mrs. Brown."
        Dickensian, 56 (1960), 29-33.

        Cardwell works from Forster's marginal notation of Mrs.
        Brown as the possible prototype for Rosa and traces
        connections between Dickens's character and this companion
        of Angela Burdett-Coutts. She concludes that Rosa, though
        possessing some of Mrs. Brown's traits, is not an exact
        portrait of her.

601.   Carlton, William J. "A Companion of the *Copperfield* Days."
        Dickensian, 50 (1953), 7-16.

        When giving James E. Roney a set of his books, Dickens
        called him "a companion of my *Copperfield* days." Carlton
        fills in material concerning this friend, who shared
        lodgings with Dickens in Buckingham Street, site of David's
        London residence.

602.   ————. "An Echo of the Copperfield Days." *Dickensian*,
        45 (1949), 149-152.

        Documents Dickens's visits to his uncle's Norwood house
        in 1833-1834 and suggests they were the prototype for
        David's visit to Mr. Spenlow's country residence.

603.   Chancellor, E. Beresford. "*David Copperfield*." In *The
        London of Charles Dickens*. London: Grant Richards,
        1924 pp. 183-199.

        Claims the novel is so autobiographical that the author
        drew "on a memory rich enought to be ... a substitute for
        inspiration." Chancellor presents a description of places
        mentioned in the novel and includes an illustration of
        Doctors' Commons. He notes the topographical changes that
        take place during the time of the story.

604.   Clair, Collin. *Charles Dickens: Life and Characters*.
        Bruce and Gawthorn, 1963. 71 pp.

        An illustrated guide to Dickensland, especially useful
        in tracing changes in Charing Cross-Hungerford Stairs-
        Adelphi from the time of *David Copperfield* and before the
        construction of Trafalgar Square. A chapter on the Dickens
        countryside identifies Dickens's nurse, Mary Weller, as
        the prototype for Clara Peggotty. Clair gives close atten-
        tion to Rochester and Canterbury as favorite locations
        for Dickens.

605. Clark, Cumberland. *Dickens and Talfourd, With an Address
      and Three Unpublished Letters to Talfourd, the Father
      of the First Copyright Act which Put an End to the
      Piracy of Dickens's Writings.* London: Chiswick Press,
      1919. 43 pp.

      Useful details about Talfourd, the likely prototype of
      Tommy Traddles. Born in 1795, Talfourd was considerably
      older than Dickens. According to Clark, Traddles reflects
      Talfourd's "loyal and lovable nature." He was a bit of a
      Bohemian, but by 1849 he was awarded a judgeship. Clark
      thinks that the novel's mention of the bench as Traddles's
      destiny is an allusion to Talfourd's recent appointment.

606. Collins, P.A.W. [Collins, Philip]. "The Middlesex Magis-
      trate in *David Copperfield.*" *N&Q*, 206 (1961), 86-91.

      Collins protests that despite reviewers' notice of
      similarities between Thomas Carlyle's pamphlet "Model
      Prisons" and Chapter 61, "I Am Shown Two Interesting
      Penitents," no notice has been taken of Dickens's specific
      but inaccurate association of the novel's prison with
      Middlesex prototypes.

607. Collins, Philip. "*David Copperfield* and East Anglia."
      Dickensian, 61 (1965), 46-51.

      Shows that Dickens's knowledge of the Yarmouth area
      rested on only a few hours of observation and concludes
      that various anecdotes about his visit to Blundeston are
      apocryphal. Collins hypothesizes that Dickens may have
      chosen the East Anglian setting rather than his native
      Kent to avoid strict autobiography.

608. ————. *Dickens and Education.* London: Macmillan, 1963,
      passim.

      Discusses Salem House and Dr. Strong's school, summariz-
      ing information about their possible prototypes and using
      them as examples of Dickens's views of childhood and of
      education. Collins shows Creakle, though vicious, to be
      more like actual schoolmasters than was the monstrous
      Squeers of *Nicholas Nickleby.* He finds no clear model
      for Strong or his school and thinks it likely that Dickens
      practiced some wish fulfillment in the portrayal. Collins
      shows that Dickens echoes some contemporary opposition
      to corporal punishment in characterizing the Murdstones
      and that on the whole Dickens does an effective job of
      presenting the visual and mental recreation of childhood.
      Reviews: Trevor Blount, *RES*, NS 17 (1966), 219-221; R.D.

McMaster, *NCF*, 19 (1964), 306-308; Harry Stone, *VS*, 8
(1965), 371-372.

609. Cooper, T.P. *The Real Micawber. With a Batch of His Re-
      markable Letters.* London: Simpkin, Marshall, Hamilton,
      Kent, [1922]. 34 pp.

      Pamphlet reprinted from the *Newcastle Weekly Chronicle*,
      9 and 16 April 1904. Cooper contends that the resemblance
      of Micawber to John Dickens is only superficial. He also
      discounts F.G. Kitton's suggestion that Thomas Powell was
      the prototype for Micawber--see Kitton (743) and Wright
      (766). Cooper's candidate is Richard Chicken of York, a
      friend of Dickens's younger brother. Cooper traces Dickens's
      associations with the city of York and with his brother,
      Alfred Dickens, who lived there while Dickens was writing
      Copperfield. According to Cooper, Chicken had a local
      reputation as one of York's genteel oddities, and his
      career was beset with misfortune. Cooper regards the
      novel's deportation of Micawber as unrealistic, for Chicken
      died in a poorhouse. See also Cooper's "Who Was Mr.
      Micawber?" *Dickensian*, 14 (1918), 186-187, quoting the
      Yorkshire Evening Post on Chicken as the Micawber proto-
      type.

610. Corfield, Wilmot. "The Golden Cross of *Pickwick* and
      Copperfield." *Dickensian*, 11 (1915), 158-160.

      Culminates a series of articles identifying the Golden
      Cross Inn of the novel. See also Walter Dexter, "Along
      the Strand with Dickens," *Dickensian*, 18 (1922), 31-35.

611. Cramp, K.R. "Dr. Strong of Canterbury." *Dickensian*, 48
      (1952), 117-119.

      Suggests a connection between Dr. Strong and King's
      School, Canterbury, where a headmaster was forced to re-
      sign in 1832 because of trouble with his wife. See also
      Collins's *Dickens and Education* (608).

612. "David Copperfield's Birthplace." *Black and White*, 7 Sept.
      1895, p. 316.

      Article with sketches of Blundeston scenes to announce
      news of planned alterations to Blundeston Hall.

613. Dexter, Walter. "The London of *David Copperfield*."
      Dickensian, 27 (1931), 113-119, 221-229.

      Lists sixty-five London settings as described in the
      novel and comments occasionally on their appearances in

1930. Dexter notes that a number of the buildings have disappeared or have been modified since World War II. Useful inclusion of a few illustrations.

614.   ————, and Percy T. Carden. "Roundabout Doctors' Commons." *Dickensian*, 27 (1930-1931), 7-17, 127-129.

Supplies information about the various law courts and legal practices mentioned in the novel.

615.   Dickens, Cedric, and John Greaves. "The *David Copperfield* Country." *Dickensian*, 72 (1976), 52.

Reports extant buildings in Yarmouth area generally thought to be mentioned in the novel.

616.   [Fielding, K.J.]. "*David Copperfield* and Dialect." *TLS*, 30 April 1949, p. 288.

Demonstrates that Dickens had a fine ear for East Anglian dialect even though he visited the area only briefly. Fielding notes a number of dialect words in the novel and identifies some of Dickens's coinages. He notes that Dickens apparently made use of Moor's *Suffolk Words and Phrases*, which made prominent mention of the sale of a caul.

617.   ————. "The Making of *David Copperfield*." *Listener*, 19 July 1951, pp. 93-95.

Studies Dickens's transformation of the originals for Miss Mowcher and Mr. Micawber. Fielding observes that although Dickens changed his intentions for Mowcher when the original complained, no change was in order for Micawber because he "was less than life-size, and John Dickens [was] larger than fiction."

618.   Fyfe, Thomas A. *Charles Dickens and the Law*. Edinburgh: William Hodge, 1910, pp. 64-67.

Observes that there are several lawyers but relatively little about the subject of law in *David Copperfield*. Fyfe thinks Tommy Traddles "is probably the outcome of Dickens' own short attempt at keeping terms."

619.   Gadd, W. Laurence. "Is This Peggotty's Boat-House?" *Dickensian*, 25 (1925), 124-126.

Proposes a cottage on the Gravesend and Higham Canal as the original; unlike other likely prototypes, this building was constructed from an inverted boat.

620.   Gordon, Elizabeth H. "The Naming of Characters in the
        Works of Charles Dickens." *Univ. of Nebraska Studies
        in Language, Literature, and Criticism,* 1 (1917), 3-35.

        Includes a few *Copperfield* characters in a general sur-
        vey of known character originals and of names, which are
        classified as directly descriptive, vaguely suggestive,
        or neutral.

621.   "Gormed!" *Dickensian,* 35 (1939), 72.

        An anonymous correspondent suggests that Mr. Peggotty's
        curious expression, "gormed," may derive from the name
        of a Viking who sacked East Anglia and may, therefore,
        mean "utter devastation." L.R.B. White and T.W. Hill make
        separate responses in the *Dickensian,* 35 (1939), 209.
        White notes that Eric Partridge's *Dictionary of Slang
        and Unconventional English* includes "gormed" as a collo-
        quial form of "god-damned." Hill doubts that East Anglians
        ever heard of the Viking Gorm. Also, *N&Q,* 177 (1939),
        118, identifies "gormed" as slang for "god-damned."

622.   Hardwick, Michael, and Mollie Hardwick. *Dickens's England.*
        J.M. Dent & Sons, 1970, pp. 34-44, 80-82.

        This attempt to tell Dickens's life story against the
        scenes he knew is helpful in understanding the autobio-
        graphical details of *David Copperfield.* The Hardwicks'
        work is distinguished from other much more painstaking
        topographical studies because it begins with the premise
        that Dickens's London and England were fantastic places
        of his own imaginative building. The Hardwicks not only
        point to favorite *Copperfield* locales but also suggest
        that various places have definite imaginative values.
        For example, in Highgate they think Charles Dickens
        "became, in essence, David Copperfield," because there
        he found "the piece of London which alone held a piece
        of his cherished, undisillusioned youth." According to
        the Hardwicks, it may have been the extremely personal
        quality of the novel which led Dickens to place David
        not in his own childhood landscape of Kent but in an area
        the author had only recently seen. This is one of the
        most intelligent discussions of the novel's locales.

623.   Hill, T.W. "Notes to *David Copperfield.*" *Dickensian,*
        39 (1943), 79-88, 123-131, 197-201; 40 (1943), 11-14.

        Chapter-by-chapter explanatory notes about usage,
        topography (very useful for places that have disappeared),
        and literary allusion. Hill's notes occasionally establish

little-known autobiographical points such as the relation
between Dickens's conjuring and some of Mr. Dick's skills
(see Chapter 17 of *Copperfield*).

624.   Hutchings, Richard J. *Dickens on an Island*. Bath: James
       Brodie, 1970. 83 pp.

       Provides details concerning Dickens's residence on the
       Isle of Wight, where in 1849 he wrote Chapters 13-18.
       Hutchings mentions a number of likely originals for the
       characters and locales. He notes a change of name from
       "Mr. Roberts" to "Mr. Dick" that may indicate a Bonchurch
       prototype for that character. His pamphlet incorporates
       "Dickens at Bonchurch," *Dickensian*, 61 (1965), 79-100.

625.   James, Henry. *English Hours*. Ed. Alma L. Lowe. London:
       Heinemann, 1960, pp. 39, 89, 179, 195-202.

       Essays first collected in 1905. James mentions *Copper-
       field* as an instance of "how in the retrospect of later
       moods the incidents of early youth 'compose', visibly,
       each as an individual picture, with a magic for which the
       greatest painters have no corresponding art." James visits
       Rochester and remembers it as the place where David rested
       on his journey from London to Dover. Also he observes that
       as with Scott and Thackeray novels, which one reads be-
       cause one feels the author's presence, one goes on "liking
       David Copperfield--I don't say you go on reading it, which
       is a very different matter, because it is Dickens." James's
       closing essay, "Old Suffolk," laments the changes in the
       county since David Copperfield's time.

626.   Lansbury, Coral. "Charles Dickens and His Australia."
       Royal Australian Historical Society Journal, 52 (June
       1966), 115-128.

       Discusses Dickens's views of Australia and the recep-
       tion of his works there. Lansbury shows that Dickens
       viewed Australia as "the working man's paradise, the
       Arcadian, egalitarian Utopia where the social distress
       of England would find immediate relief."

627.   ————. "The Micawbers." In *Arcady in Australia: The
       Evocation of Australia in Nineteenth-Century British
       Literature*. Melbourne: Melbourne Univ. Press, 1970,
       pp. 92-107.

       Traces in detail Dickens's views of Australia, shows
       Micawber had qualities fitting him for colonial life, and
       indicates Dickens was beginning to think of Australia as
       a workers' Utopia.

628. Lightwood, James T. *Charles Dickens and Music*. London:
      Charles H. Kelly, 1912, pp. 110-117.

      Notes that Dickens's original idea of the bull in the
      china shop for Mr. Dick's obsession referred to a popular
      song, "The Bull in the China Shop." Lightwood discusses
      the various songs the Micawbers mention or sing. He in-
      cludes an annotated list of songs and instrumental music
      mentioned in Dickens's works.

629. Major, Gwen. "Some Damage Has Been Reported...."
      Dickensian, 42 (1946), 92-97.

      Lists war damage to London buildings associated with
      David Copperfield. Also see *Dickensian*, 43 (1947), 99-
      101, for a list of damages to locations outside of London.

630. Manning, John. *Dickens on Education*. Toronto: Univ. of
      Toronto Press, 1959, pp. 94-99 and passim.

      Discusses the background and portrayal of Creakle's
      and Dr. Strong's schools and gives much general informa-
      tion about Dickens's own schooling and views of education.
      See also Collins (608).

631. Matchett, Willoughby. "Dickens in Bayham Street."
      Dickensian, 5 (1909), 147-152, 180-184.

      Reports the imminent demolition of the tenements Dickens
      lived in as a boy and used in the novel as the home of
      the Micawbers.

632. Matz, B.W. "Blunderstone: A Visit to David Copperfield's
      Birthplace." *Dickensian*, 2 (1906), 153-157.

      Cites Blundeston as the model for the novel's Blunder-
      stone and suggests that the rectory was the prototype for
      the Rookery. Later Dickensian biographers and topographers
      frequently challenge this view by questioning whether
      Dickens ever did visit Blundeston. See also Dickens's
      Letters (1), where he claims to have hit upon the town
      name from a signpost.

633. ————. "*David Copperfield*." In *Dickensian Inns and
      Taverns*. New York: Charles Scribner's Sons, 1922, pp.
      144-168.

      Identifies the provincial and London inns and taverns
      described or alluded to in *David Copperfield*. Matz in-
      cludes several illustrations.

634. Morten, W.V. "James Sharman and Ham Peggotty." *Dickensian*, 11 (1915), 247-248.

   Notes that a Yarmouth pictorial guidebook identifies Sharman, who assisted the wounded Lord Nelson, as a prototype for Ham.

635. "Mr. Creakle." *Dickensian*, 67 (1971), 96.

   Reproduces a sketch of William Jones, master at Wellington House Academy and likely original for Creakle.

636. "Mrs. Crupp's House." *Dickensian*, 2 (1906), 309.

   Announces the demolition of the house where Dickens first lived in London and which he used for David's lodging.

637. "Peggotty's Boat: Fact and Fiction." *Dickensian*, 56 (1960), 117-119.

   Quotes K.J. Fielding article in *Eastern Daily Press* which challenged earlier proposed prototypes and which reminded readers that Dickens probably had seen a number of boathouses, and the Peggotty hut was probably a total fiction.

638. Pugh, Edwin. *The Charles Dickens Originals*. London: T.N. Foulis, 1912, passim.

   Discursive survey of the novels and of Dickens's life, making frequent mention of *David Copperfield*. Most of the character originals Pugh mentions are discussed more fully in other *Dickensian* articles. He concludes that although Dickens was not too frank about parts of his life in *David Copperfield*, the book "introduced him to himself" and made him "more worldly wise" in later novels.

639. Rimmer, Alfred. "*David Copperfield*." In *About England with Dickens*. London: Chatto and Windus, 1883, pp. 1-39.

   Describes and comments upon the novel's settings with little effort to distinguish fiction from fact.

640. Roe, F. Gordon. "Some Remarks upon the *Copperfield* Controversy." *Dickensian*, 10 (1914), 145-147.

   The controversy is the long-standing one of the model for the Peggotty house, and Roe suggests that earlier-mentioned possibilities are less likely than a Yarmouth hut he describes.

641. ————. "Uriah Heep's Face." *Connoisseur*, 187 (1931),
      102-103.

      Suggests that the gargoyle-like bracket on a house in
      Wincheap Street, Canterbury, suggested to Dickens the im-
      pression David had of Uriah staring down at him from a
      beam-end (Chapter 15 of *Copperfield*).

642. Rushton, Joseph. "Bill Sikes and Mr. Dick." *Dickensian*,
      7 (1911), 223-224.

      Suggests, without definite evidence, the ballad of Happy
      Dick as a source for Dickens's character.

643. Savage, Oliver D. "Cheer Up, Old Mawther!" *Dickensian*,
      37 (1940), 37-38.

      Traces previous literary instances of the dialect ex-
      pression, "Old Mawther," by which Mr. Peggotty addresses
      Mrs. Gummidge.

644. Skottowe, P.F. "Thomas Talfourd and *David Copperfield*."
      Dickensian, 65 (1969), 25-31.

      Examines the evidence for Dickens's friend Talfourd as
      the prototype of Tommy Traddles and proposes a Reading
      school as the model for Dr. Strong's school. See also
      J.W.T. Ley, "Dickens and Talfourd: An Early and Deeply
      Rooted Friendship," *Dickensian*, 10 (1914), 89-94, for
      more general discussion of Talfourd as a prototype.

645. S[taples], L[eslie] C. "Dickens and Australian Emigration."
      Dickensian, 42 (1946), 75-77.

      Describes Dickens's continuing interest in the social
      question of emigration and suggests that his sending of
      the Peggottys and Micawbers to Australia may have been
      inspired by Caroline Chisholm's Family Colonisation Loan
      Society, established in 1848. See also Lansbury (626, 627).

646. "Uriah Heep's House at Canterbury." *Dickensian*, 1 (1905),
      70.

      Laments the proposed demolition of the house Dickens
      may have had in mind when describing Heep's.

647. Ward, H. Snowden, and Catherine W.B. Ward. *The Real Dickens
      Land*. London: Chapman and Hall, 1904, pp. 168-174 and
      passim.

      Identifies and publishes photographs of various *Copper-
      field* locales.

648. Wetherill, Albert. "Dr. Strong and Dr. Johnson." *Dickensian*, 31 (1934), 59-60.

    Draws admittedly far-fetched parallels between Boswell's Johnson and Dickens's Dr. Strong.

LITERARY INFLUENCES
AND PARALLELS

649. Barstow, Jane M. "Charles Dickens, Marcel Proust, and Günter Grass on Childhood." *Children's Literature*, 7 (1978), 147-168.

    This sweeping comparison of writers from different times and cultures makes some observations about the development of the literary "cult of the child." Dickens was a romantic, says Barstow, and he symbolized the conflict of a dreamlike world with reality. She notes that *Copperfield* is concerned with the proper atmosphere for learning, and she defends its affectionate protectiveness by insisting that "Dickens does not idealize innocence, he rather blames the world for putting it in constant jeopardy." One difficulty with this interpretation is that it suggests a more overt social criticism than most readers find in *Copperfield*. Barstow traces different directions the "cult of the child" took in Proust and Grass. See also her "Childhood Revisited and Revised: Perspective in the First Person Novels of Dickens, Grass, and Proust," *DAI*, 34 (1973), 1848A-1849A (Michigan, 1973).

650. Cain, Tom. "Tolstoy's Use of *David Copperfield*." *CritQ*, 15 (1973), 237-246.

    Supplements and qualifies the work of Q.D. Leavis (678) by showing Tolstoy used *David Copperfield* more extensively and subtly than Leavis had suggested. In addition to the parallel Leavis made between marriages in the novels, Cain finds similarity between Betsey Trotwood and the old prince in *War and Peace* and also between episodes involving the seduction of naive heroines. Enormous differences remain between the books, Cain admits, but both are broadly concerned with problems of human relationship.

651. Christian, R.F. *Tolstoy: A Critical Introduction*. Cambridge: Cambridge University Press, 1969, pp. 27-29.

Discusses the affinity between the early chapters of
David Copperfield and Tolstoy's *Childhood* (1852). Christian
shows that both books preserve the boyhood perspective,
portray affectionate nurses, and show the boys suffering
the pangs of first love and enduring harsh school experiences. Christian examines comparative passages with "a
fairly close correspondence in the imagery or narrative
detail."

652.   Church, Howard W. "*Otto Babendiek* and *David Copperfield*."
        Germanic Review, 11 (1936), 40-49.

        Shows Dickens to have been a favorite of Gustav Frenssen
        and draws general parallels in story, plot, characters,
        and style between *Copperfield* and *Otto Babendiek*, Frenssen's
        1926 autobiographical novel.

653.   Colburn, William E. "Dickens and the 'Life-Illusion.'"
        Dickensian, 54 (1958), 110-118.

        Mentions a number of Dickens characters who, like many
        Ibsen characters, fabricate "life-illusions." The *Copper-*
        field characters Colburn identifies include Mr. Dick, who
        hovers between eccentricity and madness as he pursues his
        illusion, and Mr. Micawber, who rises above reality by
        means of a "life-illusion."

654.   Collins, Philip. "Dorothea's Husbands." *TLS*, 18 May 1973,
        pp. 556-557.

        Suggests that David's resolution to adapt himself to
        Dora anticipates Lydgate's similar decision concerning
        Rosamond in *Middlemarch*. Collins also notes that *Copper-*
        field's Dr. Strong and *Middlemarch*'s Dr. Casaubon have
        scholarly pretensions and that both are disturbed "by
        apprehensions about a younger man who belongs to the
        family."

655.   "Dickens and Daudet." *Cornhill Magazine*, NS 17 (1891),
        400-415.

        Contrasts Dickens's use of exaggeration for moral
        purposes with the decadent French writers' floutings of
        moral codes by "strange and diseased imaginativeness."
        Despite the many differences this anonymous commentator
        acknowledges between Dickens and Daudet, he feels that
        the writers both present admirable studies of children.
        The essay specifically mentions the resemblance between
        Daudet's autobiographical account of a schoolroom incident
        and *David Copperfield*'s portrayal of Steerforth's attack

on Mr. Mell. It is unlikely that this essay was written
by George Gissing, but in his preface to the Rochester
Edition (322) Gissing compares Daudet and Dickens.

656. Dunn, Richard J. "David Copperfield's Carlylean Retailor-
ing." In *Dickens the Craftsman: Strategies of Presentation*. Ed. Robert B. Partlow, Jr. Carbondale: Southern
Illinois Univ. Press, 1970, pp. 95-114.

Compares *Sartor Resartus* and *David Copperfield* in a
discussion of the ways by which Dickens's novel "incorporates both the process and the product of self-discovery."
The essay identifies numerous parallels between the boyhood and youth of Teufelsdröckh and David: David examines
the issue of his heroism just as Carlyle's hero poses the
question of his identity; when David begins a new life
under his aunt's protection he joins what Carlyle called
the "Dandiacal Body" and he follows a false guide, Steerforth; romantic Carlylean ideas of feeling as the beginning of knowledge recur in the novel's stress on the
loving heart; David learns Carlylean modes of response
to nature; like a Carlyle hero, David redefines himself
through work.

657. Dutton, A.R. "Jonson and *David Copperfield*: Dickens and
Bartholomew Fair." *ELN*, 16 (1979), 227-232.

Shows that although Dickens does not directly mention
Jonson or his works, his admiration is manifested indirectly in *David Copperfield*. Dutton thinks that at the
point when David's life separates from Dickens's, the
story begins to run "remarkably parallel to what is
generally known of Ben Jonson's." Noting that Dickens
could have known Barry Cornwall's biography of Jonson,
and having a few textual parallels in mind, Dutton speculates that Dickens consciously used his knowledge of
Jonson's life in *Copperfield*.

658. Fanger, Donald L. *Dostoevsky and Romantic Realism*.
Cambridge, Mass.: Harvard Univ. Press, 1967, p. 235.

Fanger notes that *Crime and Punishment*'s Marmeladov
"is a kind of literary cousin" to Mr. Micawber, but he
perceives an inversion from comedy to tragedy in the
Dostoevsky character.

659. Fleissner, Robert F. "The Indebtedness to Shakespeare
in *David Copperfield*." *Dickens and Shakespeare: A Study
in Histrionic Contrasts*. New York: Haskell House, 1965,
pp. 141-184.

Speculative discussion of Shakespearean elements in
Copperfield's plot structure and character relationships.
Fleissner suggests a "five-fold division" of the novel's
plot with each part constituting a representative whole.
Although Fleissner finds references to other plays, *Hamlet*
is the one he considers closest to Dickens's novel. Some
of the Shakespeare allusions seem far-fetched, such as
"hamlet on the sea-coast" and "Ham" as shortenings of
"Hamlet." Fleissner probably is correct in saying that
Micawber has some of Polonius's traits, but he is less
convincing about David as a Hamlet figure (the similarity
breaking down when David turns into a conventional middle-
class hero). Steerforth, Fleissner writes, has "the
strongest Hamlet potential," and he is Dickens's "most
exquisite creation."

660. Friedman, Stanley. "Kotzebue's 'The Stranger' in *David
      Copperfield*." *DSN*, 9 (1978), 49-50.

      Notices some plot similarities between Kotzebue's *The
      Stranger*, the sentimental drama David mentions attending,
      and *Copperfield*, but Friedman cannot prove a definite
      link.

661. Gelpi, Barbara. "The Innocent I: Dickens' Influence on
      Victorian Autobiography." In *The Worlds of Victorian
      Fiction*. Ed. Jerome H. Buckley. Cambridge, Mass.: Har-
      vard Univ. Press, 1975, pp. 57-71.

      Discusses Dickens's creation of an image of the child,
      which affected Ruskin's, Mill's, and Pater's views of
      themselves as Dickensian waifs. Gelpi thinks Dickens and
      these autobiographers failed "to dissociate the archetypal
      symbol of the child from memory's image of their child-
      hood self." She presents no direct discussion of *David
      Copperfield*.

662. Gilmour, Robin. "Dickens, Tennyson, and the Past."
      Dickensian, 75 (1979), 131-142.

      Shows Dickens's "subtle sense of personal time and of
      the persistence of the past in human memory" as similar
      to Tennyson's fascination with the past. Gilmour finds
      lines in the novel's opening chapter echoing Tennyson's
      mention of his father in "To J.S." and notes a more
      general affinity between the novel's nostalgia in the
      "Retrospect" chapters and the poet's "Tears, Idle Tears."

663. Grylls, David. "Jane Austen and Dickens." In *Guardians
      and Angels: Parents and Children in Nineteenth-Century
      Literature*. London: Faber and Faber, 1978, pp. 111-152.

      Contrasting Dickens with Jane Austen, Grylls sees him
      as the more influential champion of the young. *David
      Copperfield* represents the turning point in Dickens's
      treatment of innocence, says Grylls, for it shows trust-
      fulness to be a liability. Grylls finds the book ambivalent
      in its criticism of undisciplined affection, especially
      that of parents. Grylls's discussion covers various
      Dickens works, noting that Dickens revered childhood
      innocence, although he became more alert to its limita-
      tions in *Copperfield*.

664. Gusev, N. "Dickens and Tolstoy." Trans. Edward Bernstein.
      Dickensian, 28 (1931), 63-64.

      Quotes Tolstoy's diary, "How delightful is *David
      Copperfield*." Gusev also notes that Tolstoy, having read
      a translation in 1852, the next year ordered an English
      version.

665. Hall, William F. "Caricature in Dickens and James." *UTQ*,
      39 (1970), 242-257.

      Little direct discussion of *Copperfield*. Hall notes
      that James, in *The Art of Fiction*, appreciated Micawber
      as an effective caricature. Hall also finds an ironic
      complication in David's being an artist who must remain
      aware of his fictional world as caricature.

666. Harbage, Alfred B. *A Kind of Power: The Shakespeare-
      Dickens Analogy*. Philadelphia: American Philosophical
      Society, 1975, passim.

      Discusses the interpenetration of animate and inanimate
      worlds in both writers, citing Dickens's description of
      Uriah Heep as an example. Harbage also uses various
      Copperfield passages to demonstrate Shakespearean rhetoric,
      comedy, and sympathy in Dickens. Despite his several
      pages claiming Micawber to be "as complex and enigmatic
      as Hamlet," Harbage's discussion of Dickens and Shakes-
      peare is generally more cautious than Fleissner's (659).
      Reviews: Walter Allen, *DSN*, 7 (1976), 88-90; B[ryan]
      H[ulse], *Dickensian*, 71 (1975), 174-175; James R. Kincaid,
      NCF, 30 (1976), 535-538.

667. Harris, Stephen L. "The Mask of Morality: A Study of the
      Unconscious Hypocrite in Representative Novels of Jane

Austen, Charles Dickens, and George Eliot." *DA*, 25
(1965), 4699A (Cornell, 1964).

Comparisons of characters "morally defective but ostensibly respectable" who, while remaining well within the
law, cause more "suffering and injustice in society than
does the criminal or calculating hypocrite." Edward
Murdstone is one of Harris's examples.

668.   Harvey, William R. "Charles Dickens and the Byronic Hero."
       NCF, 24 (1969), 305-316.

General essay of interest because it suggests Dickens
may have been inspired by Byron to blend the good and bad
in a single character. Harvey says little about *David
Copperfield* but does acknowledge Steerforth as the first
of several Byronic figures in Dickens.

669.   Helm, W.H. "Balzac and Dickens." In *Aspects of Balzac*.
       London: Eveleigh Nash, 1905, pp. 121-150.

Considers differences and similarities between the
novelists. Helm acknowledges that Dickens's handling of
the young-man-coming-to-town theme in *Copperfield* differs
greatly from Balzac's, but he thinks there is a parallel
between Uriah Heep and Jean Goupil, the notary's clerk
in *Ursule Mirouët*. Helm observes how seldom Dickens's
good people come to a bad end, and he explains Steerforth's
death in the storm as an instance of Dickens's preference
for the dramatic rather than an instance of his intention
to portray inevitable punishment for evil. This study
grants that close comparison of the two novelists is
impossible.

670.   Herbert, Christopher. "DeQuincey and Dickens." *VS*, 17
       (1974), 247-263.

Defines "a complex of subjects" common to these writers
and finds *David Copperfield* "fully DeQuincean in its
exploration of the world of memory" and in its mood of
unappeased longing. Memory is paradoxical, writes Herbert,
because it mixes joys and pains. Herbert thinks that
David's relationship to Uriah Heep brings to mind DeQuincey's
theory of alien internal doubles, as David is both drawn
to and repelled by Heep.

671.   James, Henry. "Preface." *The Ambassadors*. New York: Charles
       Scribner's Sons, 1909, pp. xvii-xviii.

Notes that first-person narration in a long work "is a
form foredoomed to looseness." James says that he did not

throw the reins on his narrator's neck to flap as freely
as Dickens had permitted in *David Copperfield*. James did
not make his narrator both historian and hero because James
wished to forbid what he considered "the terrible *fluidity*
of self-revelation."

672. Jones, Ernest. *The Life and Work of Sigmund Freud. Volume
I, 1856-1900: The Formative Years and the Great Dis-
coveries*. New York: Basic Books, 1953, p. 174.

Quotes from an unpublished Freud letter of 5 October
1883. Freud speaks of Dickens's usually oversimplified
distinctions between virtue and vice, comments on "his
easy toleration of feeble-mindedness," and mentions the
presence of a philanthropist character in each novel.
Freud says that "*Copperfield* has the least of all this.
The characters are individualized; they are sinful without
being abominable."

673. Katov, George. "Steerforth and Stavrogin: On the Sources
of *The Possessed*." *Slavonic and East European Review*,
27 (1949), 469-488.

Finds "that the basic scheme of *The Possessed*, as far
as Stavrogin and the intrigue centered in him is concerned,
was built up from reminiscences of the reading of Dickens's
David Copperfield," although Dostoevsky did not admit a
relationship. Katov thinks the Russian writer tried to
avoid "cheap and shallow solutions" to problems his characters shared with Dickens's characters.

674. Kearney, Anthony. "A Borrowing from 'In Memoriam' in
'David Copperfield.'" *N&Q*, NS 26 (1979), 306-397.

Points out a resemblance between a passage in Chapter
forty-seven expressing Martha's sense of guilt and loss
over the corruption of Little Em'ly and the seventh section of *In Memoriam*. Kearney shows that the writers
"shared imagery of despair and guilt seen in terms of
night wanderings through deserted streets." He thinks
it likely that Dickens had read Tennyson's poem before
composing Chapter forty-seven, which was written a month
or so after the first appearance of *In Memoriam*.

675. Kitchen, Paul C. "Dickens, *David Copperfield*, and Thomas
Holcroft." In *Schelling Anniversary Papers by His Former
Students*. Ed. A.H. Quinn. New York: Century, 1923,
pp. 181-188.

Presents a speculative and dubious case for Holcroft's *Memoirs* as a germ for Dickens's novel. Kitchen says Mr. Micawber admittedly resembles Dickens's father but thinks the character also has much in common with Holcroft's father. Also, Kitchen notes that Dickens and Holcroft retained similar views of childhood; the most striking resemblance he cites is between the episode of a stolen dinner in the *Memoirs* and David's encounter with a waiter (Chapter five).

676. Kovačević, Ivanka. "William Godwin, the Factory Children, and Dickens's *David Copperfield*." *Filoški pregled*, 3-4 (1970), 29-40.

Notices striking similarities between Godwin's portrayal of childhood suffering in *Fleetwood* and Dickens's portrayal in *David Copperfield*. This essay shows a number of parallel details and claims that both writers seem to have understood "the social message of their narratives when they allowed the young heroes to overcome the adversities of their condition."

677. Lary, N.M. "Steerforth and Stavrogin." In *Dostoevsky and Dickens: A Study of Literary Influence*. London: Routledge and Kegan Paul, 1973, pp. 119-123.

Supports Katov's claim that Stavrogin derives from Steerforth (673), but he finds Katov's discussion confused by "circular and illusory explanations." Lary considers David's admiration for Steerforth as the crucial point and speaks of a compelling force in Steerforth's apparent freedom from ordinary laws.

678. Leavis, Q.D. "Dickens and Tolstoy: The Case for a Serious View of *David Copperfield*." In *Dickens the Novelist*. By Q.D. Leavis and F.R. Leavis. London: Chatto and Windus, 1970, pp. 34-117.

The single most complete discussion of the regard Tolstoy had for Dickens, especially for *David Copperfield*, which he read first in its Russian translation in the early 1850's, and which he ordered in English in 1853. Leavis notes that Tolstoy in old age said that *David Copperfield* was the English book he thought highest of. For additional annotation of Leavis's chapter, see earlier reference (386).

679. Lucas, John. "Dickens and Shaw: Women and Marriage in *David Copperfield* and *Candida*." *Shaw Review*, 22 (1979), 13-22.

Argues that Shaw missed the point in dismissing the novel because it did not reveal much about Dickens's own marriage (477). Lucas says *David Copperfield* might be subtitled "Marriage Under Three Heads," because it is crucially concerned with the relationships between men and women. He notes that as Shaw did with Morell, Dickens punctures sentimental male complacency by displaying his hero's awakening to his heroine's inadequacies. Lucas also defends Dickens's presentation of Agnes, because she makes possible David's existence as a social being.

680. Lupton, E. Basil. "Oliver Goldsmith as the Prototype of Mr. Mell." *Dickensian*, 16 (1920), 133.

Suggests that Dickens drew on Forster's *Life of Oliver Goldsmith* to characterize Mr. Mell as a flute-playing usher.

681. Mason, Leo. "*Jane Eyre* and *David Copperfield*." *Dickensian*, 43 (1947), 172–179.

Compares the manners of storytelling; shows the shared themes of loneliness, adult bullying, and school experience; and notes the more limited range of Charlotte Brontë's fictional world. For Mason, Brontë's novel reaches a depth of passion while love of humanity remains Dickens's dominant note. This article deals more with *Jane Eyre*'s uniqueness than with its similarities to *Copperfield*.

682. Meckier, Jerome. "Some Household Words: Two New Accounts of Dickens's Conversation." *Dickensian*, 71 (1975), 5–20.

Includes, on the authority of an anonymous note-taker the information that Dickens claimed never to have read *Jane Eyre*. Thus Meckier argues that any similarities critics find between Brontë's novel and *Copperfield* may be coincidental.

683. Monkshood, pseud. [William J. Clarke]. "Mr. Micawber: Typically Considered." *Bentley's Miscellany*, 56 (1864), 286–291.

Cites Micawber as the representative man "of those who never by any chance have (or at least hold) a bird in the hand." This observer finds "Micawberism" not only in Micawber but also in other Dickens characters and in such characters as the husband of Fielding's Amelia, Bulwer-Lytton's Captain Higginbotham (*My Novel*), and Thackeray's James Gann (*A Shabby Genteel Story*). The list extends to real people including Gilbert Gurney, Leigh Hunt's father, and William John Wells.

684. Oddie, William. *Dickens and Carlyle: The Question of
      Influence*. London: Centenary Press, 1972, pp. 130-136.

      Discusses the "I Am Shown Two Interesting Penitents"
      chapter, considering the extent to which it echoes Car-
      lyle's "Model Prisons" (*Latter-Day Pamphlets*) and con-
      cluding that the influence probably was less than has
      been suggested. Oddie notes that although "both writers
      represented a substantial section of public opinion,"
      Dickens did not share Carlyle's severity toward the prison
      reform issue.

685. Poston, Lawrence. "Uriah Heep, Scott, and a Note on
      Puritanism." *Dickensian*, 71 (1975), 43-44.

      Suggests a resemblance between Heep and Andrew Skurlie-
      whitter in *The Fortunes of Nigel*. Poston not only finds
      physical similarities between the characters but also
      finds that both of them comically secularize Puritan
      humility.

686. Schweitzer, Joan. "*David Copperfield* and *Ernest Pontifex*."
      Dickensian, 63 (1967), 42-45.

      Compares *Copperfield* with *The Way of All Flesh*, consider-
      ing both as efforts to come to terms with unhappy child-
      hood experiences. Although parallels "are not conclusive,"
      Schweitzer thinks it likely Butler was influenced by his
      childhood reading of *David Copperfield*.

687. Sharrock, Roger. "A Reminiscence of *In Memoriam* in *David
      Copperfield*." *N&Q*, 201 (1956), 502.

      Finds in Chapter 47 a brief but striking echo of the
      final stanza of the seventh section of *In Memoriam*.
      Sharrock cannot prove an influence but notes that this
      forty-seventh chapter appeared a month after the first
      edition of Tennyson's poem.

688. Spilka, Mark. "Kafka and Dickens: The Country Sweetheart."
      AI, 16 (1959), 367-378.

      Shows Tedlock's explanations of the country sweetheart
      parallel in Kafka and Dickens (691) to be inadequate.
      In both novels Spilka sees the sweetheart theme fusing
      with economic concerns as "economic experience is expressed
      through sexual immaturity." See also Spilka's more ex-
      tensive subsequent discussion in *Dickens and Kafka* (487).

689. ————. "Kafka's Sources for *The Metamorphosis.*" *CL*,
11 (1959), 289-307.

Suggests, in this study of various sources, that the
fourth chapter of *David Copperfield* provided Kafka with
a bewildering childhood experience, which he used centrally
in *Amerika* and *The Metamorphosis*. See also Spilka's subsequent *Dickens and Kafka* (487).

690. Sullivan, Patricia R. "A Student Response to the Genuine:
Fear and Pain in *Mort à crédit* and *David Copperfield.*"
Recovering Literature, 7 (1979), 42-55.

Compares the Murdstones' behavior and David's reaction
to the conduct of Auguste and Ferdinand's response in
Louis F. Destouches' *Mort à crédit*.

691. Tedlock, E.W., Jr. "Kafka's Imitation of *David Copperfield.*"
CL, 7 (1955), 52-62.

Finds *Amerika* "not so fragmentary or difficult a work
as to be incapable of comparison with" *David Copperfield*.
Tedlock claims that Kafka followed Dickens's method of
presenting perplexing experiences that could not be re-
duced to systematic religious or social explanations.
Tedlock cites a theme shared by Dickens and Kafka--the
idea of the country sweetheart. See Spilka (487) for a
significant extension of Tedlock's argument.

692. Tolstoy, Leo. *What Is Art?* Trans. Aylmer Maude. London:
Oxford Univ. Press, 1938, p. 243.

First published in Russian in 1898. Tolstoy briefly
mentions *David Copperfield* (with *Don Quixote* and *The
Pickwick Papers*) as an example of "good universal art,"
distinguished by "the exceptional nature of the feelings"
it transmits as well as by "the superfluity of special
details of time and locality." Tolstoy says this kind of
art differs from the highest art mainly because "of the
poverty ... of subject-matter in comparisons with examples
of universal ancient art."

693. Wierstra, Frans D. *Smollett and Dickens*. Amsterdam: C. de
Boer, Jr., 1928, pp. 56-58, 75-77.

Gives brief attention to specific comparisons of *Pere-
grine Pickle* and *Roderick Random* with *David Copperfield*.
Wierstra says that Miss Murdstone resembles Pickle's
sister, and he thinks Mr. Creakle may have had a prototype
in *Pickle*'s Mr. Keypstick. Wierstra thinks *David Copper-*

field's opening chapters may show the influence of
Roderick Random, because superstition is much in evidence
in each.

694. Willey, Basil. "A Nineteenth-Century Intellectual Novelist:
Basil Willey on George Eliot." *Listener*, 43 (1950),
352-353.

Brief comparison of *The Mill on the Floss* with *David
Copperfield* to show that Eliot presents a broader social
and spiritual predicament, whereas Dickens portrays "mere
stage types." Willey takes care to observe that Eliot,
the more documentary social historian, is not necessarily
the superior creative artist.

695. Wilson, Angus. "Dickens and Dostoevsky." In *Dickens
Memorial Lectures 1970*. *Dickensian*, 65, Supplement
(September 1970), 41-61.

Thinks *David Copperfield* must have had a strong influence on Dostoevsky because *Crime and Punishment*'s Marmeladov resembles Mr. Micawber and because a passage from
The Idiot suggests Micawber's reappearance as General
Ivolgin.

STUDY GUIDES AND HANDBOOKS

696. Brightfield, Myron P. *Victorian England in Its Novels*.
4 vols. Berkeley: Univ. of California Library, 1968,
passim.

Useful anthology of brief quotations arranged by subject from major and minor novels. It includes *Copperfield* quotes under the following headings: "Flavors of
Victorian Life"--descriptions of the Thames, of the
shoddy Golden Square area of London, and of Mr. Wickfield's substantial old house; "Servants"--Littimer as
an instance of the valet who appears to be a pillar of
society; "Coach Travel"--David's trip to Yarmouth, and
the departure of the Australian emigrant ship; "Continental"--David in Switzerland; "Boys' Schools"--Creakle
as a pathological specimen and Dr. Strong's responsibly
run school; "Conflict of the Ideal and Real in Marriage"--
David and Dora with notice of how the husband's burden
increased when the wife was not able to manage the household. These *Copperfield* quotations usually are surrounded

by a number of similar passages from other writers. Brightfield's objective is social history; he does not suggest
influences or plagiarisms.

697. Carrington, Norman T. *Brodies Notes on Charles Dickens's
David Copperfield.* London: Pan Educational, 1977. 99 pp.

Revision of Wilfred Eastwood's study guide (698); keyed
to the Pan Edition (70). This is an intelligent guide referring readers frequently to Forster (730), Gissing (321),
and Chesterton (253). Carrington provides a map of locales,
considers structural implications of the serial form and
first-person narration, and discusses the importance of
the illustrations. He says that thematically *Copperfield*
is concerned with problems of courtship and marriage and
with David's development, and he considers David "a real
creation," possessed with "extreme sharpness of observation." This guide presents crisp commentaries about the
Micawbers, Betsey, Heep, Mr. Dick, Steerforth, Traddles,
Dora, Agnes, and Clara Peggotty, and there is an extensive
index to more minor characters. Carrington retains Eastwood's section on style and his tabular comparison between the novel and Dickens's life. His chapter summaries
are concise and include explanatory notes.

698. Eastwood, Wilfred. *Charles Dickens. David Copperfield.*
London: James Brodie, 1947. 84 pp.

Excellent study guide later revised by Norman Carrington (697). The biographical section makes more connection
with earlier and contemporary writers than is usual in
a study aid.

699. Frankel, Bernice, ed. *David Copperfield: Chapter Notes
and Criticism.* New York: American R.D.M., 1963, 74 pp.

Provides an outline of biographical information, a brief
introduction to the novel, and chapter-by-chapter notes.
Frankel's notes seem geared for beginning students and
include a self-tutoring mastery test and a short bibliography. Her critical appraisal acknowledges a disparity
among critics and notes that in many ways Dickens attacked
Victorian moral foundations.

700. Kraus, W. Keith. *Charles Dickens. David Copperfield.*
Barnes and Noble Book Notes. New York: Barnes and Noble,
1966. 96 pp.

Contains a brief biographical summary and a short
synopsis and discussion for each chapter. The quality of

Kraus's discussion and of his questions is uneven and
seems geared for the youngest readers (typical questions
are ones of what will happen in coming chapters). His
brief critical analysis of structure, style, and themes
is weakened by his opening misstatement that the novel
"first appeared as a newspaper serial." His character
sketches provide the most elementary identification.
(Jane Murdstone is Mr. Murdstone's sister. "She runs the
Copperfield household and incessantly harasses David.")
A series of multiple-choice study questions, a brief
synopsis of critical commentary, and a short bibliography
conclude this pamphlet.

701. McMurtry, Jo. *Victorian Life and Victorian Fiction: A
      Companion for the American Reader*. Hamden, Conn.: Archon,
      1979, passim.

      Useful for readers seeking information about the Vic-
      torian educational and legal systems; customs of marriage
      and courtship and mourning; and facts about and public
      attitudes toward prostitution. McMurtry mentions many
      characters from *Copperfield* as typical of the Victorian
      Age, and much of the information she includes helps to
      explain the social condition of other characters. For
      example, McMurtry's discussion of disreputable hospitals
      helps us to understand the desperate condition of Betsey
      Trotwood's husband when he dies in such a place. McMurtry
      does have some mistaken identities such as "Jarvis" for
      "Barkis."

702. *Notes on Charles Dickens' David Copperfield*. London:
      Methuen, 1969. 69 pp.

      Includes a biographical introduction, a story outline
      that attempts stylistically to preserve the presence of
      the first-person narrator, a commentary on characters in
      the order of their appearances, general observations, and
      typical examination questions. It mistakes the date of
      Dickens's death as 9 January rather than 9 June 1870.
      It insists David is passive but grants that the point may
      be arguable. This guide recognizes the importance of
      memory and gives it more attention than is common in study
      guides. These notes seem directed to very young readers.

703. Ochojski, Paul M. *Review Notes and Study Guide to Dickens'
      David Copperfield*. New York: Monarch Press, 1964. 92 pp.

      Justifies himself by claiming to enable "the average
      student to read with perception and understanding a work
      he might otherwise have found hopelessly perplexing and

therefore distasteful." Ochojski's introduction describes
the life and career of Dickens by quoting and acknowledg-
ing major biographers and critics. A detailed chapter-by-
chapter summary follows a short synopsis of the novel.
His brief, but usually informative comments appear within
the chapter summaries. A section of "Critical Commentary"
summarizes some of the early reactions to *Copperfield* as
well as the modern views of various histories of English
fiction and of Edgar Johnson (738), André Maurois (415),
and Bruce McCullough (396). The study guide concludes
with a list of characters, review questions and answers,
and a short bibliography. All in all, it is one of the
more reliable study guides.

704.　Pierce, Gilbert A. *"David Copperfield."* In *The Dickens
　　　Dictionary. Boston: Houghton, Osgood, 1878, pp. 290-
　　　331.

　　　Lists all of the characters, provides descriptive summaries of their roles, and gives chapter-by-chapter summaries of principal incidents.

705.　Roberts, James L. *David Copperfield: Notes*. Lincoln, Neb.:
　　　Cliff's Notes, 1959. 89 pp.

　　　Includes a biographical note and several pages summarizing general critical opinions without identifying any of
the critics. Roberts outlines pros and cons of Dickens's
style and provides the *Oxford Companion to English Literature* story synopsis, a chapter-by-chapter summary, and a
series of character sketches. He makes clear that the
notes are intended as supplementary to the serious student's
note-taking and reading, but without clear reference to
authoritative biographical or critical studies and with
only a survey of the action and thought of *David Copperfield*, these notes are of questionable value.

706.　Seeley, Harold M. *David Copperfield Notes*. London: Coles,
　　　1963. 89 pp.

　　　Surveys Dickens's works and summarizes critical comments
about *David Copperfield* and Dickens's style without
identifying the critics whose views are summarized. Seeley
is guilty of some ludicrous errors such as his observation that toward the end Dickens "very rapidly illuminates
[eliminates?] burdensome characters." He lists characters
alphabetically by sex and provides brief chapter summaries.
He also provides a final "synopsis" of Dickens's style
and a series of study questions.

707.   Short, Wilsie G.N. *David Copperfield: Notes, Appreciation
       and Exercises*. Sydney: College Press, 1966. 80 pp.

       Cited in the 1967 *Modern Humanities Research Association
       Bibliography* but not available now for annotation.

708.   Stevenson, R.W. *Charles Dickens. David Copperfield*. York
       Notes. London: Longman, 1980. 80 pp.

       Unique among study guides in declaring itself aimed at
       non-British readers. Stevenson supplies a biographical
       summary. He discusses the Victorian era, the novel's set-
       ting (treating Blunderstone as if it were a real place),
       and the literary background. The textual note misleadingly
       suggests that all Dickens's later novels were monthly
       serials. Stevenson's commentary accompanying chapter-by-
       chapter summaries attempts comprehensiveness by stressing
       various themes and by considering plot, style, humor,
       pathos, and unity. The hints for study are better than most
       found in study guides because they suggest ways of read-
       ing and not just facts to consider when reading. Also
       Stevenson guides readers to the work of major Dickens
       critics.

709.   Stockwell, N. *Notes on Dickens's David Copperfield*.
       London: Normal Press, n.d. 50 pp.

       Evidently designed for examination study, although
       Stockwell expresses a desire to "contribute to a critical
       knowledge and an intelligent appreciation of Dickens'
       interesting work." Stockwell includes a biographical sketch,
       plot and character surveys, notes (explanatory, historical,
       etymological), and sample test-paper topics. Although
       undated, this clearly is an earlier twentieth-century
       study aid, lacking much of the detail found in more recent
       guides.

Part III
BIOGRAPHY AND BIBLIOGRAPHY

BIOGRAPHICAL STUDIES

710. Adrian, Arthur A. *Georgina Hogarth and the Dickens Circle*.
      London: Oxford Univ. Press, 1957, pp. 24-26.

      Suggests that the characterization of Dora blends
      qualities of Maria Beadnell from Dickens's past with those
      of Catherine Dickens from his present. Adrian argues that
      just as David comes to depend on Agnes, so did Dickens
      turn "to his sister-in-law [Georgina] for intellectual
      companionship, sympathetic understanding, and practical
      common sense." In a perceptive explanation of the novel's
      passionless portrait of Agnes, Adrian finds the whole
      tone suggestive of "Dickens's own lack of romantic ardour
      for Agnes Wickfield's prototype [Georgina]." As a further
      point, Adrian notes that Georgina may have also inspired
      the self-denying Sophy Traddles.

711. Aldington, Richard. "The Underworld of Young Dickens."
      In *Four English Portraits, 1801-1851*. London: Evans
      Brothers, 1948, pp. 147-189.

      Notes that *David Copperfield* retains the essence of
      Dickens's childhood, "telling it with intense self-pity
      and graphic indignation." Aldington follows Forster (730)
      in paralleling life and novel, but he makes serious
      mistakes such as claiming Dickens spent two years at a
      blacking factory. His general point is that because of his
      tendency toward fantasy Dickens failed to present accurate
      pictures of the Victorian underworld in *Copperfield* but
      gave more factual accounts in his *Household Words*.

712. Archer, Thomas. *Charles Dickens: A Gossip about his Life,
      Works and Characters*. London: Cassell and Co., [1902].
      92 pp.

      Contains illustrations by well-known artists and includes
      eighteen full-page photogravure character sketches by
      Frederick Barnard of Micawber, Betsey Trotwood, Mr.
      Peggotty, Uriah Heep, and others. The reader will be
      primarily interested in the illustrations rather than in
      Archer's comments.

713.   "The Author and Himself. Dickens and *David Copperfield*."
       Academy, 6 December 1902. Two-page clipping in Dickens
       House, London.

       Brief discussion noting that although Dickens had many
       kindly solutions for difficult human problems, he "still
       found the individual life an enigma inexplicable by any
       formula." This commentator thinks Dickens's best literary
       presentation of the enigmatic personal life is in *Great
       Expectations*, but because of its autobiographical nature
       David Copperfield remains his most personal work. Sounding
       more like later twentieth-century critics, this observer
       remarks that "in no other book do ghosts glide so per-
       sistently across the stage, challenging the renewal of
       dead dreams," and nowhere else in Dickens is there such
       an antithesis between characters elucidated by their ac-
       tion in the plot (e.g. Steerforth) and those whose exist-
       ence seems to depend on Dickens's personal fascination
       with them (e.g. Micawber).

714.   Axon, William E.A. "Charles Dickens and Shorthand."
       Manchester Quarterly, 43 (1892), 291-300.

       Shows Gurney's "Brachygraphy" as a leading system of
       shorthand at the time Dickens was a reporter. Only a few
       pages of Dickens's shorthand survive in the Forster Col-
       lection of the Victoria and Albert Museum, London, which
       also has a notebook made by Dickens while teaching his
       son shorthand. See also Carlton (718).

715.   Barker, George P. *Charles Dickens and Maria Beadnell:
       Private Correspondence*. Boston: Bibliophile Society,
       1908. 151 pp.

       With an introduction by Henry H. Harper. Only 493 copies
       of Barker's book were published in the 1908 limited edi-
       tion. This was the first publication of these letters,
       which show that David's love affairs were those of Dickens
       himself and that traits of Maria are portrayed in Dora.
       The letters also suggest originals for Julia Mills and
       for the troublesome servant, Mary Anne. B.W. Matz describes
       these letters in an article in the *Strand Magazine* for
       December 1922.

716.   Becker, May L. *Introducing Charles Dickens*. London: George
       F. Harrap, 1941, pp. 183-191.

       A sentimental appreciation of Dickens as "a banner in
       the sun" and of his novels as "dancing shadows." Becker
       sees *Copperfield* as Dickens's arrival at the point where

"he, a novelist like David, could write this book." En-
trapped by the circularity of her arguments, Becker also
claims but does not prove that John Dickens enjoyed the
character Micawber.

717. "The Boyhood of Dickens: II London." *Dickensian*, 26 (1929),
61-66.

Compares Mrs. Micawber's boarding school scheme to the
similar project of Dickens's mother and shows that the
novel's fictionalized vision of boyhood kept Dickens's
actual experience secret.

718. Carlton, William J. *Charles Dickens: Shorthand Writer.*
London: Cecil Palmer, 1926. 149 pp.

Supersedes Axon's account (714) of Dickens learning
Gurney's "Brachygraphy" and includes the passages from
Copperfield describing David's mastery of shorthand.

719. ———. "The Deed in *David Copperfield.*" *Dickensian*, 48
(1952), 101-106.

Establishes parallels between the debts of John Dickens
and those of Mr. Micawber and shows a "certain deed"
possessed by Micawber most likely originating from a
particular recollection from Dickens's boyhood.

720. ———. "In the Blacking Warehouse." *Dickensian*, 60
(1964), 11-16.

Provides many details on the state of the blacking
business in the early nineteenth century and corrects
Forster (730) concerning the Lamberts, the relations who
suggested that Dickens take the job at Warren's Blacking.

721. Collins, P.A.W. [Philip Collins]. "Bruce Castle: A School
Dickens Admired." *Dickensian*, 51 (1955), 174-181.

Presents Dickens's favorable opinion of a school he considered for his own son as a contrast to his inadequate
portrayal of a good school (Dr. Strong's) in *Copperfield.*

722. Cooper, Lettice. *A Hand Upon the Time: A Life of Charles
Dickens.* London: Pantheon Books, 1968, pp. 115-121.

A brief discussion of events surrounding the genesis
and composition of *Copperfield.* Cooper makes little critical
commentary but does acknowledge the importance of the
theme concerning "no disparity in marriage like unsuita-
bility of mind and purpose." Cooper considers this theme

a comment on Dickens's dream of Maria Beadnell and also
possibly on his marriage.

723.   "David Copperfield and Charles Dickens." *Spectator*, 44
       (1871), 1490–1491.

       Reviews the first volume of Forster's *Life of Dickens*
and closely considers the mixture of autobiography and
fiction in *David Copperfield*. This reviewer finds Forster's
revelations about Dickens's early life pointing up a
"decided tendency which imaginative men often show to
exaggerate in retrospect the receptive and passive side
of their own life as distinguished from the hard grit
of will and judgment underneath it." The reviewer's point
is that the easily-imposed-upon young David only partially
resembles the young Dickens, because Dickens exaggerated
the boy's passivity and left out the "shrewd, hard, acute
side" of Dickens himself that becomes public in Forster's
biography. Generalizing about Dickens's methods of characterization, the reviewer claims that the novelist's principal successes were in surface features: "Dickens could
paint and illustrate in a well-marked *manner* with the most
wonderful fertility of variation, with the richest humour
of fancy; but he never could get down to the core of any
subtle or complex character, not even his own. David Copperfield is only a poor surface wax impression of Charles
Dickens."

724.   Dexter, Walter. "Charles Dickens––One Hundred Years Ago."
       Dickensian, 20 (1924), 12–17.

       Corrects Forster's dating of Dickens's boyhood employ-
ment in the blacking warehouse.

725.   ————. *Dickens: The Story of the World's Favourite
       Author*. London: The Dickens Fellowship, 1927. 90 pp.

       Draws frequently on *David Copperfield* to describe
Dickens's early years and includes numerous photographs
and illustrations.

726.   ————. *The Love Romance of Charles Dickens Told in His
       Letters to Maria Beadnell (Mrs. Winter)*. London: Argo-
       naut Press, 1931. 125 pp.   ·

       Publishes letters which Stonehouse drew upon for his
study (77) and which Barker had printed in a limited
American edition (715). Dexter dates the letters as most
likely beginning when Dickens was twenty and continuing
for three years. Barker and Stonehouse had assumed that
they were written when Dickens was eighteen.

727. ————. "What Dickens Thought of *David Copperfield*."
      Dickensian, 27 (1931), 230.

      Compiles from Dickens's letters ten brief comments con-
      cerning the novel.

728. DuCann, C.G.L. "The Pocket Venus: Maria Beadnell." *The
      Love-Lives of Charles Dickens*. London: Frederick Muller,
      1961, pp. 28-44.

      Traces details of Dickens's early love for Maria and
      observes that from his state of "wretchedness" he years
      later "idealized the cause of it all in Dora ... destined
      to die rather than to grow up and be other than the Maria
      he had known and desired so passionately." DuCann also
      notes that Agnes may be an idealized portrait of Georgina
      Hogarth--see Adrian (710). See also Dexter's *The Love
      Romance of Charles Dickens* (726).

729. Fitzgerald, Percy. *The Life of Charles Dickens As Revealed
      in His Writings*. 2 vols. London: Chatto and Windus,
      1905, passim.

      Frequent mention of *David Copperfield*'s biographical
      details and character originals. Fitzgerald includes
      personal recollections, such as receiving a gift copy of
      David Copperfield from Dickens. His annotated table of
      contents provides easy reference.

730. Forster, John. *The Life of Charles Dickens*. 3 vols.
      London: Chapman and Hall, 1872-1874, passim.

      Originally published in three volumes between 1872 and
      1874, Forster's work is now available in 2 vols., edited
      by A.J. Hoppé (London: Dent, 1966). Forster's was the
      standard Dickens biography until the appearance of Edgar
      Johnson's biography in 1952 (738). Forster's early chap-
      ters draw heavily upon *David Copperfield*, and his second
      chapter is based largely on Dickens's fragmentary auto-
      biography. Although not clear about when Dickens wrote
      it, Forster claims first to have seen the fragment on
      20 January 1849. A footnote quotes Forster's diary and
      adds information about the quote: "'The description may
      make none of the impression on others that the reality
      made on him.... Highly probable that it may never see
      the light. No wish. Left to J.F. or others.' The first
      number of *David Copperfield* appeared five months after
      this date; but though I knew, even before he adapted his
      fragment of autobiography to the eleventh number, that
      he had now abandoned the notion of completing it under

his own name, the '*no wish*,' or the discretion left me,
was never in any way subsequently modified." Forster
claims that Dickens had kept the details of his childhood (and also the autobiography revealing them) secret
from his family, but Charles Dickens the Younger some
years later states that his mother had known of the fragment and approved Dickens's decision not to publish it
(283). Following the many quotations from the autobiographical fragment, Forster echoes the opening of *Copperfield* to strike his own keynote: "In what way these strange
experiences of his boyhood affected him afterwards, the
narrative of his life must show." In his later chapter
on *David Copperfield* and *Bleak House* (308), Forster
identifies many prototypes for the novel's people and
places, but although he mentions Dickens's disappointment in young love that prompted his characterization of
Dora, he does not name Maria Beadnell, and her identity
remained unknown for a number of years. In discussing the
events leading to Dickens's 1858 separation from his
wife, Forster states that the psychological compensation
Dickens received from his works up to the date of the
completion of *Copperfield* was "an all-sufficient resource."
But, as Forster shows, during the mid-1850's Dickens's
letters indicate growing discontent, and in one of them
he alludes to *Copperfield* to describe his state of mind,
speaking of an old "unhappy loss or want of something"
and of "the happy and yet so unhappy existence which seeks
its realities in unrealities, and finds its dangerous
comfort in a perpetual escape from the disappointment of
heart around it." For additional annotation, see Forster
(308).

731. [Friswell, J. Hain]. *Charles Dickens: A Critical Biography.*
      London: Blayney and Fryer, 1858, pp. 54-56.

      Friswell's work was clearly inspired by Dickens's
      1858 separation from his wife, and he claims that the
      most painful passages of this study "have been supplied
      by the hand of Mr. Dickens himself" (i.e. Dickens's
      statements about the separation). In his survey of Dickens's
      writing, Friswell somewhat grudgingly terms *Copperfield*
      his most finished and natural book and thinks the Micaw-
      ber family as original a group as Dickens ever drew.
      Friswell writes, "The dark and weird character of Rosa
      Dartle, and the more disgusting one of Uriah Heep are
      the only painful ones in the book. But they are full of
      fine touches of nature, which also illumine the dark draw-
      ing of the Murdstones." These specific comments about

Rosa Dartle and Uriah Heep, along with some of Friswell's other views, were repeated with only general acknowledgment by R. Shelton Mackenzie (747). Much of Friswell's commentary was reprinted in his *Modern Man of Letters Honestly Considered* in 1870. This book was soon suppressed when G.A. Sala won a defamation of character suit against Friswell. Forster owned both Friswell's and Mackenzie's books, but neither copy has any markings, and Forster mentions neither in his biography.

732. Hammond, R.A. *The Life and Writings of Charles Dickens. A Memorial Volume.* Toronto: A.H. Hovey, 1871, pp. 265-272.

Very unreliable in details but interesting because of its pre-Forster claim that Dickens's novel is not very autobiographical because the author "never had a stepfather who ill-treated him; never ran away from home, to be brought up by an eccentric aunt; never groaned under the sway of a brutal flogging schoolmaster like Crinkle [sic]; was never employed to wash bottles in a wine merchant's cellar; and never was articled to a proctor in Doctors Commons." Hammond regards this as Dickens's best work, even in the portrayal of David as a modest hero.

733. Hanaford, Phebe A. "His Masterpiece." In *The Life and Writings of Charles Dickens: A Woman's Memorial Volume.* Boston: B.B. Russell, 1871, pp. 307-323.

Draws on an 1863 *Christian Examiner* article, "The Reality of Fiction," to uphold Hanaford's claims for imaginative literature against mechanistic thought. She has great praise for the "Tempest" chapter (quoting much of it) and also thinks highly of Halliday's play, *Little Em'ly* (90). But despite the subtitle, Hanaford's book does not attempt a female critical perspective and has nothing to say about any of the novel's women.

734. Harrison, Michael. *Charles Dickens: A Sentimental Journey in Search of an Unvarnished Portrait.* London: Cassell, 1953, passim.

Provides little that is useful because Harrison makes only a few curious references to *Copperfield* (including his idea that Phiz knew what he was doing when he inverted Peggotty's house even though the textual description has it rightside-up). Assuming *Copperfield* to be too literally autobiographical, Harrison finds *Our Mutual Friend* a more personal book: "Any other writer as great as Dickens could

have told the story of Copperfield, given the facts; only
Dickens could have written *Our Mutual Friend*, unburdening
obligations great and small to the confessional of the
blank page."

735.   Hibbert, Christopher. *The Making of Charles Dickens.* New
        York: Harper and Row, 1967, passim.

        Frequently mentions *Copperfield* in telling the story
        of Dickens's early years and in showing "how he inter-
        preted his youthful experiences both to the reader and
        to himself." Hibbert concentrates on Dickens's first
        thirty-two years and therefore does not present any
        account of him at the time of *David Copperfield.* He offers
        no new views of the novel's prototypes or biographical
        sources and summarizes much of the information provided
        by other biographers.

736.   Hill, T.W. "David's Confidences." *Dickensian,* 45 (1949),
        145-148.

        Considers the impetus the autobiographical fragment gave
        to *Copperfield* but notes that the book remains preeminently
        fictional. Hill also observes that *Household Words* (35)
        began as a forum for Dickens's thoughts on current events
        while the novel was halfway through its serial run and
        points out that both the novel and the periodical satis-
        fied Dickens's need for personal contact with his public.

737.   Hutter, Albert D. "Reconstructive Autobiography: The
        Experience at Warren's Blacking." *DSA,* 6 (1977), 1-14.

        Although he does not directly deal with *David Copper-
        field,* Hutter observes that in regarding the trauma of
        Dickens's childhood, critics and biographers have not
        noted the "normal and even healthy aspects" which Hutter
        thinks possible in Dickens's childhood employment. A
        shorter version of Hutter's argument appeared in "Psycho-
        analysis and Biography: Dickens' Experience at Warren's
        Blacking," *HSL,* 8 (1976), 23-37. There Hutter points out
        distortions and short-sightedness in Forster's (730),
        Lindsay's (390), and E. Wilson's (536) discussions of
        Dickens's experience. Hutter thinks "Warren's tells us
        more about Dickens' character and its formation than
        about pathological behavior."

738.   Johnson, Edgar. *Charles Dickens: His Tragedy and Triumph.*
        2 vols. New York: Simon and Schuster, 1952, passim.

The standard modern biography, which has been revised
and abridged (New York: Viking, 1977). Following and often
supplementing Forster, Johnson stresses the formative
effect of Dickens's childhood experiences and draws
heavily on the autobiographical fragment, which he dates
as sometime between September 1845 and May 1846. Of the
blacking factory experiences, Johnson writes, "Dickens
projected them, both in the fragment of autobiography ...
and in their fictional guise in *David Copperfield*....
No emphasis can overstate the depth and intensity with
which these experiences ate into his childish soul....
In a final sense, the great and successful effort of his
career was to assimilate and understand the blacking
warehouse and the Marshalsea, and the kind of world in
which such things could be." Johnson's book is especially
useful in describing the many other activities of Dickens
while he was writing the novel, and Johnson includes
quotations from many of Dickens's letters in Part VII,
Chapter 5, "Myself Into the Shadowy World." Reviews: John
E. Butt, *NCF*, 8 (1953), 151-153; W.J. Carlton, *Dickensian*,
49 (1952), 53-58; Philip Collins, *TLS*, 21 April 1978, p.
446; Angus Easson, *Dickensian*, 75 (1979), 37-38; James
Olney, *DSN*, 10 (1979), 23-27; Gordon N. Ray, *VQR*, 29
(1953), 297-302. See also Johnson's critical chapter on
David Copperfield (357).

739. Jones, Charles H. "From Birth to Manhood" and "*David
Copperfield*." In *A Short Life of Charles Dickens*. New
York: D. Appleton, 1882, pp. 7-34, 166-172.

Traces autobiographical elements and reprints the autobiographical fragment from Forster (730). Jones realizes
that the novel contains much more than the mere facts
of Dickens's life, for in light of his family experiences
the novel lays bare "the real tendency of his thoughts
and feelings." Jones provides little critical analysis to
support this assertion.

740. Kitton, F[rederic] G. "The Autobiographical Element in
David Copperfield." *Good Words*, June 1904, pp. 386-392;
July 1904, pp. 473-481.

Provides many autobiographical details but notes that
the sequence of events does not correspond exactly between life and novel. Most of Kitton's information concerns the boyhood and young manhood years, events, places,
and people that may have been sources for the fiction.
Kitton makes no speculation about deliberate changes such
as Dickens's transplanting of his hero's birthplace to

East Anglia. He seems alone in the conjecture that Agnes
may have been modeled on the novelist's wife.

741. ———. *Charles Dickens by Pen and Pencil*. 2 vols. London:
      Frank T. Sabin, 1890, passim.

      Draws heavily on Forster (730) and Langton (744) to
      trace Dickens's early years. Kitton includes a lady's
      recollection of reading current serial numbers of *David
      Copperfield* while picnicking at Bonchurch with Dickens.
      According to her, Dickens would call out, "Mind and give
      me my own knives; they are marked 'Brooks of Sheffield!'"
      Leech's cartoon of the picnic appeared in *Punch* on 25
      August 1849.

742. ———. *"David Copperfield."* In *The Novels of Charles
      Dickens*. London: Elliot Stock, 1897, pp. 112-130.

      Draws heavily on Forster (730) and on various letters
      for biographical backgrounds; summarizes the early recep-
      tion, but ventures no critical assessment of *Copperfield*.

743. ———. *"David Copperfield."* In *Charles Dickens: His
      Life, Writings, and Personality*. London: Caxton, n.d.,
      pp. 166-193. Also published in two volumes in Edinburgh,
      1902.

      Discusses Forster's account of the novel's origins (730)
      and follows Charles Dickens the Younger's claim that Mrs.
      Dickens was aware of the autobiographical fragment (283)
      and tried to dissuade her husband from using it because
      it spoke too harshly of Dickens's parents. Kitton thinks
      Forster was indiscreet in having published the autobio-
      graphical fragment but doubts that he knew of what may
      have passed between Dickens and his wife. Kitton not only
      cites John Dickens as a prototype for Mr. Micawber but
      also names Thomas Powell of Boston and Richard Chicken
      of York as possible sources. For Clara Peggotty, Kitton
      says Dickens found an original in his childhood nurse,
      Mary Weller.

744. Langton, Robert. *The Childhood and Youth of Charles
      Dickens*. London: Hutchinson, 1891. 260 pp. Revision
      and enlargement of privately printed (Manchester, 1883)
      edition.

      Supplements Forster's biography (730) with a few
      details. Langton suggests Dickens's childhood neighbor,
      George Stroughill of Chatham, as the prototype for Steer-
      forth, and Mr. Taylor, English master at Wellington House

and a flute player, as the prototype for Mr. Mell. Langton mentions that Dickens probably never saw Canterbury in his boyhood and in his novel may have used it as a disguise for his familiar Rochester. He notes that Miss Trotwood's thinking Peggotty a "heathenish name" may be ill-founded, for the name was used as a Christian name in Chatham.

745. Leask, William K. "Biographical Introduction." In 1900 Gresham Edition, pp. v-xvi (46).

Questions the appropriateness of great writers attempting their own biographies by citing a number of cases (Thackeray, Browning) against it. Leask concludes, however, that *David Copperfield* is "the best biography" of Dickens and is an example of Carlyle's doctrine "regarding the artistic superiority of fact to fiction."

746. Mackenzie, Norman, and Jeanne Mackenzie. *Dickens: A Life.* New York: Oxford Univ. Press, 1979, pp. 213-226.

Traces the changes in Dickens's life in the late 1840's that brought him back to long-buried events of his childhood. The Mackenzies relate the themes of *The Haunted Man*, Dickens's 1848 Christmas Book, to *Copperfield*'s stress on memory. They believe there is "real forgiveness" in the portrayal of John Dickens as Mr. Micawber. Although their book is more recent than Johnson's (738), the additional information they draw upon does not lead them to any startling new conclusions. Reviews: David Parker, *MLQ*, 40 (1979), 319-322; Andrew Sanders, *Dickensian*, 76 (1980), 44-45; Harry Stone, *NCF*, 34 (1980), 438-443.

747. Mackenzie, R. Shelton. *Life of Charles Dickens.* Philadelphia: T.B. Peterson, [1870], pp. 183-184, 203.

Cites Dickens's father as the Micawber prototype but curiously regards Traddles as "scarcely complimentary" to Dickens's truest friend, Talfourd--see Clark (605). Mackenzie's summation of *David Copperfield* comes directly from Friswell (731), but Mackenzie identifies his source only by saying, "It was critically reported" that *David Copperfield* is "the most finished and natural of his works," with Rosa Dartle, Uriah Heep, and the Murdstones well done. This book seems hastily composed and is unreliable.

748. McNulty, J.H. "*Copperfield*, Fact or Fiction?" *Dickensian*, 45 (1949), 153-155.

Appreciative survey of the novel as one of Dickens's
greatest books. McNulty finds the autobiographical elements "the least happy" part of a novel which begins as
fact and changes to fiction. For more considered study
of this point, see Collins (263).

749.   Major, Gwen. "'Into the Shadowy World.'" *Dickensian*, 40
       (1943), 15-18.

Suggests that in its details the novel does not follow
Dickens's life very closely. Major discusses a number of
events and characters that do have partial prototypes in
Dickens's life, and she thinks there is no question that
"Charles is David, in the real incidents and associates
and the fancied."

750.   Marzials, Frank T. *Life of Charles Dickens*. London: Walter
       Scott, 1887, pp. 111-113.

Portrays Dickens's early interests and sufferings by
drawing freely upon *David Copperfield*, as did Forster
(730), upon whom Marzials greatly depends. He considers
Copperfield the culmination of Dickens's career and
defends the portrayal of Steerforth and Em'ly against
the French critics' demands for more stress on "the mad
force and irresistible sway of passion"--see Taine (199).

751.   Nicoll, Sir W. Robertson. "The True History of Dora
       Copperfield." In *Charles Dickens*. *Bookman Extra Number*.
       London: Hodder and Stoughton, 1914, pp. 26-32.

Outlines George P. Barker's *Charles Dickens and Maria
Beadnell* (715), considering it a significant addition to
Forster's biography (730). Nicoll states that Dickens lost
courage and burned his autobiographical manuscript when
he arrived at the point of describing his futile infatua-
tion with Maria.

752.   Pearson, Hesketh. "C.D. and D.C." In *Dickens: His Charac-
       ter, Comedy, and Career*. New York: Harper and Brothers,
       1949, pp. 154-173.

Discusses *David Copperfield* in the context of Dickens's
busy life and finds David possessing prominent temperamental traits of Dickens. Pearson believes Dickens ranked
this as his favorite work because in it he was able to
relive his past. Pearson acknowledges the burden of Victorian conventionality in Dickens's portrayal of sexual
attitudes. Although Pearson presents one of the more
complete modern discussions of the David-Dickens resemblance, his study is superseded by Johnson's (738).

753. Perkins, F.B. *Charles Dickens: A Sketch of His Life and Works*. New York: G.P. Putnam, 1870, pp. 82-86.

Relies upon the early reviews and general suppositions that *Copperfield* was autobiographical but is more original when recognizing the intensity and psychological truthfulness of both the humorous and pathetic parts of the novel. In a unique but unsupported remark, Perkins suggests that a gentleman's modesty keeps the first-person narrator "more of a lay-figure than otherwise."

754. Pope-Hennessey, Una. *Charles Dickens*. London: Chatto and Windus, 1945, pp. 270-274, 342-344.

Like other biographies in its high regard for *David Copperfield* as one of Dickens's greatest works; unlike many in raising the question of why Dickens frequently found facing the past so painful.

755. Pratt, Branwen. "Dickens and Father: Notes on the Family Romance." *HSL*, 8 (1976), 4-19.

Argues, in her discussion of various novels, that Dickens protected his ego by creating noble images of himself and his father while projecting "aggressions onto the substitute tyrants of his novels." Pratt thinks that the fragmentary autobiography shows Dickens's struggle both to conceal and to confront his resentment against his father. For a different view of Dickens's treatment of his father, see Hutter (737).

756. Priestley, J.B. *Charles Dickens and His World*. London: Thames and Hudson, 1969, pp. 75-79.

A reprint of *Charles Dickens: A Pictorial Biography*, 1961. Priestley thinks *David Copperfield* is declining in modern critical favor because of the new critical interest in structure. He considers *Copperfield* one of Dickens's most important works; as a complicated mixture of memory and invention, "it stands by itself." Priestley reproduces a sheet of W. Wilson's music for "The David Copperfield Polka" (158).

757. Pugh, Edwin. "*David Copperfield*." In *Charles Dickens: The Apostle of the People*. London: The New Age Press, 1908, pp. 164-176.

An unconvincing attempt "to prove Dickens a Socialist in all but name." Although Pugh does not examine *Copperfield* critically, he declares that he does not find it

didactic. Pugh thinks Dickens is at his best when shedding
the light of his genius "upon the lowly and the rude."

758. Rees, Richard. "Dickens, or the Intelligence of the Heart."
      In *For Love or Money: Studies in Personality and Essence*.
      London: Secker and Warburg, 1960, pp. 89-112.

      Little-known essay with no separate discussion of *Copper-
      field* but relevant to that novel because of its recogni-
      tion that the "intelligence of the heart" is a major
      element of Dickens's genius.

759. Stephen, Leslie. "Charles Dickens." In *Dictionary of
      National Biography*. London: Smith, Elder, 1908, Vol. V,
      pp. 925-937.

      Appreciates *David Copperfield* as "in many respects the
      most satisfactory" of Dickens's novels and as remarkable
      for the autobiographical element. Stephen notes that John
      Dickens's character is "more or less represented by Mr.
      Micawber."

760. Stone, Harry. "Dark Corners of the Mind: Dickens' Child-
      hood Reading." *Horn Book Magazine*, 39 (1963), 306-321.

      Treats the general effect of Dickens's childhood read-
      ing and elaborates *Copperfield*'s passing remarks about
      the stories David remembers and the books he cherished.
      As Stone remarks, Dickens "was able to take the literary
      flotsam and jetsam of his childhood--the terror stories,
      essays, nursery rhymes, comic songs, and recitations--
      and ... transmute them to a highter form." For a more
      extensive discussion of this subject see Stone's disserta-
      tion "Dickens's Reading" (UCLA, 1955).

761. Stonehouse, John H. "Dickens's Contemplated Autobiography"
      and "Agnes." In *Greeen Leaves: New Chapters in the Life
      of Charles Dickens*. London: The Piccadilly Fountain
      Press, 1931, pp. 51-57, 105-112.

      Argues that the fragmentary autobiography Dickens gave
      Forster "bears very little relationship to the life of
      himself Dickens contemplated before writing *David Copper-
      field*." Stonehouse's comparison of *David Copperfield*
      with Thomas Holcroft's *Memoirs* (written in 1816 and men-
      tioned much later by Dickens to Forster) suggests that
      Dickens may have followed Holcroft's lead in describing
      youthful hardships in the novel. Stonehouse's arguments
      remain tenuous but intriguing, for Dickens and Holcroft
      give similar descriptions of their fathers, and also

David's adventure with the friendly waiter has a parallel in the *Memoirs*. A separate chapter presents an extensive case for Mary Hogarth as the original for Agnes Wickfield-- see Adrian (710). Stonehouse finds that "*purity* is the one word that expresses the quality in" all of Dickens's idealized women.

762. Strange, Kathleen H. "Blacking-Polish." *Dickensian*, 75 (1979), 7-11.

Describes articles from the *Penny Magazine* (1842) which provided an account of a day's work in a blacking-polish factory. Also, Strange quotes a ballad in the *Aberdeen Chronicle* advertising Warren's blacking in 1817.

763. Straus, Ralph. *Dickens: The Man and the Book*. London: Thomas Nelson and Sons, 1936, pp. 123-132.

Provides no new biographical or critical material but intends "to send any reader back again to Dickens's own works." Straus uses generous quotations from Mr. Micawber and from the description of David's first meeting with Betsey Trotwood.

764. Wagenknecht, Edward. *The Man Charles Dickens: A Victorian Portrait*. Boston: Houghton Mifflin, 1929. New and revised edition. Norman: Univ. of Oklahoma Press, 1966, passim.

Examines Dickens's ideas about art, humanity, love, and religion, resisting Edgar Johnson's suggestions of a darkening, Dostoevskian world view in Dickens (738). Wagenknecht's first edition includes an appendix describing his "psychographic" critical method. Concerned with his subject's inner life and disregarding chronology, he tries to outline important biographical events. The revision in 1966 is less self-descriptive of Wagenknecht's critical theories and takes into account more recent Dickens criticism and biography.

765. Waugh, Arthur. "Biographical Introduction." In 1903 Biographical Edition, pp. ix-xxi (49).

Considers the novel's mixture of autobiography and fiction, repeating Kitton's (743) and Charles Dickens the Younger's (283) contentions that the novelist's wife talked him out of publishing the autobiographical fragment. Waugh insists that there is nothing "even vaguely unfilial" in Dickens's portrayal of his father as Mr. Micawber. He notes Dickens's change of intention with Mr.

Dick to include the detail of King Charles's head. Waugh
exudes enthusiasm for *Copperfield* as Dickens's comic
masterpiece, assimilating his "typical qualities with an
artistic breadth and harmony beyond the reach of criticism."

766.   Wright, Thomas. *The Life of Charles Dickens*. London:
       Herbert Jenkins, 1935, pp. 197-206.

Follows and updates Forster (730) on a number of points.
On the question of Micawber's prototype, Wright quotes
one Thomas Gunn, who claims Thomas Powell as well as John
Dickens as Micawber prototypes, Gunn also provided Wright
with a grim meaning for Mr. Peggotty's "gormed" (see 621),
for "Gorm" was a name of a Scandinavian Cerebus, a fact
probably unknown to Dickens.

SELECTED BIBLIOGRAPHY

767.   Churchill, R.C. *A Bibliography of Dickensian Criticism,
       1836-1975*. New York: Garland, 1975. 314 pp.

Attempts comprehensiveness but omits much important
material, commits numerous errors, and is less reliable
than Nisbet (777), Collins (769), and Gold (774). This
bibliography lists general criticism chronologically in
sections on the nineteenth and twentieth centuries,
criticism of particular works (the *David Copperfield*
section includes brief quotations from a number of commentators), and critical comparisons of Dickens and other
writers. Review: Alan M. Cohn, *DSN*, 7 (1976), 120-122.

768.   Cohn, Alan M. "The Dickens Checklist." *DSN*, 1 (1970),
       21-25. Appears in every issue of *DSN*, which is published
       quarterly.

A compilation of editions, secondary studies, and miscellaneous items pertaining to Dickens. Cohn's work is
valuable because it is the most current bibliographical
record and because it is thorough, including many out-of-
the-way items. Cohn includes dissertations, reviews, and
all forms of adaptations.

769.   Collins, Philip. "Charles Dickens." In *New Cambridge
       Bibliography of English Literature*. Ed. G. Watson.
       Cambridge: Cambridge Univ. Press, 1969, Vol. III, pp.
       779-850. Also can be purchased in offprint form from
       Dickens House, London.

Lists a number of the collected editions of Dickens's works, studies of *David Copperfield*, many personal recollections and memoirs about Dickens, a number of general studies of Dickens, topographical studies, commentary on Dickens's illustrators and illustrations. Collins is more selective in his list of critical commentary on *David Copperfield* than in his coverage of more general studies.

770. ————. "Charles Dickens." In *Victorian Fiction: A Second Guide to Research*. Ed. George H. Ford. New York: Modern Language Association, 1978, pp. 34–113.

A bibliographical essay supplementing Nisbet (777) and changing some of her subject categories. Collins divides the criticism section into general criticism, studies of special aspects, and studies of individual novels. His *David Copperfield* section (pp. 94–96) mentions a number of studies and supplies very concise annotation. Together Nisbet and Collins provide the most comprehensive modern bibliographic survey of Dickens; the scope of both of their works imposes limits upon their commentary and upon their comprehensiveness. Collins, for example, regrets that he cannot discuss adaptations of Dickens's works, and neither bibliography includes nonacademic writing about Dickens.

771. Dunn, Frank T. *A Cumulative Analytical Index to The Dickensian, 1905–1974*. Hassocks: The Harvester Press, 1976, pp. 37–38 and passim.

A useful author-subject guide to *Dickensian* articles about *David Copperfield*. Besides the main *Copperfield* entry (pp. 37–38), Dunn elsewhere in his volume includes entries for articles concerning many of the characters and locales.

772. Dunn, Richard J. "*David Copperfield*." In *The English Novel: Twentieth Century Criticism. Volume I, Defoe Through Hardy*. Chicago: Swallow, 1976, pp. 36–38.

A selective list of major articles and sections of books concerning *David Copperfield*. This bibliography is designed for the reader seeking major critical information about individual novels.

773. Fenstermaker, John J. "*David Copperfield*." In *Charles Dickens, 1940–1975: An Analytical Subject Index to Periodical Criticism of the Novels and Christmas Books*. Boston: G.K. Hall, 1979, pp. 123–136.

Excellently cross-referenced subject index to articles
concerned with characterization, characters, composition,
critical assessment, explanatory notes and backgrounds
and sources, illustrations, influences, language and
style, literary parallels, plot, point of view, setting,
structure/unity, techniques, text, themes. Fenstermaker's
criterion for inclusion in his alphabetical listing of
articles is whether an article bears directly on the
critical assessment of the novel, on Dickens's literary
reputation, or on his influence on other writers. Review:
Richard J. Dunn, *Analytical & Enumerative Bibliography*,
4 (1980), 67–73.

774.   Gold, Joseph. "*David Copperfield.*" In *The Stature of
       Dickens: A Centenary Bibliography*. Toronto: Univ. of
       Toronto Press, 1971, pp. 142–150.

       Gold covers the years 1870–1968, but he also lists a
       number of earlier reviews and studies. He is selective
       in attempting to include only what he considers to be
       of "lasting, scholarly value or interest." In the instance
       of *David Copperfield* he lists various introductions, study
       guides, notes on topography and dialect, as well as most
       major critical studies. There is no annotation for these
       entries. Gold also includes a chronologically arranged
       list of general studies of Dickens and a list of disser-
       tations on Dickens. Reviews: Richard D. Altick, *NCF*, 17
       (1972), 107–110; Duane DeVries, *Dickensian*, 68 (1972),
       188–191; Robert Partlow, *DSN*, 2 (1971), 103–105.

775.   Kitton, Frederic G. *Dickensiana: A Bibliography of the
       Literature Relating to Charles Dickens and His Writings*.
       London: George Redway, 1886. 510 pp.

       The most inclusive early listing of biographical and
       critical studies, reviews of Dickens and of Forster (730),
       poetic tributes, anthologized passages from Dickens,
       musical numbers relating to Dickens, stage adaptations,
       parodies, plagiarisms, and testimonies to Dickens. Kitton
       provides generous excerpts from some of the rarer early
       items, and he annotates many of his entries. His exten-
       sive scrapbooks, from which he excerpted much of the
       material for this book and which he continued until his
       death in 1904, are owned by the Dickens House, London.
       Miller (776) supplements much of Kitton's work.

776.   Miller, William. *The Dickens Student and Collector: A
       List of Writings Relating to Charles Dickens and His
       Works, 1836-1945*. Cambridge, Mass.: Harvard Univ. Press,
       1946. 351 pp.

Miller updates Kitton (775) and follows Kitton's format but with less annotation. Miller has many errors and omissions, but he includes materials not usually listed. These include poetic tributes, adaptations, musical compositions, anthologies with selections from Dickens, parodies, and plagiarisms.

777. Nisbet, Ada. "Charles Dickens." In *Victorian Fiction: A Guide to Research*. Ed. Lionel Stevenson. Cambridge, Mass.: Harvard Univ. Press, 1964, pp. 44-153.

Bibliographic essay arranged by general subjects rather than according to Dickens's individual works. Nisbet includes sections on manuscripts, bibliography, editions, letters, biography, and criticism. The criticism section is subdivided into social realism, imagination and symbolism, craftsmanship, precursors and imitators, foreign influence, foreign criticism, epilogue on humor. Nisbet's commentary is informative, and her survey of foreign influence and criticism is the most extensive work to date on Dickens's international stature. See Collins (770) for a supplement to this bibliography. Nisbet has in progress a massive international Dickens bibliography.

778. Wilkins, William G. *First and Early American Editions of the Works of Charles Dickens*. Cedar Rapids: Torch Press, 1910, p. 51.

A reasonably detailed listing of American editions published in Dickens's lifetime. The first hard-cover American edition, according to Wilkins, was Wiley's 1850 two-volume collection of the monthly numbers (39), and the *National Union Catalogue* also lists a G.P. Putnam single-volume edition in 1850 set from the same plates as the Wiley Edition.

AUTHOR AND SUBJECT INDEX

Arabic numbers refer to numbered entries, small Roman numbers to pages in the Introduction. Italic numbers indicate main entries.

Oddie, William *440*, *684*
The Old Curiosity Shop 387
Oliphant, Margaret *441*
Oliver Twist 231, 386, 387, 527
Olney, James review 738
O'Mealy, Joseph H. *442*
Omer, Mr. 374
Optimism xvi, xix, 238, 255, 295, 318, 456, 515, 531. *See also*
    Comedy
Originals. *See* Autobiographical fragment; Autobiography; *indi-*
    vidual characters such as Agnes Wickfield, prototypes;
    Prototypes; Topography
Orphan 306, 325, 351, 464
Orr, J.W., and Brother 39
Orwell, George *443*
Other novels. *See individual names such as Bleak House*
Other writings 34, 35, 520
Our Mutual Friend 364, 734

Parker, David reviews 527, 746
Parker, Louis N. *105*, 117
Parody 161, 170, 775, 776
Partington, Wilfred *196*
Partlow, Robert B., Jr. reviews 500, 774
Passnidge 27
Pater, Walter 661
Pathos 371, 540. *See also* Sentimentality
Patten, Robert L. *195*, *444*, reviews 189, 324, 331, 489, 508,
    527
Pattison, Robert *445*
Pavese, Cesare *446*
Pearlman, E. *447*, *448*, *449*
Pearson, Hesketh *450*, *752*
Peggotty, Clara 78, 197, 218, 314, 353, 361, 427, 467, 539,
    590, 697, 744
  prototypes 604, 743
Peggotty, Daniel
  and family 78, 218, 353, 361, 377
  commentary on 197, 280, 324, 353, 386, 449, 519, 522, 573,
    645
  dialect of 621, 643, 766
  in illustrations 18, 38, 712
  in music 154
  in plays 88, 90, 98, 99, 100
  prototypes 271, 595, 619, 637, 640, 744
Peggotty, Ham 78, 218, 353, 361, 401, 634, 659
Pemberton, T. Edgar *120*
Pendennis. *See* Thackeray, William M.

THE GARLAND DICKENS
BIBLIOGRAPHIES

Duane DeVries, Polytechnic Institute of New York
General Editor

This series of annotated bibliographies of the individual novels and miscellaneous writings of Charles
Dickens is intended for both student and established
scholar. Each volume lists the manuscript materials,
important editions, adaptations, contemporary reviews, critical analyses, and other scholarly studies of
its subject—with full annotation.